WHERE WAS GOD?

Theological Perspectives on the Holocaust

WHERE WAS GOD?

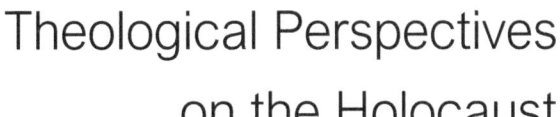

Theological Perspectives on the Holocaust

BARRY R. LEVENTHAL, TH.M., PH.D.

Where Was God?
Theological Perspectives on the Holocaust
(Author: Barry R. Leventhal, Th.M., Ph.D.)

First Edition © 2023 by Ariel Ministries
ISBN: 978-1-958552-09-4
Library of Congress Control Number: 2023923742

Edited and produced by Christiane K. Jurik, M.A.
Cover design by Jesse and Josh Gonzales
Printed in the United States of America

Unless otherwise noted, all biblical quotations are from the New American Standard Bible of 1977.

All rights reserved. No part of this publication may be translated, reproduced, distributed, or transmitted in any form or by any means, including photocopying, recording, or other electronic or mechanical methods, without the prior written permission of the publisher, except in the case of brief quotations embodied in critical reviews and certain other non-commercial uses permitted by copyright law. For permission requests, write to the publisher at the address below.

Published by Ariel Ministries
P.O. Box 792507
San Antonio, TX 78279-2507
www.ariel.org

This work is dedicated to the six million,
especially to those who are of the household of faith
(Gal. 6:10).

Table of Contents

FOREWORD XI
EDITOR'S NOTE: HOW THIS BOOK DEVELOPED XV
    Permission to Edit xvi
INTRODUCTION 1
    The Nature of the Study... 2
    The Purpose of the Study... 3
    The Reasons for the Study... 3
    The Method of the Study 8
    The Limits of the Study 9
THE PERSPECTIVE OF CONTEMPORARY JUDAISM 11
    Finding God and Losing God 12
    Questioning God from Different Spheres 13
    Survey of Varying Religious Responses Within Contemporary Judaism 22
    The Traditional Perspective 24
        The Hidden Purpose... 25
        Kiddush Hashem... 29
        The World to Come 31
        The Suffering Servant.. 33
        The Hiding of the Face 36
        The Price of Redemption... 39
        Loving Punishment by God 42
        Because of Our Sins... 43
        Summary of the Traditional Perspective.................... 51
    The Radical Perspective 52
        The Impotence of God's Omnipotence 53
        The Breaking of the Covenant................................... 56
        The Death of God 58
        Summary of the Radical Perspective.......................... 67
    The Moderate Perspective... 67

    The Unanswerable Mystery 68
    God Suffering with Israel 70
    Contending with God 73
    The Presence of Two Histories 76
    Dialectical Faith 81
    Human Freedom—Human Depravity 84
    Israel Must Live 91
    Summary of the Moderate Perspective 98
  Conclusion 99

THE PERSPECTIVE OF THE BIBLICAL COVENANTS 103

  The Abrahamic Covenant 106
    The Nature of the Abrahamic Covenant 106
    The Provisions of the Abrahamic Covenant 108
    The Protection in the Abrahamic Covenant 109
    Stated Fulfillment 112
    Unstated Fulfillment 120
    The Unity of the Abrahamic Covenant 124
  The Land Covenant 128
    The Provisions of the Land Covenant 129
    The Character of the Land Covenant 130
    The Outworking of the Land Covenant 132
    The Dispossessions 133
    The Restorations 137
  The Davidic Covenant 139
    The Provisions of the Davidic Covenant 140
    The Character of the Davidic Covenant 142
    The Outworking of the Davidic Covenant 142
  The New Covenant 148
    The Provisions of the New Covenant 148
    The Character of the New Covenant 150
    The Outworking of the New Covenant 150
  The Mosaic Covenant 154
    The Provisions of the Mosaic Covenant 155
    The Character of the Mosaic Covenant 156
    The Outworking of the Mosaic Covenant 159
  Conclusion 179
    The Security of the Covenants 179
    The Sensitivity of the Covenants 180

THE PERSPECTIVE OF THE NATION ISRAEL 183

  Israel's Election 185
    The Nature of the Election 186

The Purposes of the Election	189
The Results of the Election	193
Israel's Remnant	198
The Remnant Chronologically Developed	201
The Remnant Considered Historically	201
The Remnant Considered Prophetically	203
The Remnant Considered Contemporarily	205
The Remnant Systematically Developed	209
Israel's Adversary	214
The Old Testament Perspective	215
The New Testament Perspective	217
The Attack on the Man-child at the First Advent	217
The Attack on the Woman at the Second Advent	218
Conclusion	222
THE PERSPECTIVE OF A BIBLICAL THEODICY	**225**
A Philosophical Perspective of Theodicy	232
Unacceptable Philosophical Positions	232
Illusionism	232
Dualism	233
Finitism	234
Sadism	234
Impossibilism	235
Atheism	235
Acceptable Philosophical Positions	237
Theism	237
Depravity	241
Conclusion	243
A Theological Perspective of Theodicy	244
Specific Doctrinal Positions	244
Specific Biblical Purposes	250
Summary and Conclusion	252
CONCLUDING THOUGHTS	**255**
INDEX OF NAMES	**261**
BIBLIOGRAPHY	**265**
Articles	265
Books	269
Other items	282
SCRIPTURE INDEX	**283**

Foreword

In response to the atrocities committed during the Holocaust, many Jews have become atheists. The central question that drives them first to doubt and then to vehemently deny God's existence is "Where was He during the Holocaust?" A second question is "How could a good God justify permitting evil?" My friend Dr. Barry Leventhal made the difficult topic of theodicy in the face of the Holocaust the focus of his doctoral dissertation, which he submitted in the 1980s to Dallas Theological Seminary. It was actually Barry's doctoral advisor, Dr. Charles Ryrie, who proposed this topic. At the time, there were no substantial theological works on the Holocaust, no dissertations or books written from an evangelical perspective, let alone a dispensational perspective. Barry was at first adamant that he would never enter that vast void—the horrors of the Holocaust—but after much prayer and discussing the idea with his wife, Mary, he took on the challenge. We are all very grateful to him and the entire Leventhal family for their sacrifice—the sacrifice of time and life energy it took to accomplish this task. This book is based on Barry's excellent dissertation.

Barry was a much-beloved teacher at Ariel's School of Messianic Jewish Studies at the Shoshanah Campus, and one of the topics he taught was the Holocaust. He often conveyed to his students that people who bring up the problem of evil in discussions about God can inadvertently create a barrier against the gospel. For many Jewish people, this barrier becomes even more formidable

Above: Dr. Arnold Fruchtenbaum is standing behind two of his favorite co-lecturers, Mottel Baleston (left) and Dr. Barry Leventhal (right) at the Shoshanah Campus, in 2014 (picture courtesy of Mottel Baleston).

when the lens is focused on the horrific reality of the Holocaust. Responding to the Holocaust with resolute religious atheism or existential conflict can render these barriers nearly insurmountable. How can the believer in Yeshua, the Jewish Messiah, break through these spiritual walls?

Barry's work offers biblically based explanations for the existence of evil in a world that was created by an omnipotent, omniscient, and all-loving God. It provides a solid biblical response to the most haunting of all questions: Where was God in the Holocaust? In doing so, the book does not shy away from putting Israel's responsibility in its proper place—a sobering point that becomes all the more powerful because the author of this work was a Jew, born to Jewish parents and four Jewish grandparents. Understanding the struggle can increase our empathy for Jews who experience comparable anguish.

Studying the reasons why believers in Messiah Yeshua continue to believe in God in the face of evil may enhance our ability to help break down the barrier in the hearts of unbelievers. As we carefully dismantle their walls of resistance and propose solid biblical answers to their most pressing question, we will be able to present Messiah to the Jewish people in a loving and effective manner.

Arnold G. Fruchtenbaum, Th.M., Ph.D.
Founder and Director of Ariel Ministries
September 2023

Right: Dr. Barry Leventhal teaching at Ariel's School of Messianic Jewish Studies in New York, in 1989 (photo: Mottel Baleston)

Editor's Note

How This Book Developed

In the fall of 2022, Dr. Arnold Fruchtenbaum, founder and CEO of Ariel Ministries, flew from Texas to Georgia to visit his friend Dr. Barry Leventhal. Barry was quite sick at the time, and it had become clear to all that he would soon pass into glory. During the visit with Arnold, Barry drifted in and out of sleep, but when he was awake, he kept up a good conversation with his old friend. The two men shared considerable history, as they had labored side by side in the Lord's field for many years. Barry had taught at Ariel's School of Messianic Jewish Studies in New York multiple times, and joy filled the room as the men reflected on the many fond memories they had created together.

Eventually, the conversation led to Barry's doctoral dissertation, which was presented to the faculty of the Department of Systematic Theology at Dallas Theological Seminary (DTS) in 1982. The dissertation is still available at the Turpin Library, located in

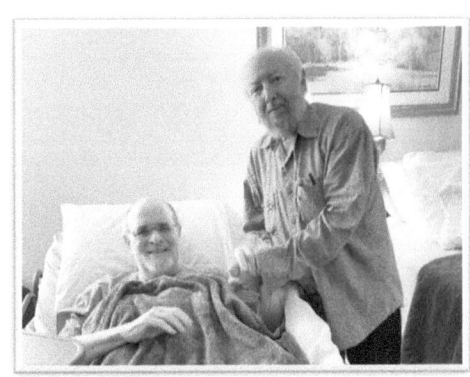

Above: Dr. Fruchtenbaum receives Dr. Leventhal's approval for the publication of this book (picture courtesy of Mrs. Mary Leventhal).

the seminary, and can be accessed there. For the longest time, Arnold had wanted Barry to publish this important work through Ariel Ministries, and so during his visit with his friend, he brought up the topic one more time. The reason you are reading this preface today is because Barry wholeheartedly said yes to the proposal.

Permission to Edit

As a follow-up to his conversation with Arnold, Barry contacted me and gave me permission to edit his work however I saw fit. The driving force behind any changes my team and I made to the original text may be summarized in the following question: How can we best present Dr. Leventhal's research in such a way that everyone—believer and unbeliever alike, Jew and Gentile alike, academic and non-academic alike—could benefit from reading this work while maintaining the author's intended voice? The edits that were made primarily pertained to the readability of the text. Some information that the author presented in the footnotes but that seemed less important for the non-academic reader was removed. Efforts were made to include more recent studies, when applicable, because by now forty years have passed since Dr. Leventhal's original research. Overall, the edits were minor. For those readers who would like to review the results of all of Dr. Leventhal's doctoral research, especially the information he included in the footnotes, we ask you to contact DTS for a copy of the original dissertation.

On December 13, 2022, Dr. Leventhal went home to be with the Lord. He was a giant of a man, and his passing has left his beloved wife, Mary, his four children, and multiple grandchildren, as well as the entire team of Ariel Ministries, in tears. He lived a life worth living for the risen Savior, Yeshua the Jewish Messiah. He served as the Offensive Captain of the 1965 UCLA Football Team, winning the Rose Bowl in 1966. He was a family man at heart and a tremendous academic researcher and respected professor of theology. Whatever Barry touched, he touched with fervor. To work on his insightful and groundbreaking study on God's goodness in light of the Holocaust has been a tremendous honor and formidable responsibility for the entire publishing team. We believe that God honored the prayers that went into this project and each and every edited passage, and we are confident that the author would have been content with the outcome.

Dr. Fruchtenbaum and I would like to extend our gratitude to Michele Ormand, Julie Peterson, and a friend who wishes to remain anonymous for their efforts in peer-reviewing, copyediting, and proofreading this work. Our thanks also go to Mottel Baleston for providing some of the images in this book.

Christiane K. Jurik, M.A.
Editor-in-Chief
Ariel Ministries
December 2023

Introduction

> I believe in the sun when it is not shining.
> I believe in love even when feeling it not.
> I believe in God even when He is silent.[1]

These almost tragic words were anonymously inscribed on the walls of a cellar in Cologne, Germany, where several Jews were hidden from the Nazis. In a most profound way, they raise the eternal issue of faith in a loving God both during and since the Holocaust. Seymour Cain, the senior editor for religion and philosophy in the making of the 15th edition of *Encyclopaedia Britannica*, states the matter straight to the point:

> Auschwitz, or "the Holocaust," looms as the stumbling block of contemporary Jewish theology. Whatever may be the case with Christian theologians, for whom it seems to play no significant generative or transformative role, the Jewish religious thinker is forced to confront that horror, the uttermost evil in Jewish history.[2]

This work will seek to confront the horror of the Holocaust not from an evangelical posture but, more specifically, from a Messi-

---

[1] Eliezer L. Ehrmann, ed., *Readings in Modern Jewish History: From the American Revolution to the Present: Sources* (New York City, NY: Ktav for the BJE of Metropolitan Chicago, 1977), p. 232.

[2] Seymour Cain, "The Question and the Answers After Auschwitz," *Judaism* 20 (Issue 3, Summer 1971): 263.

anic Jewish dispensational stance. It is based on the author's dissertation, which was presented to the faculty of the Department of Systematic Theology at the Dallas Theological Seminary in August 1982.

The Nature of the Study

This study will seek to investigate certain theological perspectives on the Holocaust. It is not possible to investigate every viewpoint, for they are multitudinous. Nevertheless, it is imperative that an evangelical and, in particular, a dispensational response be directed toward the horror of the Holocaust.

What is meant, then, when the term "Holocaust" is used in this book?[3] Jacob Robinson, in the *Encyclopaedia Judaica*, gives the following definition:

> The "Holocaust" (also known as the Catastrophe, the *Sho'ah*, the *Hurban*) is the most tragic period of Jewish Diaspora history and indeed of modern mankind as a whole. It started in Germany on Jan. 30, 1933, with the accession of the Nazis to power, and ended on May 8, 1945, with the unconditional surrender of Nazi Germany.[4]

The Holocaust spread like a cancer through Europe, destroying in its wake all of Eastern European Jewry—some six million Jews, including over one million Jewish children. This study of the Jewish suffering during that tragic period assumes the complete authority and reliability of the Scriptures in their totality, both the

---

[3] The term "Holocaust" is derived from the Greek word *holokauston*. In the ancient world, Jewish scholars used *holokauston* to translate the Hebrew term עֹלָה (*'ōlāh*, "ascent") into Greek. In 1 Samuel 7:9, *'ōlāh* is used for a "burnt offering" sacrifice offered whole to God.

[4] Jacob Robinson, "Holocaust," in Cecil Roth, Geoffrey Wigoder, eds., *Encyclopedia Judaica*, 1st ed., (Jerusalem, Israel: Keter Publishing House, 1971), Vol. 8: He-Ir, p. 459.

Hebrew Bible and the New Testament. Unless otherwise indicated, the New American Standard Bible will be used.[5]

The Purpose of the Study

The purpose of this study is threefold. First, it will investigate the major religious responses to the Holocaust from within contemporary Judaism. These responses will be reviewed from Jewish philosophers, theologians, and rabbis. Second, it will demonstrate that only a consistent and biblical theology can answer the many questions and problems with which modern Judaism is wrestling concerning the Holocaust. This consistent and biblical theology must be both evangelical and dispensational. Third, this study will demonstrate that only biblical theism can adequately provide the answers to the perennial question of theodicy (a rational defense of the justice of God in view of the presence of evil in the world), especially with regard to the evil and suffering of the Holocaust.

The Reasons for the Study

There are several major reasons for this particular study. First, the Holocaust was a life-shattering experience for Jews and non-Jews alike. In many respects, it caused a unique kind of suffering for the Jewish people, a kind of suffering never before experienced by any people or group. A total of roughly eleven million people died in the Holocaust. However, Clark Williamson, Indiana Professor Emeritus of Christian Thought at Christian Theological Seminary, suggests four specific reasons why the slaughter of the six million Jews was unique and different:

---

[5] For details regarding the number of Jewish victims mentioned, see: Lucy S. Dawidowicz, *The War Against the Jews: 1933–1945* (New York City, NY: Bantam Books, 1975), pp. 543-544. For a more recent study, see: Yitzhak Arad, *The Holocaust in the Soviet Union* (Lincoln, NE: University of Nebraska and Yad Vashem, 2009)

(1) The Nazi resolution to exterminate the Jews targeted all Jews. All 18 million Jews in the world—men, women, and children—were to be destroyed for having been born into a Jewish family. Young and old were to receive the "final solution" to the Jewish question.

(2) While the Nazis planned final solutions for other groups (such as Gypsies and communists), they decided that these groups could wait until the end of the war. Not so with the Jews. They had to go.

(3) The war against the Jews took precedence over all other enemies. It was more important to murder Jews than to win the war.

(4) Regarding the murder of Jews, there were no economic, military, or other competing considerations to take into account. No matter the expense, the Jews had to disappear.[6]

Such a unique catastrophe for the Jews, God's chosen people, with all of its magnitude and intensity, certainly demands a response from within evangelicalism.

A second reason for this study is that one of the major sources of the rise of Nazism in Germany came from within the church. It is only fitting that an evangelical answer be heard from within the church as well. It was the growing interest in the evolutionary and destructive higher criticism of the Bible in Germany that fueled the anti-Semitic Nazi war machine.[7] In fact, Germany has had a long history of so-called "Christian anti-Semitism" not only from within the Roman Catholic Church but even from within the Protestant Church. It was Martin Luther (1483–1546) who, in his later years, turned upon the Jews with a religious fury and

---

[6] See: Clark M. Williamson, *Has God Rejected His People? Anti-Judaism in the Christian Church* (Eugene, OR: Wipf & Stock, 2017), p. 125.

[7] See: Cyril M. Abelson, "Bias and the Bible," in Aryeh Carmell and Cyril Domb, eds., *Challenge: Torah Views on Science and Its Problems* (Jerusalem/New York: Feldheim Publishers, 2nd edition, 1978), pp. 412-420.

thus paved the way for an Adolf Hitler (1889–1945) to consummate the Reformer's great desire for the elimination of the Jewish people.[8] Is it any wonder that Hitler could say in his *Mein Kampf*: "Hence today I believe that I am acting in accordance with the will of the Almighty Creator: by defending myself against the Jews, I am fighting for the work of the Lord,"[9] and then later in the same work cite Martin Luther as one of the great heroes of the German people?[10] The frightening connection seems obvious.

This is not to imply that Nazi anti-Semitism was Christian at its core. Quite the contrary, Nazi anti-Semitism was also anti-Christian. However, as Professor for Systematic Theology at Fuller Theological Seminary Paul Jewett rightly acknowledged, centuries of Christian persecution of the Jews certainly paved the way for the Hitlerian extermination of the six million Jews:

> Of course Nazi anti-Semitism was not Christian in its essence; in fact it was anti-Christian. Next to the Jews, there was no one Hitler hated more than the Christians. And what resistance the Nazi did encounter was largely inspired by the church. But these palliating reminders of Christian suffering and heroism can hardly alleviate the reproaches which the Christian conscience must feel when it views Auschwitz in the light of all the centuries of Christian persecution of the Jews.[11]

Holocaust historian Raul Hilberg, in his masterful work *The Destruction of the European Jews*, agrees that the Holocaust did not happen in a theological vacuum but rather was the inevitable result

---

[8] See: Martin Luther, *Luther's Works*, 55 vols. (St. Louis, MN: Concordia Publishing House, Fortress Press, 1957–86), Vol. 54, Table Talk, pp. 239, 426.

[9] Adolf Hitler, *Mein Kampf* (New York and London: Hutchinson Publ. Ltd., 1969), p. 60.

[10] Ibid., p. 194.

[11] Paul K. Jewett, "X. Concerning Christ, Christians, and Jews," in E. R. Geehan, ed., *Jerusalem and Athens: Critical Discussions on the Philosophy and Apologetics of Cornelius Van Til* (Phillipsburg, NJ: Presbyterian and Reformed Publishing Company, 1971), p. 222.

of three consecutive anti-Jewish policies that were pursued throughout Western history:

> Since the fourth century after Christ, there have been three anti-Jewish policies: conversion, expulsion, and annihilation. The second appeared as an alternative to the first, and the third as an alternative to the second...
>
> The Nazi destruction process did not come out of a void; it was the culmination of a cyclical trend. We have observed the trend in three successive goals of anti-Jewish administrators. The missionaries of Christianity had said in effect: you have no right to live among us as Jews. The secular rulers who followed had proclaimed: You have no right to live among us. The German Nazis at last decreed: You have no right to live.
>
> These progressively more drastic goals brought in their wake a slow and steady growth of anti-Jewish actions and anti-Jewish thinking. The process began with the attempt to drive the Jews into Christianity. The development was continued in order to force the victims into exile. It was finished when the Jews were driven to their deaths. The German Nazi, then, did not discard the past; they built upon it. They did not begin the development; they completed it.[12]

A third reason for this study is that there is a growing movement among neo-Nazis who deny that the Holocaust ever happened. This is both an alarming and appalling trend in our day. These so-called historical revisionists are anti-Holocaust to the core and are feeding the rapidly growing problem of anti-Semitism in our day. Many conservative people are being taken in by this non-historical attack against contemporary Judaism, as well as modern-day Israel. It is indeed frightening to imagine that a few non-historians can come along years after the historical event of the Holocaust

---

[12] Raul Hilberg, *The Destruction of the European Jews* (New York, NY: Harper & Row, 1979), pp. 3-4.

and rewrite that terrifying period as a "Jewish myth." This study will hopefully help to set the record straight, at least from a theological perspective.

The fourth reason for this study on the Holocaust is that there is really no major evangelical or dispensational work currently available on the subject.[13] There are several works from within Judaism as well as from within Roman Catholicism and liberal Protestantism. Except for two works within conservative Protestantism (both non-dispensational),[14] the field is empty. This study, hopefully, will be a beginning, for what God has to say in His infallible Word is certainly more important and vital than what either dogma or humanism has to say, especially in regard to the Jews and their plight.

The fifth reason for this particular study is that Jewish missions have suffered a tremendous blow since the evil and suffering of the Holocaust. Many Jewish people are no longer ready to consider the Messiahship of Jesus, for they have rejected a personal view of God after the Holocaust.[15] If God allowed six million Jews to be slaughtered, over one million of whom were children, then He is no longer worthy of personal consideration, let alone able to send

---

[13] As mentioned in the Editor's Note, this work is based on the author's 1982 dissertation. Since then, several evangelical authors have addressed the topic of theodicy in light of the Holocaust.

[14] These two works are: Jakob Jocz, *The Jewish People and Jesus Christ After Auschwitz: A Study in the Controversy Between Church and Synagogue* (Grand Rapids, MI: Baker House, 1981); Ulrich Simon, *A Theology of Auschwitz: The Christian Faith and the Problem of Evil* (London, England: Gollancz, 1967). Both authors are Messianic Jews.

[15] For the problems Jewish people have had with the gospel since the Holocaust, see: Charles L. Feinberg, *Israel at the Center of History & Revelation*, 3rd edition (Portland, OR: Multnomah Press, 1980), pp. 199-200; Arnold G. Fruchtenbaum, *Jesus was a Jew*, rev. ed. (San Antonio, TX: Ariel Ministries, 2021), pp. 79-91; Louis Goldberg, *Our Jewish Friends* (New York, NY: Loizeaux Brothers, 1983), pp. 40-41, 154; Arthur W. Kac, *The Rebirth of the State of Israel: Is it of God or of Man* (Chicago, IL: Moody Press, 1958), pp. 232-233, 287-290; Arthur W. Kac, *The Spiritual Dilemma of the Jewish People: Its Cause and Cure* (Chicago, IL: Moody Press, 1963), pp. 29-35.

His own Messiah to deliver the chosen people. Why did He not send the Messiah when He really was needed—during the horror of the Holocaust? It is hoped that this study will provide some of the answers needed in Jewish missions today.

The sixth reason for this study of the Holocaust is that the generation of survivors is quickly passing off the scene. Few of those who survived the atrocities of the Nazis are still alive today. With each passing year, more die and pass into the eternal judgment of God Himself. They need an evangelical and dispensational response to the Holocaust. Hopefully, it might serve to prepare them to hear the good news of the gospel before they depart this earth.

The seventh and last reason for this study is that a dispensational theology is uniquely qualified to respond to the many problems raised by the evil and suffering of the Holocaust. It has the highest and most consistent view of Israel and the Jews of any theology. Therefore, it is most able to deal with "the Jewish question." Dispensationalism maintains a consistent and comprehensive view of the divine plan and purpose for the nation of Israel. Therefore, a dispensational response to the Holocaust is long overdue.

The Method of the Study

In order to investigate the various theological perspectives on the Holocaust, this study will confine itself first of all to what Jewish religious leaders have said concerning the *Shoah*. These religious leaders include Jewish philosophers, theologians, and rabbis. Most studies involving this kind of survey draw only from a few sources or from many sources in a cursory way. At the time of writing, this was the first treatise to survey eighteen major responses from within three major Jewish categories.

Second, this study will then investigate the major biblical covenants that God initiated with the nation Israel: i.e., the Abrahamic, the Land, the Davidic, the New, and the Mosaic covenants. These covenants establish the eternal relationship between God and the Jewish people. It is, therefore, incumbent to see their contribution to an understanding of the Holocaust.

Third, this study will then investigate the nature of Israel as a unique and special people. While the covenants establish the broad parameters of Israel's relationship with God, many other scriptures (the Prophets in particular) lay out the details and specifics of that relationship. In order to study these particulars of Israel's peoplehood, three major areas will be surveyed: (1) Israel's election; (2) Israel's remnant; and (3) Israel's adversary. These three areas will then be applied to a clearer understanding of the Jewish people in the Holocaust.

Fourth, this study will investigate the area of theodicy, providing a justification of God's character in view of the evil in the world, in particular the evil of the Holocaust. If God were a God of love, He certainly would have halted the suffering of the Holocaust; and if He were a God of power, He certainly could have stopped the evil of the Holocaust. Yet He did not stop the Holocaust. Therefore, is it possible that He is either not all-loving or not all-powerful? These issues deserve a biblical and theological response. It will be seen that only biblical theism can produce an adequate response to the evil of the Holocaust.

The Limits of the Study

This study is limited to three basic focal points. First, it is limited to what Jewish religious leaders (i.e., philosophers, theologians, and rabbis) have said concerning the Holocaust. A survey of what Jewish laymen have said is beyond the scope of this work. Second, it is limited to what the Bible has to say concerning the Holocaust.

More specifically, it is limited to an evangelical and dispensational approach to the Bible. Therefore, the study itself will not investigate what the Catholic and Protestant churches did during the Holocaust (i.e., in response to the great Jewish need in Europe) nor what they have said since in response to the Holocaust. Third, this study is limited to a brief survey of the philosophical and theological options for establishing an adequate theodicy regarding the Holocaust. Rather, it seeks to establish a detailed response from biblical theism in this regard—a biblical theism that is both evangelical and dispensational.

A final word is in order. The author is greatly indebted to the Messianic Jewish scholar Arnold G. Fruchtenbaum for his constant encouragement and insight into this whole subject. His assistance is greatly appreciated.

Above: The American Sculptor Kenneth Treister explains what was going through his mind when he created the "Holocaust Memorial Miami Beach": "The totality of the Holocaust cannot be created in stone and bronze... but I had to try... The murder of one and a half million children whose joys turned to sorrow suddenly on September 1, 1939, when World War II broke out, cannot be sculpted... but I had to try. Six million moments of death cannot be understood... but we must all try." (www.holocaustmemorialmiamibeach.org; photo: © AdobeStock)

The Perspective of Contemporary Judaism

The Holocaust has permanently scarred the face of contemporary Judaism. This excruciating experience will probably never heal. It will last as long as Judaism itself. Every facet of Jewish life feels the pain of the scar, from the simplicity of childhood to the complexity of old age.

The simplicity of childhood is reflected in the innocent faith of an Anne Frank (1929–1945): "Who has inflicted this upon us? Who has made us Jews different from all other people? Who has allowed us to suffer so terribly up till now? It is God that has made us as we are, but it will be God, too, who will raise us up again."[1] This simplicity is also mirrored in the intriguing thought of a Hasidic rabbi: "For the faithful, there are no questions; for the nonbeliever, there are no answers."[2]

The complexity of old age, on the other hand, is reflected in the words of Elie Wiesel, himself a survivor and Holocaust storyteller.

---

[1] Anne Frank, *The Diary of a Young Girl: The Revised Critical Edition* (New York, NY: Doubleday, 2003), p. 622.

[2] Azriel Eisenberg, ed., *Witness to the Holocaust* (New York, NY: Pilgrim Press, 1981), p. 628.

He says the Holocaust "could not have been without God, nor could it have been with God. It cannot be conceived on any level."[3]

Finding God and Losing God

For some, the Holocaust was a religiously shattering experience; for others, it was a religiously developing experience. Viktor Frankl, a psychotherapist as well as a survivor, supports this thesis:

> The truth is that among those who actually went through the experience of Auschwitz, the number of those whose religious life was deepened—in spite of, not because of, this experience—by far exceeds the number of those who gave up their belief. To paraphrase what La Rochefoucauld once remarked with regard to love, one might say that just as the small fire is extinguished by the storm while a large fire is enhanced by it—likewise a weak faith is weakened by predicaments and catastrophes, whereas a strong faith is strengthened by them.[4]

The thesis regarding the religious impacts the Holocaust had on its victims is also graphically illustrated by the Orthodox theologian Eliezer Berkovits:

> There were really two Jobs at Auschwitz: the one who belatedly accepted the advice of Job's wife and turned his back on God, and the other who kept his faith to the end, who affirmed it at the very doors of the gas chambers, who was able to walk to his death defiantly singing his *"Ani Ma'amin*—I Believe." If there were those whose faith was broken in the death camp, there were others who never wavered. If God was not present for many, He was not lost to many more. Those who rejected did so in authentic rebellion;

---

[3] Elie Wiesel, "Freedom of Conscience—A Jewish Commentary," *Journal of Ecumenical Studies* 14 (Fall 1977): 643.

[4] Victor E. Frankl, *Man's Search for Ultimate Meaning* (New York, NY: Basic Books, 2000), p. 19.

those who affirmed and testified to the very end did so in authentic faith.[5]

The Jewish philosopher and survivor Emil Fackenheim has said that both religious and non-religious survivors are unique witnesses:

> Why hold fast to the God of the covenant? Former believers lost Him in the Holocaust Kingdom. Former agnostics found Him. No judgment is possible. All theological arguments vanish. Nothing remains but the fact that the bond between Him and His people reached the breaking point but was not for all wholly broken. He is a witness whose like the world has not seen.[6]

Finally, Wiesel confesses that although both kinds of religious experience occurred, the mystery of the Holocaust remains:

> Loss of faith for some equaled discovery of God for others. Both answered the same need to take a stand, the same impulse to rebel. In both cases, it was an accusation. Perhaps some day someone will explain how, on the level of man, Auschwitz was possible; but on the level of God, it will forever remain the most disturbing of mysteries.[7]

Questioning God from Different Spheres

Before surveying the varying religious responses from within contemporary Judaism, it will prove helpful to review some of the profound and perplexing spiritual questions that the mystery of the

---

[5] Eliezer Berkovits, *Faith After the Holocaust* (Brooklyn, NY: KTAV Publishing House, 1973), p. 69.

[6] Emil L. Fackenheim, "The Human Condition After Auschwitz," in Jacob Neusner, ed., *Understanding Jewish Theology: Classical Issues and Modern Perspectives* (New York, NY: KTAV, 1973), p. 171.

[7] Elie Wiesel, *Legends of Our Time* (New York, NY: Schocken Books, 1982), p. 6.

Above: The inscription over the main gate of Auschwitz reads "Arbeit macht frei" ("Work sets free"; photo: © AdobeStock).

Holocaust has raised. These heartrending quests have arisen from many different spheres of contemporary Jewish life, some from those who have survived the Holocaust and some from those who reflect back on it.

Alexander Donat, a survivor of the Warsaw ghetto and Hitler's death camps, wrote to his grandson years later concerning his religious questioning:

> The Holocaust was for every survivor a crucial religious experience. Day-in and day-out we cried out for a sign of God's presence. In the ghettoes and in the death camps, before gallows and the doors of gas chambers, when confronted with ultimate incredible evil, we cried: "Lord, where art Thou?" We sought Him, and we didn't find Him. The acute awareness of God's puzzling and humiliating absence was always with us. Memory of this experience is always with us… The far-reaching religious implications of the Holocaust have by no means been explored, nor has the process of coming to grips with its meaning been completed. It

implies a profound revolution in the basic tenets of Judaism, and the rise of a new set of Judaic values.[8]

Another survivor, Werner Weinberg, explains the two kinds of religious faith he observed in the concentration camp, both of which he personally rejected:

> And then there was the question of religious faith in the camp, of belief in God's providence—in one of two forms. One was resignation: all he does is for the good; if he has decreed that I be among the dead of this place, so be it. The other was that of invoking personal privilege. God will hear my prayer and save me alive from this hell. I have seen both of these attitudes among believing Jews (I was never imprisoned together with Christians).[9]

Again, Donat, in his personal memoirs, records the anguish of the thousands trapped in the Warsaw ghetto:

> It was an agonizing self-appraisal. We were bitter to the point of self-flagellation, profoundly ashamed of ourselves, and of the misfortunes we had endured. And those feelings intensified our sense of being abandoned alike by God and man. Above all we kept asking ourselves the age-old question: why? why? What was all that suffering for? What had we done to deserve this hurricane of evil, this avalanche of cruelty? Why had all the gates of Hell opened and spewed forth on us the furies of human vileness? What crimes had we committed for which this might have been calamitous punishment? Where, in what code of morals, human or divine, is there a crime so appalling that innocent women and children must expiate it with their lives in martyrdoms no Torquemada ever dreamed of?[10]

---

[8] Alexander Donat, "A Letter to My Grandson," *Midstream* 16 (June 1970): 43-44.

[9] Werner Weinberg, "On Being a Survivor," *The Christian Century*, Volume XCVIII, Number 12, April 8, 1981, p. 380.

[10] Alexander Donat, *The Holocaust Kingdom: A Memoir* (New York, NY: Holocaust Library, 1965), p. 100.

The spiritual and psychological impact of the Holocaust on the Jews is further stated by Jewish historian Shmuel Ettinger:

> The Holocaust was a dreadful blow for the Jewish People, more savage and inhuman than anything it had ever suffered—both in numbers and in agony. It was also a stunning spiritual and psychological shock. All the achievements and innovations of modern science and technology had been enlisted for the extermination of an entire nation; Nazi propaganda had endeavored to reduce the Jews to the status of vermin, to exterminate them by gas and fire in order to 'purify the world.'[11]

Conservative rabbi, historian, and educator Jacob Neusner recalls both the religiously similar as well as dissimilar aspects of the Holocaust and other tragic events of Jewish history:

> The events of 1933 to 1948 constitute one of the decisive moments in the history of Judaism, to be compared in their far-reaching effects to the destruction of the First and Second Temples, 586 B.C. and 70 A.D.; the massacre of Rhineland Jewries, 1096; and the aftermath of the Black Plague, 1349, the expulsion of the Jews from Spain, 1492, or the Ukrainian massacres of 1648-9. But while after the former disasters, the Jews responded in essentially religious ways, the response to the Holocaust and the creation of the State of Israel on the surface has not been religious. That is to say, while in the past people explained disaster as a result of sin and therefore sought means of reconciliation with God and atonement for sin, in the twentieth century the Jews superficially did not.[12]

Reformed rabbi, educator, and radical theologian of the Holocaust Richard L. Rubenstein asserts that the Holocaust stands as the greatest contemporary challenge to modern Jewish theology:

---

[11] Shmuel Ettinger, "The Modern Period," in H. H. Ben-Sasson, ed., *A History of the Jewish People* (Cambridge, MA: Harvard University Press, 1976), p. 1033.

[12] Neusner, *Understanding Jewish Theology*, p. 179.

> I believe the greatest single challenge to modern Judaism arises out of the question of God and the death camps. I am amazed at the silence of contemporary Jewish theologians on this most crucial and agonizing of all Jewish issues.[13]

Michael Brown, Professor Emeritus and Senior Scholar at the Israel and Golda Koschitzky Centre for Jewish Studies at York University, likewise admits that the Holocaust has sparked theological questioning that cannot fall back on the explanations of past Jewish generations:

> However much one might regret it, few can fail to sympathize with, and even to participate in, the theological questioning which the Holocaust has sparked. The survivors—and, in a sense, we are all survivors—need ways of understanding. Yet the explanations which past generations have offered for Jewish suffering do not satisfy. Some Jews have been relatively unaffected, but others have lost their belief in God entirely and not regained it. Still others see the Holocaust as the symbol of God's ultimate rejection of Judaism and have become Christians.[14]

Jewish American critic and author Alfred Kazin maintains that the perplexing problems of the Holocaust are evidence that, for the Jew, the war has really never ended:

> At the core of our existence as Jews lies the *fact* of the Holocaust: a whole people, once called "God's people," condemned to death; the indifference to this, by which one really means the inability to take it in; the savage joy of the many who as foolishly believed that here was a "final solution" to the Jewish problem. Year by year

---

[13] Richard L. Rubenstein, "Symposium of Jewish Belief," in Jerry V. Diller, ed., *Ancient Roots and Modern Meanings: A Contemporary Reader in Jewish Identity* (New York, NY: Bloch, 1978), p. 240.

[14] Michael Brown, "On Crucifying the Jews," *Judaism* 27 (Fall 1978): 476.

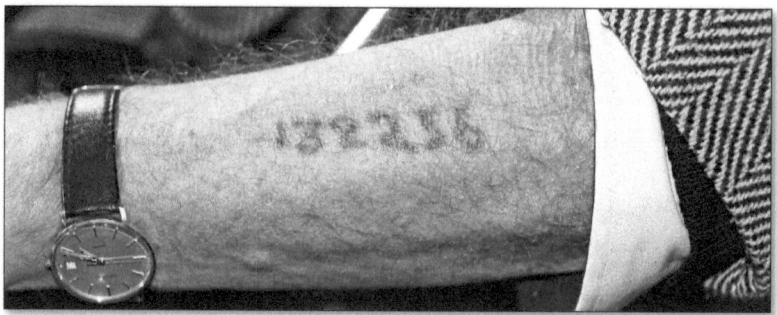

Above: Arm tattoo of a Holocaust survivor (photo: Frankie Fouganthin; wikimedia.org)

these terrible events press themselves more tightly on our minds. The war has never ended.[15]

Not only have Jewish survivors, historians, and educators wrestled with the religious perplexity of the Holocaust, but so have Jewish philosophers, rabbis, theologians, and poets. Leroy Howe, Professor Emeritus of Pastoral Theology at Southern Methodist University in Dallas, Texas, maintains that the Holocaust is an event that forces each person to examine life if he is to live it:

> Let us… consider Auschwitz as [an] event. A "happening" of the most grotesque kind, it cannot be easily understood, for only the inhumane could contemplate it unfeelingly. Yet it must be comprehended. Whatever else one may learn from the death camps, Auschwitz demonstrates with terrible clarity that it is no longer possible for the unexamined life to be lived, much less to be worthwhile.[16]

Dan Magurshak, professor of philosophy at Carthage College in Wisconsin, maintains that not only does all of life need to be examined in light of the Holocaust, but the very nature of God itself:

---

[15] Alfred Kazin, "The Heart of the World," in Eva Fleischner, ed., *Auschwitz: Beginning of a New Era? Reflections on the Holocaust* (New York, NY: KTAV, 1977), p. 71.

[16] Leroy T. Howe, "Theology and the Death Camps," *Christian Century* 86 (19 February 1969): 252.

Believers in Israel's God of history or in the Christian God of the resurrection have often asked how God—omnipotent, omniscient, benevolent—could let the children burn under the blue and empty sky. The event demands a rethinking of speculations about God's nature, its relationship to humankind, the plausibility of its existence, and its purpose in at least allowing, if not willing, such carnage.[17]

Reuven Pinchas Bulka, Orthodox rabbi and former co-president of the Canadian Jewish Congress, reiterates the same tragic effect of the Holocaust on the status quo of modern Judaism:

> No event, save the destruction of the Temple, has had such a shattering effect on Jewish life and thought as the holocaust. With the exception of atheists, who could use the holocaust as proof that there is no God, and the devoutly religious, who could point to the holocaust as an indication that any salvation for the world is possible only through faith, the status quo has been demolished.[18]

Neusner takes the problem a step further, identifying the Holocaust as the central obstacle to contemporary Jewish belief:

> The murder of the nearly six million Jews in Europe constitutes the single predominant issue in, and obstacle to, Jewish belief… It is contained in the key-word "Auschwitz," which is used to refer to the terrible experience of European Jewry from 1933 to 1945, the extermination of men and women and children only on account of their having been born to a Jewish parent (or, in fact, having had a single Jewish grandparent). To put it simply: Where was God when these things happened?[19]

---

[17] Dan Magurshak, "The 'Incomprehensibility' of the Holocaust: Tightening Up Some Loose Usage," in Michael R. Marrus, ed., *The Nazi Holocaust – Part 1: Perspectives on the Holocaust* (Westport, CT: Meckler, 1989), p. 92.

[18] Reuven P. Bulka, "Logotherapy As a Response to the Holocaust," *Tradition: A Journal of Orthodox Jewish Thought*, Vol. 15, No. 1/2 (Spring-Summer 1975): 89.

[19] Neusner, *Understanding Jewish Theology*, pp. 150, 163.

The Reformed rabbi Harold Schulweis also probes the dilemma of the Holocaust with penetrating and disturbing questions:

> That men who sin are punished is understandable; but that millions of innocent should be destroyed is not. What role does God play here? Is His permissiveness morally justifiable? If the monumental catastrophe belongs to man, what relevance does God have if He washes His hands of the whole matter and sets Himself apart as a spectator?[20]

Even the Hebrew poet voices his perplexity at the lack of answers to the great riddle of the Holocaust. Following a reminder of the miraculous rescue of the three Hebrew youths in Daniel 3, Shlomo Tana vents his poetic rage at the fact that the six million did not deserve the same miracle:

> Nowadays, bereft of lore and legend
> So many have been thrown into the burning pit,
> Their bodies were consumed, only ashes remained,
> Not even one was saved.
> No angel did come.
> How great was the betrayal.
> And every time we tried to escape or obstruct,
> The fumes of fires would kill us at once,
> And God's way remains a riddle.[21]

Every Jew, in some way, small or large, feels the weight of the impact of the Holocaust, perhaps none more than the Messianic Jew. Jakob Jocz, theologian and author, aptly summarizes the post-Auschwitz venture for the modern Jew:

---

[20] Harold M. Schulweis, "Suffering and Evil," in Abraham E. Millgram, ed., *Great Jewish Ideas* (Washington, D.C.: B'nai B'rith Department of Adult Jewish Education, 1964), p. 217.

[21] Shlomo Tana, "Reyach Ha'esh," in Murray J. Kohn, *The Voice of My Blood Cries Out: The Holocaust as Reflected in Hebrew Poetry* (New York, NY: Shengold Publishers, 1979), pp. 148-149.

Auschwitz casts a black pall upon the civilized world. Not only is man's humanity put under a question mark, but God himself stands accused. Jews are asking insistently: Where was God when our brothers and sisters were dragged to the gas ovens?...

Faith in the God of Israel, in the God of the Covenant, in the God of history, is always a test and a challenge, but after Auschwitz it is an agonizing venture for every thinking Jew.[22]

Above: The impenetrable fences of Auschwitz (photo: Mottel Baleston)

---

[22] Jocz, *The Jewish People and Jesus Christ After Auschwitz*, pp. 23, 34.

Survey of Varying Religious Responses Within Contemporary Judaism

Having reviewed some of the questions raised from different spheres concerning the Holocaust, a detailed survey of the varying religious responses from within contemporary Judaism will now be developed. These religious responses are many and varied. The founding director of the Elie Wiesel Center for Judaic Studies at Boston University, Steven Katz, reflects this truth when he summarizes them into nine configurations:

> Out of the still nascent and still uncertain conversation of the Holocaust several general responses, with their various combinations and configurations, have emerged. They can be enumerated as follows: (1) the Holocaust is like all other tragedies and merely raises again the question of theodicy and "the problem of evil," but it does not significantly alter the problem or contribute anything new to it. (2) The classical Jewish theological doctrine of *Mi-penei hata'einu* ("because of our sins we were punished") which was evolved in the face of earlier national calamities can also be applied to the Holocaust. According to this account, Israel was sinful and the Auschwitz is her just retribution. (3) The Holocaust is the ultimate in vicarious atonement. Israel is the "suffering servant" of Isaiah (ch. 53ff.)—she suffers and atones for the sins of others. Some die so that others might be cleansed and live. (4) The Holocaust is a modern *Akedah* (sacrifice of Israel)—it is a test of our faith. (5) The Holocaust is an instance of the temporary "Eclipse of God"—there are times when God is inexplicably absent from history or unaccountably chooses to turn His face away. (6) The Holocaust is proof that "God is dead"—if there were a God, He would surely have prevented Auschwitz; if He did not, then He does not exist. (7) The Holocaust is the maximization of human evil, the price mankind has to pay for human freedom. The Nazis were men, not gods; Auschwitz reflects ignominiously on man; it does not touch God's existence or perfection. (8) The Holocaust

is revelation: it issues a call for Jewish affirmation. From Auschwitz comes the command: Jews survive! (9) The Holocaust is an inscrutable mystery; like all of God's ways it transcends human understanding and demands faith and silence.[23]

The survey of religious responses within contemporary Judaism will be divided into three major categories: (1) the traditional perspective; (2) the radical perspective; and (3) the moderate perspective. These three categories do not reflect the three major divisions of modern Judaism: Orthodox, Reformed, and Conservative. In fact, there is some overlap between these divisions in the various responses. The Holocaust is so traumatic to contemporary Judaism that many of the recognized religious boundaries have been obliterated in certain aspects of this topic.

The traditional perspective of the survey reflects, by and large, the thinking of Orthodox and Rabbinic Judaism. Many of the traditional categories of Talmudic thought are brought to bear on the Holocaust, while some are rejected.

The radical perspective reflects the opposite end of the spectrum from the traditional perspective. Most of the Orthodox and Talmudic responses are thrown off. Some categories, such as religious atheism and secular nationalism, begin to appear.

The moderate perspective falls into the large space between the two extreme ends of the spectrum (i.e., between the traditional and radical perspectives), attempting to restore religious meaning to Judaism without adopting rabbinic and Talmudic categories as well as humanistic religious categories.

---

[23] Steven T. Katz, "Jewish Faith After the Holocaust: Four Approaches," in *Encyclopedia Judaica Yearbook 1975-6* (Jerusalem, Israel: Encyclopaedia Judaica, 1976), p. 93.

The Traditional Perspective

Several different perspectives are brought to bear on the Holocaust from within more traditional Jewish religious thought. Many of them reflect former Talmudic and rabbinic ideas and are still thought to be relevant to this present catastrophe. Neusner reaffirms this classical position:

> Classic Judaic theology was not struck dumb by evil, and neither changed its apprehension of the divinity, nor claimed in its own behalf a renewed demand on the Jews, on account of disaster. To be sure, important theological issues require careful, indeed meticulous attention. But to debate those issues outside of the classic tradition and under the impact of grief can produce few lasting, or even interesting results.[24]

Neusner then goes on to ask what the implications of the Holocaust are from within this tradition and comes to the following conclusion:

> I claim there is *no* implication—none for Judaic theology, none for Jewish community life—which was not present before 1933... Jews find in the Holocaust no new definition of Jewish identity because we need none. Nothing has changed. The tradition endures.[25]

The Jewish theologian Michael Wyschogrod maintains that Israel's historic faith has always centered on the saving acts of God, of which the Holocaust is not one:

> Israel's faith has always centered about the saving acts of God: the election, the exodus, the Temple, and the Messiah. However more prevalent destruction was in the history of Israel, the acts of

---

[24] Neusner, *Understanding Jewish Theology*, p. 192.

[25] Ibid., p. 193.

destruction were enshrined in minor fast days while those of redemption became the joyous proclamations of the Passover and Tabernacles, of Hanukkah and Purim. The God of Israel is a redeeming God; this is the only message we are authorized to proclaim, however much it may not seem so to the eyes of non-belief. Should the Holocaust cease to be peripheral to the faith of Israel, should it enter the Holy of Holies and become the dominant voice that Israel hears, it could not but be a demonic voice that it would be hearing. There is no salvation to be extracted from the Holocaust, no faltering Judaism can be revived by it, no new reason for the continuation of the Jewish people can be found in it. If there is hope after the Holocaust, it is because to those who believe, the voices of the Prophets speak more loudly than did Hitler, and because the divine promise sweeps over the crematoria and silences the voice of Auschwitz.[26]

On the following pages, eight of the numerous perspectives from the traditional category will be examined.

The Hidden Purpose

The first perspective from within the traditional category is that the God of Israel is a rational and purposeful God and that although the Holocaust appears to be without meaning, it must have a purpose even if it is not clearly perceived. Jocz defines this perspective in the following manner:

> Jewish tradition allows no room for absolute chaos in the order of things. Such a world would contradict the purposefulness of a good and intelligent God. Behind even the most grotesque events in history is some purpose; otherwise life ceases to make sense. The questions about Auschwitz are, therefore, in the last analysis,

---

[26] Michael Wyschogrod, *Abraham's Promise – Judaism and Jewish Christian Relations*, ed. R. Kendall Soulen (Grand Rapids, MI: Eerdmans, 2004), p. 119.

questions about God. In what sense is he still the *ribono shel olam* ("the Lord of the Universe")?[27]

Nachum Eliezer Rabinovitch, the *rosh yeshiva* (dean) of Yeshivat Birkat Moshe in Ma'ale Adumim, Israel, concludes that in light of this unanswerable mystery, the only valid response is submissive silence:

> Nothing can explain the terrible God-forsakenness of the Holocaust years. It is not given to man to understand "Why dost Thou hide Thyself at times in trouble?" [Ps. 10:1]. The man of faith is also the faithful man, and so he does not mock the Hiding God by false attributes. Nor can there be any recompense in this world for the rivers of blood shed to sanctify His Name [religious martyrdom]. In the face of the terrifying mystery of endless *Akedot* ["bindings" of Isaac], when the Heavens are shut fast against both heartrending pleas for pity and outraged demands for justice, the true believer can only "sit alone in silence... and put his mouth in the dust" [Lam. 3:28-29].[28]

Rabbi Emeritus Melvin Granatstein reiterates this same counsel in light of the incomprehensibleness of divine governance:

> We can claim no comprehension of the nature of Divine governance at all. All statements regarding the nature of God as compassionate, gracious, and just arise only from the experience of God's presence in the moments of Divine descent into our midst. In short, our knowledge of God is restricted to what God Himself reveals within the constricted contexts of His revelations to us. On all other questions we can only remain silent... Our formulation of classical Jewish belief can be expressed thus: God reveals Himself to us in the context of our history as the executor of justice, but every such revelation is a violation of the norm and for this

---

[27] Jocz, *The Jewish People and Jesus Christ After Auschwitz*, p. 33.

[28] Nachum L. Rabinovitch, "The Religious Significance of Israel," *Tradition: A Journal of Orthodox Thought* 14 (Fall 1974): 24.

reason, we must conclude that "there is no reward in this world." [*b. Chullin* 142a][29]

Joseph Soloveitchik, an important American Orthodox rabbi, Talmudist, and modern Jewish philosopher, also details the Jewish struggle to comprehend certain catastrophic events, such as the Holocaust:

> Judaism, even as it knew and tried to comprehend catastrophic events which cruelly destroy man's dreams and hopes, could not accept the existence of the ultimately irrational in human life. Events which we label as accidents belong to a higher Divine order into which man has not been initiated. Not decrees of fate, but rather reasons beyond our comprehension, operate in such instances. We have been granted the opportunity of gaining insights and of accumulating scientific knowledge about the regular course of events and physical nature, but we are excluded from the realm of *goral* [divine "elective"] understanding. The relationship between the individual and his environment eludes our grasp. To God there are no accidents, though they often appear so to us. Essentially, this is the reply which God gave to Job, who sought to reconcile his painful plight with his faith in God's justice. There is no deterministic fate; all operates on a transcendental plane which is beyond the grasp of man's finite mind.[30]

Rabbi Hershel Jonah Matt sees this mystery bound up with the fact that God has chosen to limit His power to allow for the human freedom that He Himself created. The answer, Rabbi Matt affirms, lies within the concept of divine providence:

---

[29] Melvin Granatstein, "Theodicy and Belief," *Tradition: A Journal of Orthodox Thought* 13.3 (Winter 1973): 40.

[30] Abraham R. Besdin, *Reflections of the Rav: Lessons in Jewish Thought – Volume One Adapted from Lectures of Rabbi Joseph B. Soloveitchik* (Hoboken, NJ: KTAV, 1993), p. 48.

> The only adequate key to resolving the above-mentioned dilemmas [the genuineness of both God's power and man's freedom] lies in the concept of divine providence (*hash-gaḥah*). "Providence" affirms that God has a plan and purpose for man, for Israel, for the world—but that in forming this plan and carrying out this purpose God has chosen to limit the operation of His own power by granting men the power to choose, to decide, and to act... The full measure of revelation, however—involving full judgment and recompense by God and full awareness by man—is reserved for the world- and age-to-come. Only then-and-there will the true measure and true consequences of human freedom in the here-and-now be made known... Until the coming of that Final Day, however, we are able to know in faith the only two truths we need to know: that our freedom to distinguish and choose between right and wrong, however limited, is genuine; and that every use we make of that freedom is of genuine significance for furthering God's design and affecting our own destiny.[31]

Abraham Joshua Heschel, rabbi, theologian, philosopher, and professor of Jewish mysticism at the Jewish Theological Seminary of America, likewise attests to the fact that Israel has a unique destiny—a destiny that will be ultimately fulfilled, even though through many harsh tribulations. Israel is God's stake in human history:

> Our life is beset with difficulties, yet it is never devoid of meaning. The feeling of futility is absent from our souls. Our existence is not in vain. There is a Divine earnestness about our life. This is our dignity. To be invested with dignity means to represent something more than oneself. The gravest sin for a Jew is to forget what he represents.
>
> We are God's stake in human history. We are the dawn and the dusk, the challenge and the test. How strange to be a Jew and

---

[31] Hershel J. Matt, "Man's Choice and God's Design," *Judaism* 21 (Spring 1972): 219-221.

to go astray on God's perilous errands. We have been offered as a pattern of worship and as a prey for scorn, but there is more still in our destiny. We carry the gold of God in our souls to forge the gate of the kingdom. The time for the kingdom may be far off, but the task is plain: to retain our share in God in spite of peril and contempt. There is a war to wage against the vulgar, against the glorification of the absurd, a war that is incessant, universal. Loyal to the presence of the ultimate in the common, we may be able to make it clear that man is more than man, that in doing the finite he may perceive the infinite.[32]

Finally, Wyschogrod again echoes the fact that, though Israel must suffer unjustly at times, the Jew himself can trust the God of heaven to eventually redress these injustices:

> If, after the holocaust, we have children who, in turn, beget children, if we can smile and laugh at jokes and satisfy our normal human appetites, if, in short, we have not gone mad, it is because we trust in the God of our fathers. He will reward those who have perished and punish those who have committed the evil. He watches over this nation even when it does not seem so. We believe this fairly steadily and not only for moments.[33]

Kiddush Hashem

The second perspective from within the traditional line of thinking is *Kiddush Hashem*, or "the sanctification of the Name." This rabbinic concept concerns the holiness of martyrdom, which values dying for the Name of God and as His servant.

---

[32] Abraham Joshua Heschel, *The Earth Is the Lord's: The Inner World of the Jew in Eastern Europe* (Woodstock, VT: Jewish Lights Publishing, 2011, fifth printing), p. 109.

[33] Michael Wyschogrod, "Auschwitz: Beginning of a New Era? Reflections on the Holocaust," *Tradition: A Journal of Orthodox Thought* 17 (Fall 1977): 78.

In his novel *A Beggar in Jerusalem*, Elie Wiesel describes *Kiddush Hashem* in the following manner:

> What you should fear is to inflict evil, to cause death. To die for God and His commandments is nothing: our ancestors, the saints and the martyrs, did just that. But to kill for God, to cause blood to flow in His name, is serious and difficult. It is alien to us; it goes against our nature and tradition: that is what should frighten you.[34]

As this excerpt from Wiesel's novel shows, fear is removed in *Kiddush Hashem*. For the religious Jew, during the Holocaust, it became a duty and a privilege to die for the God of the Jews.[35] Donat graphically portrays the attitude of the pious Jews in the Warsaw ghetto as they awaited eventual martyrdom:

> Still others were religious Jews, committed to the tradition of *Kiddush Hashem*: that is, a martyr's death in the name of God. They believed that, when the enemy came for us, we should be dressed in our prayer shawls and phylacteries, poring over the holy book, all our thoughts concentrated on God. In that state of religious exaltation, we should simply ignore all Nazi orders with contempt and defiance; resistance, violence, only desecrated the majesty of martyrdom in sanctification of the Lord's name.[36]

---

[34] Elie Wiesel, *A Beggar in Jerusalem* (New York, NY: Schocken Books, 1970), p. 138.

[35] Both during and after the Holocaust, rabbis were occupied with determining whether a specific *Kiddush Hashem* was valid or not. For an example of this discussion, see: Irving J. Rosenbaum, *The Holocaust and Halakhah* (Jerusalem: Ktav Publishing, 1976), pp. 61ff.

[36] Donat, *The Holocaust Kingdom: A Memoir*, p. 103.

While many of those who were killed during the Holocaust undoubtedly were not of this form of Orthodox persuasion, history records many heroic examples of religious Jews, in particular rabbinic leaders, who went joyously to their deaths as martyrs for the Name of God. Their examples brought home to others (even, in some cases, the Nazis themselves) a living awareness of God and His presence.

Closely related to *Kiddush Hashem* is the concept of *Kiddush Ha-Ḥayyim*, "the sanctification of life." The latter became increasingly important during the Holocaust years, as the Nazis attempted to liquidate not only the very life of Judaism, but also the God of Judaism. Israeli Holocaust scholar Shaul Esh states that the concept of *Kiddush Ha-Ḥayyim* was "the general reaction of the Jewish masses, especially in Eastern Europe, to the Nazi horror." It was "the overwhelming impulse to preserve life in the midst of death."[37]

The World to Come

The third perspective from the traditional Jewish viewpoint is life in the world, or age, to come. Undoubtedly, those who suffered as martyrs (i.e., *Kiddush Hashem*) rested their case on this central concept. Although this life brings much suffering and tribulation, the world to come will find justice made perfect for the faithful.[38] Granatstein summarizes this rabbinic concept aptly:

> Our formulation of classical Jewish belief can be expressed thus: God reveals Himself to us in the context of our history as the executor of justice, but every such revelation is a violation of the

---

[37] Shaul Esh, "The Dignity of the Destroyed: Towards a Definition of the Period of the Holocaust," *Judaism* 11 (Spring 1962): 106.

[38] For a summary of Talmudic and rabbinic thought on "the world to come," see: Abraham Cohen, *Everyman's Talmud: The Major Teachings of the Rabbinic Sages* (New York, NY: Schocken Books, 1975), pp. 346-389; C. G. Montefiore and H. M. J. Loewe, eds., *A Rabbinic Anthology* (Cambridge: Cambridge University Press, 2012).

norm, and for this reason, we must conclude that "there is no reward in this world."[39]

Heschel makes it clear that the concept of perfect justice in the world to come was the focus of the older, pious Jews of Eastern Europe: "The Jew of older days often overlooked this world because of his preference for the other world. Between man and world stood God. In the meantime, however, persecutions, pogroms, and murders shattered the ground under the feet of the people."[40]

Rabbi George Schlesinger argues that the suffering of the Holocaust victims will be more than compensated in the coming world, even if one can assume that this suffering was designed to elicit a virtuous response:

> Another question which may be raised: is it fair to the victim to be singled out as the instrument to increase the opportunities for VRS [virtuous response to suffering]? To this it might be replied that such a person will be amply compensated to his own satisfaction if not in this world—like Job—then in the world to come where opportunities for compensation are limitless.[41]

Schulweis develops this line of thinking in relation to rabbinic theodicy:

> Taken as a whole, rabbinic theodicy adheres to the basic principle that the world is well conducted by a supernatural moral power. Suffering is either a disguised blessing or an overt malediction. The face of justice embarrassed in this world may be saved in the tribunal of the other world.[42]

---

[39] Granatstein, "Theodicy and Belief," p. 40.

[40] Heschel, *The Earth Is the Lord's*, pp. 101-102.

[41] George N. Schlesinger, "Arguments from Despair," *Tradition: A Journal of Orthodox Thought* 17 (Spring 1979): 18.

[42] Schulweis, "Suffering and Evil," p. 208.

Finally, Berkovits admits that although recompense may come to Israel as her eternal purpose is fulfilled, the awful suffering of millions of Jews during the Holocaust must still find its resting place in God:

> The sorrow will stay, but it will become blessed with the promise of another day for Israel to continue on its eternal course with a new dignity and a new self-assurance. Thus, perhaps in the awful misery of man will be revealed to us the awesome mystery of God…
>
> Yet all this does not exonerate God for all the suffering of the innocent in history. God is responsible for having created a world in which man is free to make history. There must be a dimension beyond history in which all suffering finds its redemption through God. This is essential to the faith of a Jew. The Jew does not doubt God's presence, though he is unable to set limits to the duration and intensity of his absence. This is no justification for the ways of providence, but its acceptance. It is not a willingness to forgive the unheard cries of millions, but a trust that in God the tragedy of man may find its transformation. Within time and history that cry is unforgivable.[43]

The Suffering Servant

The fourth perspective from the realm of traditional Jewish thought is that of the Suffering Servant of Isaiah 53. Rather than interpreting this passage to refer to a personal Messiah, modern Orthodox thinkers see in it a reference to a national messiah.[44] The nation Israel is seen as the innocent sufferer, who suffers at the hands of the unrighteous Gentile nations. Orthodox Rabbi Irving

---

[43] Berkovits, *Faith After the Holocaust*, pp. 70, 136.

[44] For an extensive overview of the history of interpretation of Isaiah 53 in the Jewish tradition, see: Arnold G. Fruchtenbaum, *Ariel Bible Commentary: The Book of Isaiah* (San Antonio, TX: Ariel Ministries, 2022), pp. 546–581.

Greenberg summarizes this concept and relates it to the Holocaust and post-Holocaust traditions:

> The servant suffers because of the evils of the world which are visited on his/her head. Such a model makes clear that after the Holocaust, the correct response is not to justify God, but to challenge the world's evils and sins. Furthermore, this model implies that God allows human freedom and will not prevent the assault on the servant.[45]

Berkovits maintains that when the Suffering Servant experiences suffering, God Himself suffers along with Him. This is the partnership between God and man as history moves towards its Messianic fulfillment:

> God's chosen people is the suffering servant of God. The majestic fifty-third chapter of Isaiah is the description of Israel's martyrology through the centuries… God suffers not on account of what man does to Him. What could man do to God? He suffers because of what man does to himself and to his brother. He suffers the suffering of His servant, the agony of the guiltless. In all their affliction, He is afflicted… God's servant carries upon his shoulders God's dilemma with man through history. God's people share in all the fortunes of God's dilemma as man is bungling his way through toward messianic realization. The status of the dilemma at any one moment in history is revealed by the condition of Israel at that moment. God's people is God's challenge to man. God, who leads man "without might and without power," sent His people into the world without the might and power. This is the essence of the confrontation between Israel and the world.[46]

---

[45] Irving Y. Greenberg, "Orthodox Judaism and the Holocaust," *Gesher* 7 (1979): 60.

[46] Eliezer Berkovits, "The Hiding God of History," in: Yisrael Gutman and Livia Rothkirchen, eds., *The Catastrophe of European Jewry: Antecedents, History, Reflections* (Jerusalem, Israel: Yad Vashem, 1976), pp. 692, 694.

Yet, while history moves toward its "messianic realization," Greenberg stresses that the Suffering Servant of Isaiah 53 (i.e., Israel) stands both as a confronter to the world and a warning about the world:

> The Suffering Servant in Isaiah 53 sounds like a passage out of Holocaust literature...
>
> By its existence, Israel testifies to the God who promises ultimate redemption and perfection in an unredeemed world. Thus it arouses the anger of all who claim already to have found absolute perfection...
>
> The Holocaust warns us that our current values breed their own nemesis of evil when unchecked—even as Nazi Germany grew in the matrix of modernity. To save ourselves from such error, we will have to draw on the warning of the experiences of the Suffering Servant. The Holocaust suggests a fundamental skepticism about all human movements, left and right, political and religious—even as we participate in them. Nothing dares evoke our absolute, unquestioning loyalty, not even our God, for this leads to possibilities of SS[47] loyalties.[48]

Shalom Carmy, an Orthodox rabbi teaching Jewish studies and philosophy at Yeshiva University, handles the Suffering Servant passage of Isaiah 53 in a different manner, and yet sees it as giving courage to those suffering.[49] He does not identify the Servant with the nation Israel but rather as "an anonymous figure,"[50] actually a

---

[47] The abbreviation SS stands for the German word "Schutzstaffel." From the time of the Nazi Party's rise to power until the regime's collapse in 1945, the SS was the foremost agency of "security," mass surveillance, and state terrorism within Germany and German-occupied Europe.

[48] Irving Y. Greenberg, "Cloud of Smoke, Pillar of Fire: Judaism, Christianity, and Modernity after the Holocaust," in: Eva Fleischner, ed., *Auschwitz: Beginning of a New Era? Reflections on the Holocaust* (New York, NY: Ktav, 1977), pp. 36-38.

[49] Shalom Carmy, "The Courage to Suffer: Isaiah 53 and Its Context," *Gesher* 7 (1979): 102-124.

[50] Ibid., p. 111.

"paradigm of selfless suffering."[51] The Servant becomes the model for suffering, one who suffers without any desire for reward or vindication. He suffers merely for the sake of God Himself:

> The servant is more than merely apprehensive or uncertain about his fate in death and burial; he is actually indifferent to it. He stands before God, and his resolution, his emptying out of self, leaves no room for concern over the ultimate disposition of his life-story, whether to be "buried" among the wicked or dignified among the tombs of the wealthy…
>
> In a word, the Suffering Servant is characterized by his transcendence of the human desire for the satisfaction derived from self-justification, by the anonymity of his personal sanctity, by the lack of self-dramatization.[52]

The Hiding of the Face

The fifth perspective from traditional Judaism is the concept of "the hiding of the face" (*hester panim*). In the words of Berkovits, this is "God's hiding of his countenance from the sufferer. Man seeks God in his tribulation but cannot find him."[53] Rabbi Soloveitchik summarizes this concept and the fear that accompanies it:

> There are moments in history and in the life of the individual when it seems as if God has relinquished all concern with the course of human affairs. The Torah calls this state *Hester Panim* (lit. "hiding the face") and describes such periods as fraught with terrors. Man feels forlorn and helpless in the face of life's fearful possibilities.[54]

---

[51] Ibid., p. 108.

[52] Ibid., pp. 108, 111.

[53] Berkovits, *Faith After the Holocaust*, p. 94.

[54] Joseph B. Soloveitchik, "Chapter III: The World Is Not Forsaken," in: Besdin, *Reflections of the Rav*, p. 35.

Having briefly described this "hiding of the face," Soloveitchik gives its biblical basis and then applies its awesomeness to the Holocaust while maintaining that it terminated in the establishment of the State of Israel:

> In Deut. 31:17, the Torah describes the ultimate punishment of *Hester Panim*: "Then My anger will flare up against them in that day and I will abandon them and *hide My face from them*, and they shall be devoured, and many evils and distress shall befall them; so that they will say in that day, 'Are not these evils come upon us, because our God is not in our midst?'"
>
> *Hester Panim* involves a temporary abandonment of the world, a suspension of His active surveillance… He turns His back, so to speak, on events and leaves matters to chance. Under such circumstances, the usual vulnerability of the Jew invites the threat of total extermination…
>
> *Hester Panim*, the Torah indicates, is related to Israel's waywardness and may be regarded as an ultimate punishment. It is terrifying because it signifies rejection…
>
> The Holocaust… was *Hester Panim*. We cannot explain the Holocaust, but we can, at least, classify it theologically… even if we have no answer to the question, "why?" … This is how the world appears when God's moderating surveillance is suspended. The State of Israel, however, reflects God's return to active providence, the termination of *Hester Panim*.[55]

Heschel speaks of this same phenomenon but refers to it as "the hiding God":

> The prophets do not speak of the *hidden God* but of the *hiding God*. His hiding is a function not His essence, an act not a permanent state. It is when the people forsake Him, breaking the Covenant which He has made with them, that He forsakes them and hides His face from them [Deuteronomy 31:16-17]. It is not God

---

[55] Ibid., pp. 35-37.

who is obscure. It is man who conceals Him. His hiding from us is not in His essence: "Verily Thou art a God that hidest Thyself, O God of Israel, the Savior!" (Isaiah 45:15). A hiding God, not a hidden God. He is waiting to be disclosed, to be admitted into our lives.[56]

The hiding God is the silent God, the God who elicits faith in one sufferer and doubt in another. The response of faith is simply, but graphically, recorded in the quotation with which this book began: "I believe in the sun even when it is not shining. I believe in love even when feeling it not. I believe in God even when He is silent."[57] Likewise, the response of doubt is recorded in the complaint of Hebrew poet Kalman Bartini (1903–1995):

> And the children of my people
> Who have been chosen forever,
> The voice of the slaughtered for generations.
> Rise from the depths of the earth,
> Once again have they been "chosen" to be sacrificed
> And the Lord is silent and
> Hides behind the scenes.[58]

The impact of God's silence during the Holocaust cannot be stressed enough. It has had a paralyzing effect on all of contemporary Judaism. Berkovits calls it *Galut Ha'shkhina* ("the Exile of the Divine Presence") and states that in the generation of Nazism, it reached "its nadir, its most tragic intensification in history."[59]

---

[56] Abraham Joshua Heschel, *Man Is Not Alone: A Philosophy of Religion* (New York, NY: Farrar, Straus and Giroux, 1979), pp. 153-154.

[57] Ehrmann, *Readings in Modern Jewish History*, p. 232.

[58] Kalman Aharon Bartini, "Shir V'heydo," in *The Voice of My Blood Cries Out: The Holocaust as Reflected in Hebrew Poetry* (New York, NY: Shengold Publishers, 1979), p. 147. Bartini was also known under the name K. A. Bertini.

[59] Eliezer Berkovits, "Crisis and Faith," *Tradition: A Journal of Orthodox Thought* 14 (Fall 1974): 14.

The Price of Redemption

The sixth perspective within traditional Judaism is the concept of the price of redemption for national rebirth. The Holocaust was "the labor pains" of Israel's rebirth as a nation. Greenberg maintains that the rebirth and present struggle of the nation Israel are part of "the Messianic life-force":

> The reborn State of Israel is this fundamental act of life and meaning of the Jewish people after Auschwitz. To fail to grasp that inextricable connection and response is to utterly fail to comprehend the theological significance of Israel. The most bitterly secular atheist involved in Israel's upbuilding is the front line of the Messianic life-force struggling to give renewed testimony to the Exodus as ultimate reality. Israel was built by rehabilitating a half-million survivors of the Holocaust. Each one of those lives had to be rebuilt, given opportunity for trust restored...
>
> The real point is that after Auschwitz, the existence of the Jew is a great affirmation and an act of faith. The recreation of the body of the people, Israel, is renewed testimony to [the] Exodus as ultimate reality, to God's continuing presence in history proven by the fact that his people, despite the attempt to annihilate them, still exist...
>
> The re-creation of the state is the strongest suggestion that God's promises are still valid and reliable.[60]

The price of Israel's redemption was the Holocaust itself, when God hid His presence, when He apparently broke His promises. But the nation, alive and thriving, assures the Jew that God and His promises are still a viable option. His honor has been restored. This is Rabinovitch's confident assertion: "There is one simple basic fact which is there for all the world to see. It is so utterly simple and so totally obvious that... millions of people all over the

---

[60] Greenberg, "Cloud of Smoke, Pillar of Fire," pp. 43, 48, 50.

globe know it and see it. Israel *is*, and it bears God's Name, and it has restored God's crown!"[61]

Berkovits asserts that without the return to Israel, Jewish history becomes meaningless. Hence, the return was "a messianic moment":

> The return is the counterpart in history to the resolution in faith that this world is to be established as the Kingdom of God. The thought has its roots in the very foundations of Judaism, but might have been mere wishful thinking had it had been supported by the reality of Israel, its existence, its survival, its return to Zion…
>
> Is this the Messiah already? It is enough to look out of the window to realize that nothing could be further removed from the truth (unless he, too, come unexpectedly "like a thief"). But it is a messianic moment, in which the unexpected fruits of human endeavor reveal themselves as the mysterious manifestation of divine guidance of whose coming the heart was forever sure.[62]

Not only does Berkovits maintain that this return to Zion was "a messianic moment," but he also declares that divine providence had no other choice. The redemption of Israel's nationhood, after so radical an annihilation as the Holocaust, had to come:

> In our times, when the phase of the Exile has to be recognized as total crisis, the radically new event which… has entered Jewish history has been… the *Shoa*, the Holocaust. It is probably not the right term… The proper name for it is not *Shoa*, but *Hurban*, annihilation. For the first time in our history the Exile itself was destroyed…
>
> The rise of the State of Israel after two millennia of such Exile and at the moment when it occurred, the event itself has become

---

[61] Rabinovitch, "The Religious Significance of Israel," p. 24.

[62] Berkovits, *Faith after the Holocaust*, pp. 152-53, 156.

the reviving force, called back to life the "dry bones" of the shattered *Galut*. Divine Providence had no choice but to grant us a measure of national redemption to meet the national *Hurban*.[63]

This concept of the price of redemption in the rebirth of the nation Israel is not, however, accepted by all Jewish leaders. For example, Jacob Talmon, Professor of Modern History at the Hebrew University of Jerusalem, totally rejects this "metaphysical and theological" perspective:

> Some people profess to see the Holocaust as an ineluctable stage in Jewish history—the labour pains of national rebirth, so to speak, or the price of redemption. One hears this kind of interpretation from extreme nationalists as well as from certain extremely religious Jews.
>
> This I shall never be able to understand. I shall never be able to believe in a Guardian of Israel who claims the lives of a million children as the price of national revival. One must not confuse a metaphysical and theological question with historical and empirical statements about the role of Jewish despair after Auschwitz, the guilt feelings of the Christian world, and the fluid situation at the end of the war aiding the restoration of Jewish statehood in modern Israel. There is, of course, unparalleled grandeur in the explosion of Jewish energies and the display of an unconquerable will to live on the morrow of the most horrible bloodletting and deepest degradation and wretchedness that any people has ever experienced—in the struggle for independent Jewish nationhood.[64]

Sometimes the eye of faith and the eye of fact both focus on the same object without seeing the same thing. This is not the first

---

[63] Berkovits, "Crisis and Faith," pp. 14-15.

[64] Jacob L. Talmon, "European History as the Seedbed of the Holocaust," in *Holocaust and Rebirth: A Symposium* (Jerusalem, Israel: Yad Vashem, 1974), p. 70.

time that theologians and historians have not seen eye to eye in regard to the destruction of the six million.

Loving Punishment by God

The seventh perspective from traditional Judaism is the concept of God punishing His people because of His love for them. The suffering of the Holocaust was God's will in that it reflected His loving discipline for Israel. Of course, this perspective echoes a common biblical theme (cf. Job 5:17, Prov. 3:11-12). The New Testament scholar E. P. Sanders develops the historical background for this concept, finding it normative within much of Rabbinic Judaism, especially in the *Psalms of Solomon*[65] and the writings of Rabbi Akiba.[66] The rabbis viewed this loving punishment as a means of purifying their lives in this world and preventing suffering in the world to come.

Wiesel weaves this theme into the fabric of several of his novels. In one scene, he portrays a father and his young son being herded toward an open ditch where, a moment later, they will be shot. The father has one hand on his son's shoulder and the other hand pointing toward the sky. He is explaining the battle between love and hatred. He says to his son, "Know, my son, if gratuitous suffering exists, it is ordained by divine will. Whoever kills, becomes God. Whoever kills, kills God. Each murder is a suicide, with the Eternal eternally the victim."[67] In another scene, Wiesel portrays a young student questioning his kabbalistic master, "I can conceive

---

[65] The *Psalms of Solomon*, one of the apocryphal books, is a collection of eighteen religious songs or poems composed in the first or second centuries B.C. They are not included in any scriptural canon. However, they are present in copies of the Peshitta (standard version of the Bible for churches in the Syrian tradition) and Septuagint.

[66] E. P. Sanders, "R. Akiba's View of Suffering," *The Jewish Quarterly Review* 63, no. 4 (1973): 332-351.

[67] Elie Wiesel, *A Beggar in Jerusalem*, p. 208.

of God's wanting to punish us for reasons that are His and not necessarily ours; but why do entire nations, so many nations, aspire to become His whip, His sword?"[68] In yet another scene, Wiesel depicts a young rabbi preaching a Sabbath sermon where "he saw a punishment from God in the suffering of the Jews… God punishes the Jews because he loves them, because he is determined to make them pure and just."[69] In an interview, Wiesel stated, "If we were to hate everyone who made us suffer, we would become a people full of hate. Who didn't persecute us in history? Even God made us suffer."[70]

As one might anticipate, the majority of contemporary Jewish thinkers reject the idea that God's love was the driving force behind the Holocaust. It is not palatable with the enormity of the slaughter of six million Jews, especially with over one million being "innocent" children. Rabbi Greenberg is a representative of this rejection: "To talk of love and of a God who cares in the presence of the burning children is obscene and incredible; to leap in and pull a child out of a pit, to clean its face and heal its body, is to make the most powerful statement—the only statement that counts."[71]

Because of Our Sins

The final perspective from traditional Judaism is the most controversial. The premise is that God brought the Holocaust upon the Jewish people as a punishment for their sins. This concept is closely related to the previous one. However, while in the former

---

[68] Ibid., p. 113.

[69] Elie Wiesel, *The Town Beyond the Wall* (New York, NY: Avon Books, 1964), p. 147.

[70] Harry James Cargas, *In Conversation with Elie Wiesel* (New York, NY: Paulist Press, 1976), p. 20.

[71] Greenberg, "Cloud of Smoke, Pillar of Fire," pp. 41-42.

perspective God's loving punishment was to be remedial and disciplinary, in this view God's action is punitive and retributive. This was not an uncommon religious experience for many when they first entered a concentration camp. Thus, Wiesel reflects on many that he encountered: "If I am here, it is because God is punishing me; I have sinned, and I am expiating my sins. I have deserved this punishment that I am suffering."[72] Once again, this concept is reflected in biblical theology (cf. Lev. 26; Deut. 28-30; Amos 3:2). So it is not surprising to find it detailed in rabbinic thought. Likewise, it appears again in the words of the Hasidic masters who suffered during the Holocaust.

The problem in this perspective is defining the cause of the punishment. For what sins was Israel punished? As can be imagined, the answers vary. One model is called "The First Adam," i.e., the formula of sin and punishment. Adam, who sinned by violating God's command, is expelled from the Garden of Eden and punished. Under this model, the Israeli Orthodox Rabbi Pinchas Peli summarizes three different views of the types of sins that caused God to punish the Jews, all basically arising out of the Hasidic tradition.[73] First, there was "the sin of Zionism," meaning the attempt to hasten the final redemption by immigrating to the land of Israel en masse before the coming of the Messiah. Second, there was "the sin of opposition to Zionism." This is the exact opposite of the first view. God remembered the people of Israel in their exile, and a call went out for them to leave the exile and immigrate to the land of Israel. Yet most Jews did not heed these signs of the coming redemption and stayed where they were. Since the people did not want to end the exile, the exile ended them. Third, there

---

[72] Elie Wiesel, "Eichmann's Victims and the Unheard Testimony," *Commentary* 32 (December 1961): 515.

[73] See: Pinchas H. Peli, "In Search of Religious Language for the Holocaust," *Conservative Judaism* 32 (Winter 1979): 9-16.

was "the sin of assimilation." A direct correlation is made between the processes of alienation from and denial of Judaism that European Jewry had undergone since the *Haskalah* ("Enlightenment") and the destruction of that Jewry in the Holocaust.

Other "sins" of Judaism have been put forward as well. Rabbi Meshullam Zalman Schachter-Shalomi maintains that Jewish guilt arose out of the fact that the Jewish people did not have "enough righteousness" toward the *goyim*, meaning the Gentile nations. He goes on to explain:

> Why did we not preach to the Germans? ... Thinking that we, as victims of the Nazi German oppression, somehow had no right to preach in order to save our own necks, we kept an anguished silence. In response to Nazi hostilities, we judged *all* Germans to be inhuman, predatory beasts, and the Germans returned the compliment. They were the stronger and we, by definition, the vermin to be exterminated. In short, *the Holocaust was partially caused by Jews who did not think it worthwhile, or even possible, to reprove the Germans.*[74]

Rabbi Elliot Gertel maintains that the Holocaust must be traced back to a "pedagogical" or "constructive" guilt, which is founded in the Diaspora and which must force the Jew to look into his own conscience to find where the Jewish people have failed God.[75] Others trace the cause back to the blessings and cursings in Leviticus 26 and Deuteronomy 28-30. Israel suffered because of her national rejection of God. The curses fell upon a

---

[74] Meshullam Zalman Schachter-Shalomi, "Homeland and Holocaust: Issues in the Jewish Religious Situation-Commentary," in: Donald R. Cutler, ed., *The Religious Situation: 1968* (Boston, MA: Beacon Press, 1968), p. 81 (emphasis in the original).

[75] Elliott B. Gertel, "Because of Our Sins," *Tradition: A Journal of Orthodox Thought* 15 (Spring 1976): 75-80.

guilty nation by a faithful covenant-keeping God. While the Holocaust cannot be explained, at least it can be classified theologically.

Wyschogrod calls the Holocaust "the final circumcision of the people of God."[76] But this can only be believed if the power of God is once more displayed. He gives one final word concerning the uniqueness and all-shattering experience of the Holocaust:

> Israel's faith has always centered around the saving acts of God: the election, the Exodus, the Temple and the Messiah. However more prevalent destruction was in the history of Israel, the acts of destruction were enshrined in the minor fast days while those of redemption became the joyous proclamations of the Passover and Tabernacles, of Hannukah and Purim. The God of Israel is a redeeming God; this is the only message we are authorized to proclaim, however much it may not seem so to the eyes of non-belief. Should the Holocaust cease to be peripheral to the faith of Israel, should it enter the Holy of Holies and become the dominant voice that Israel hears, it could not but be a demonic voice that it would be hearing. There is no salvation to be extracted from the Holocaust, no faltering Judaism can be revived by it, no new reason for the continuation of the Jewish people can be found in it. If there is hope after the Holocaust, it is because to those who believe, the voices of the prophets speak more loudly than did Hitler, and because the divine promise sweeps over the crematoria and silences the voice of Auschwitz.[77]

This concept of punishment for Israel's sins is vehemently rejected by most contemporary Jewish leaders. Berkovits maintains that the exiles of the children of Israel (including the suffering of

---

[76] Michael Wyschogrod, "Faith and the Holocaust," *Judaism* 20 (Summer 1971): 293.

[77] Ibid., pp. 293-294.

Above: Auschwitz (photo: © AdobeStock)

the Holocaust) are "not God-ordained punishments but man-imposed persecution."[78] To imply that the Holocaust was a God-ordained punishment is to defame the character of God:

> Is it possible that at Auschwitz He [God] rejected Israel… [and] turned away from Israel as a punishment for its sins? To believe this would be a desecration of the Divine Name. No matter what the sins of European Jewry might have been, they were human failings. If the Holocaust was a punishment, it was a thousandfold inhuman. The only crime of man which such punishment might be conceivable would be the Nazi crime of Germany, and even there, one would hesitate to impose it.[79]

Berkovits also maintains that this approach to Israel's sins is a gross exaggeration:

> Looking at the entire course of Jewish history, the idea that all this has befallen us because of our sins is an utterly unwarranted exaggeration. There is suffering because of sins; but that all suffering is due to it is simply not true. The idea that the Jewish martyrology through the ages can be explained as divine judgment is obscene. Nor do we for a single moment entertain the thought

---

[78] Eliezer Berkovits, *God, Man and History: A Jewish Interpretation* (Middle Village, NY: Jonathan David Publishers, 1965), p. 142.

[79] Berkovits, "The Hiding God of History," p. 703.

that what happened to European Jewry in our generation was divine punishment for sins committed by them. It was injustice; injustice countenanced by God.[80]

The Conservative Rabbi Elliot Dorff maintains that the Jewish people were innocent sufferers. Therefore, rather than focus on their punishment, he focuses on God's responsibility for it in particular and for the creation of evil in general. In support of his position, he cites such biblical passages as Isaiah 45:7, Lamentations 3:37-38, and Deuteronomy 32:39, as well as several rabbinic sources.[81] After citing the rabbinic perception of the Roman dominion (A.D. 70) as an act of divine chastening, Rabbi Samuel Karff rejects such an application to the Holocaust. He boldly asserts: "No Jewish theologian of any stature has sought to understand Auschwitz in these terms."[82]

This concept is rejected not only because of its emotionally distasteful Orthodox flavor[83] but also because some have tried to link it with the Christian interpretation that says the Jews were punished because they killed the Messiah. Jewish historian Nora Levin reflects a total rejection of such an idea:

> I think with a shudder, not with reverence or fervent resignation, of the passage in Isaiah 53, passages that have justified centuries of suffering and persecution. Some Orthodox Jewish thinkers today commit the outrage of interpreting such passages and others as God's punishment during the Holocaust for our failure to keep religious law. Recently several ministers at a conference declared that Jews were punished during the Holocaust because they are

---

[80] Berkovits, *Faith after the Holocaust*. p. 94; see also pp. 89-90.

[81] Elliot N. Dorff, "God and the Holocaust," *Judaism* 26 (Winter 1977): 27-34.

[82] Samuel E. Karff, "Aggadah-The Language of Jewish 'God Talk,'" *Judaism* 19 (Spring 1970): 164.

[83] See: Marvin J. Spiegelman, "On the Holocaust and Jewish Education," *Jewish Education* 43 (Fall 1973): 36-37; Jacob B. Agus, "God and the Catastrophe," *Conservative Judaism* 18 (Summer 1964): 14-16.

no longer God's elect. The destruction of the Second Temple, similarly, if read only in the light of Scripture, continues to make Jews victims because of their sinfulness. In the work of a contemporary Christian theologian, a man of great sensitivity and liberality of spirit and intention, we have an example of the dangers of theology undisciplined and unrestrained by other forces in human culture: the death of Jesus is described as having been fore-ordained in order to fulfill God's plan. Jews are described as having been instruments in that fulfillment, as viewed by Christians. Then comes the alarming next step: Jews are again seen as suffering for the sins of mankind and suffering "in order to fulfill God's plan for Gentiles."[84]

Professor of Education at the Hebrew University Ernst Simon laments the sad truth of such an accusation when he says that "you can still hear and read, much too often, that Israel's suffering testifies to the truth of Christianity, as a punishment for the alleged sin that we never acknowledged Jesus as the Messiah."[85]

This accusation compels Michael Brown, a professor at York University in Toronto, to assert that if this kind of God existed, He would not be worthy of faith:

> Some Christians still adhere to the traditional doctrine regarding Jewish suffering and understand the Holocaust as one more manifestation of the wrath of God being visited upon the Jews for their 2000-years-ago sin. One can appreciate the desire of theological conservatives to see all events fitting into classical doctrine. Still, to an outsider, such an explanation seems unacceptable on its own terms. What kind of God would require the degradation, torture, and death of a million Jewish children in the twentieth century as

---

[84] Nora Levin, "The Human in the Holocaust: A Homily," *Sh'ma* 11 (1 May 1981): 99.

[85] Ernst Simon, "The Jews as God's Witness to the World," *Judaism* 15 (Summer 1966): 317.

atonement for the shortsightedness of their ancestors two millennia ago? How can anyone believe in such a deity?[86]

In closing this section, it is appropriate to cite Rabbi Greenberg once again. He has captured the emotional refusal of most Jews to accept the premise that during the Holocaust, the Jewish people were punished because of their sins:

> There are Jews who have sought to assimilate the Holocaust to certain unreconstructed traditional categories, to explain destruction as a visitation for evil. To account for the Holocaust as God's punishment of Israel for its sins is to betray and mock the agony of the victims. Now that they have been cruelly tortured and killed, boiled into soap, their hair made into pillows and their bones into fertilizer, their unknown graves and the very fact of their death denied to them, the theologian would inflict on them the only dignity left: that is, insistence that it was done because of their sins… this is the devil's work. God comforts the afflicted and afflicts the comforted, whereas the devil comforts and comforted and afflicts the afflicted…
>
> Moreover, summon up the principle that no statement should be made that could not be made in the presence of the burning children. On this rock, the traditionalist argument breaks. Tell the children in the pits they are burning for their sins. An honest man—better, a decent man—would spit at such a God rather than accept this rationale if it were true. If this justification is loyalty, then surely treason is the honorable choice. If this were the only choice, then surely God would prefer atheism.[87]

---

[86] Michael S. Brown, "On Crucifying the Jews," *Judaism* 27 (Fall 1978): 477.

[87] Greenberg, "Cloud of Smoke, Pillar of Fire," pp. 25, 34.

Summary of the Traditional Perspective

The following table summarizes the various Jewish positions held in the more traditional religious framework.

The Traditional Perspective	Many of the positions from within more traditional Jewish thought reflect former Talmudic and rabbinic ideas and are still thought to be relevant to this present catastrophe.
The Hidden Purpose	The God of Israel is a rational and purposeful God. Although the Holocaust appears to be without meaning, it must have a purpose even if it is not clearly perceived.
Kiddush Hashem ("Sanctification of the Name")	This rabbinic concept concerns the holiness of martyrdom, which values dying for the Name of God and as His servant. During the Holocaust, it became a duty and a privilege to die for the God of the Jews.
The World to Come	The World to Come will find justice made perfect for the faithful.
The Suffering Servant	The nation of Israel is seen as an innocent sufferer who suffers at the hands of the unrighteous Gentile nations while God Himself suffers along with him.
The Hiding of the Face	God hides His countenance from the sufferer. In his troubles, man seeks God but cannot find Him. The impact of God's silence has had a paralyzing effect on all of contemporary Judaism.
The Price of Redemption	The Holocaust was "the labor pains" of Israel's rebirth as a nation and the price of Israel's redemption.

Loving Punishment by God	The suffering of the Holocaust was God's will in that it reflected His loving discipline for Israel.
Because of Our Sins	God's action is punitive and retributive. Jewish people were innocent sufferers. Therefore, God is responsible for it in particular and for the creation of evil in general.

The Radical Perspective

The radical perspective falls on the opposite end of the spectrum from the traditional perspective. The traditional religious response will not suffice for such a devastating blow as the Holocaust. New and radical approaches must be found, and several Jewish religious leaders offer their own unique perspectives to the field of Holocaust study. Most of their concepts are rejected to one degree or another by the mainstream of Jewish religious thinkers, but their views are another, nevertheless allowed, form of free expression.

An example of the radical challenge is seen in the poem "Holocaust" by Norman Smith, published in *The Jewish Spectator* in 1973:

> When God in a moment of wrath
> Released His torrent of bitterness
> On those he chose to call "The Chosen Ones"
> His fury so blinded Him
> That before His vision cleared
> The fruit of His creation
> Were being scourged
> From the face of the earth
>
> And only the compassion
> Of His blinded faithful

Whose love for Him survived the Holocaust
Kept the heavens
From being torn asunder.[88]

Within the radical response, there are numerous subcategories and perspectives, three of which will be introduced on the following pages: the impotence of God's omnipotence, the breaking of the covenant, and the death of God.

The Impotence of God's Omnipotence

Like many of the past philosophers who wrestled with the problem of evil within a theistic framework, certain Jewish religious leaders deny the omnipotence of God during the Holocaust. In the face of the radical evil of the Holocaust, either an omnipotent God was unloving or a loving God was not omnipotent. Rather than reject the whole covenantal framework upon which Judaism itself is built (i.e., that it is founded upon the loving election of God; cf. Deut. 7:7-8), God as an all-powerful Being is rejected.

Writing from within the context of Conservative Judaism, Rabbi David Wolf Silverman steadfastly maintains that after the Holocaust, one must recognize that God is not all-powerful:

> The Holocaust has… dismissed any easy use of omnipotence as an attribute appropriate to God. After Auschwitz, we can assert with greater force than ever before that an omnipotent God would have to be either sadistic or totally unintelligible. But if God is to be intelligible in some manner and to some extent—and to this I hold firm—then His goodness must be compatible with the existence of evil, and this is only if He is not all-powerful. Only then can we maintain that He is intelligible and good, and there is yet evil in the world… The Holocaust disclosed the

---

[88] Norman Smith, "Holocaust," *The Jewish Spectator* 38 (May 1973): 17.

depths to which man had sunk and the degree to which God withdrew.[89]

Simon Friedeman, addressing himself to this same concept from within Reform Judaism as well as being a survivor himself, presents God as lacking omnipotence because of an evolutionary presupposition. God created the universe but now does not involve Himself in it at all. He doesn't need to. Evolution is carrying on the process for Him:

> God does not interfere in the events on earth *after* creation. Just as the fertilized ovum contains the features and characteristics of the future person, thus the first living cell contained all the physical, mental, and spiritual potentials of present and future men. To assume divine intervention in the evolutionary process through direct action or revelation *initiated* by God would entail defectiveness in creation and doubt in God's omnipotence and omniscience… I cannot conceive of God being capable of performing miracles and refraining from doing it. I could not worship a God capable of preventing the horrors in the Nazi death camps Who did not act.[90]

Levi A. Olan served as President of the Central Conference of American Rabbis and the rabbi of Temple Emanuel in Dallas, TX. Also writing from within the context of Reform Judaism, Olan takes the evolutionary hypothesis a step further by claiming that God Himself is evolving. He is in the process with His evolving world:[91]

---

[89] David Wolf Silverman, "The Holocaust: A Living Force," *Conservative Judaism* 31 (Fall-Winter 1976/77): 24-25.

[90] S. Simon Friedeman, "God in Buchenwald," *The Jewish Spectator* 34 (October 1969): 21.

[91] Olan's view is an example of a concept called "process theology." This theology is founded on the belief that change is the only absolute in the world. Consequently, God is also constantly changing. The Bible categorically refutes process theology. For a biblical

In fact, there is no need for God to be absolute in power to be God. God is better understood as a becoming even as is the universe and man. God struggles against evil and learns to overcome it. Man can help God and God can help man. They are co-workers in the building of the kingdom. Man needs God and God needs man. The tradition does hint at some limitations in God's power. "Everything is in the power of heaven," said the rabbis, "except the fear of heaven."[92]

Professor of Judaic Studies at the University at Albany Jerome Eckstein holds approximately the same position as Olan. God is a God of potentiality, not necessarily of actuality:

> To believe in a finite Deity with potentiality does not necessarily estrange one from the substance of Jewish or Christian faith; the Bible, especially the Jewish Bible, does not prove, or even support, the theologians' stand; and the theologians in fact draw their view from a foreign source—from ancient Greek philosophy.
>
> The Hebrew Bible's language had not evolved sufficiently to express such abstract concepts as actual infinite and potential infinite. When Moses described God's power as "great," "mighty," and "awesome," he was far from calling this force or the Lord himself an actual infinite or absolute. And when Malachi said "the Lord change[s] not" and James, allegedly Jesus' relative, said "with him [God] there is no variation," they did not mean God's plentitude allows him no potentiality for growth; the contexts of their statements reveal that they spoke only of God's steadfastness in loving good and hating evil… Thus the biblical God—whose power, for instance, is actually limited though greater than the universe's, and who develops and requires human help in making

---

evaluation of contemporary process theology, see Norman L. Geisler, "Process Theology," in Stanley N. Gundry and Alan F. Johnson, eds., *Tensions in Contemporary Theology* (Chicago, IL: Moody Press, 1980), pp. 237-284.

[92] Levi A. Olan, "An Organicist View," *Dimensions in American Judaism* 2 (Fall 1967): 27.

goodness prevail—is today a better response to the problem of evil than the God of traditional theologians.[93]

The Breaking of the Covenant

A second perspective within the radical response is that God broke His part of the Mosaic Covenant. He promised that if the Jews would keep their part of the covenant, He would keep His, namely, that He would protect them from their enemies. This certainly was not true during the Holocaust. God turned His back on His covenant people.

Speaking from within Orthodox Judaism, Rabbi Greenberg asserts that a covenant requires a covenant people and that the Holocaust itself, with its destruction of the covenant people, brings into question the very fact of the covenant itself:

> Since there can be no covenant without the covenant people, the fundamental existence of Jews and Judaism is thrown into question by this genocide...
>
> Yet surely it is God who did not keep His share of the covenant in defending His people in this generation. It is the miracle of the people of Israel that they persist in faith. Surely it is they who should be justified.[94]

However, Greenberg also asserts that if the Holocaust revealed God's failure to keep His part of the covenant, the establishment of the State of Israel reaffirmed His recommittal to the covenant:

> If the experience of Auschwitz symbolizes that we are cut off from God and hope, and that the covenant may be destroyed, then the experience of Jerusalem symbolizes that God's promises are faithful and His people live on. Burning children speak of the absence

---

[93] Jerome Eckstein, "The Holocaust and Jewish Theology," *Midstream* 23 (April 1977): 39-40.

[94] Greenberg, "Cloud of Smoke, Pillar of Fire," pp. 8, 33-34.

of all value—human and divine; the rehabilitation of one-half million Holocaust survivors in Israel speaks of the reclamation of tremendous human dignity and value. If Treblinka makes human hope an illusion, then the Western Wall asserts that human dreams are more real than force and facts. Israel's faith in the God of history demands that an unprecedented event of destruction be matched by an unprecedented act of redemption, and this has happened.[95]

This accusatory tone also runs through the many writings and novels of Elie Wiesel. For example, in a symposium on value in the post-Holocaust era, he maintained this very line of thinking:

> The Jewish people entered into a covenant with God. We are to protect His Torah, and He, in turn, assumes responsibility for Israel's presence in the world...
>
> Well, it seems that, for the first time in our history, this very covenant was broken. That is why the Holocaust has terrifying theological implications. Whether we want it or not, because of its sheer dimensions, the event transcends man and involves more than him alone. It can be explained neither with God nor without Him. Everything that happened then and there was linked to finality, to total experience. Everybody concerned was totally committed to his condition: the murderer to his crime, the victim to his fate, the bystander to his indifference. All men became identified with their image, their absolute. They turned into gods.
>
> But then, the covenant was equally revoked with regard to the relationship between Jew and man. For the first time in our history, the Jewish people were totally abandoned. God's failure was matched by man's.[96]

---

[95] Ibid., p. 32.

[96] Emil L. Fackenheim, Elie Wiesel, Steven G. Schwarzschild, "Jewish Values in the Post-Holocaust Future: A Symposium," *Judaism* 16 (Summer 1967): 281-282.

In recalling the destruction of the Jews of Lublin, Poland, the poet Jacob Glatstein graphically depicts this perspective of God breaking His covenant with Israel:

> We received the Torah on Sinai
> and in Lublin we gave it back.
> Dead men don't praise God,
> the Torah was given to the living.
> And just as we all stood together
> at the giving of the Torah,
> so did we all die together at Lublin.[97]

Another survivor, leading a group of survivors on a pilgrimage to the murder camp of Bergen-Belsen in Germany, found it raining in Hannover, the city nearest to the camp. His remark to the group also depicts the idea of God's guilt in the Holocaust: "We have revisited this place of our suffering many times: It always rains. God weeps. He weeps for the sins he has committed against his people Israel."[98]

The Death of God

A third and final perspective from radical Jewish thinkers is that the Holocaust killed God. This is the most radical response thus far demonstrated. The "death-of-God theology" has finally blasted its way into Jewish religious thought. God died during the Holocaust. He can no longer be believed in. An alternate view in the same category is that the traditional God of the fathers died and no longer remains a viable object for one's faith.

---

[97] As quoted in Alvin H. Rosenfeld, *A Double Dying: Reflections on Holocaust Literature* (Bloomington and London: Indiana University Press, 1980), p. 121.

[98] As quoted in Emil L. Fackenheim, *The Jewish Return into History: Reflections in the Age of Auschwitz and a New Jerusalem* (New York, NY: Schocken Books, 1978), p. 125.

By far, the most blatant spokesman for this position is Richard L. Rubenstein. Rubenstein held degrees from the Jewish Theological Seminary and Harvard University but later identified himself with Reform Judaism. He served as a professor of religion at Florida State University. His thinking was steeped in Rabbinic Judaism and secular philosophy, and he steadfastly maintained that after Auschwitz, man began living in the time of the death of God:

> No man can really say that God is dead. How can we know that? Nevertheless, I am compelled to say that we live in the time of the "death of God." ... When I say we live in the time of the death of God, I mean that the thread uniting God and man, heaven and earth, has been broken. We stand in a cold, silent, unfeeling cosmos, unaided by any purposeful power beyond our own resources. After Auschwitz, what else can a Jew say about God?[99]

Although Rubenstein has thrown over the traditional concept of God, he does not believe that Judaism has lost its relevance to modern man. Quite the contrary, having been freed from the traditional mold of deity, Judaism is now ready to meet the needs of modern man:

> Though I believe that a void stands where once we experienced God's presence, I do not think Judaism has lost its meaning or its power. I do not believe that a theistic God is necessary for Jewish religious life... I have suggested that Judaism is the way in which we share the decisive times and crises of life through the traditions of our inherited community. The need for that sharing is not diminished in the time of the death of God. We no longer believe in the God who has the power to annul the tragic necessities of existence; the need religiously to share that existence remains...
>
> Nevertheless, I believe the most adequate theological description of our times is to be found in the assertion that *we live in the*

---

[99] Richard L. Rubenstein, *After Auschwitz: Radical Theology and Contemporary Judaism* (Indianapolis, IN: Bobbs-Merrill, 1966), pp. 151-152.

time of the death of God. The vitality of death of God theology is rooted in the fact that it has faced more openly than any other contemporary theological movement the truth of the divine-human encounter in our times. The truth is that it is totally nonexistent. Those theologies which attempt to find the reality of God's presence in the contemporary world manifest a deep insensitivity to the art, literature, and technology of our times.[100]

If Rubenstein has buried the traditional God of the Bible, if he has put to rest the entire concept of God as a theistic Being, then with what kind of god does he propose to replace Him? He suggests a return to the gods of primordial paganism:

> It is certainly possible to understand God as the primal ground of being out of which we arise and to which we return. I believe such a God is inescapable in the time of the death of God. The God who is the ground of being is not the transcendent, theistic God of the Jewish patriarchal monotheism. Though many still believe in that God, they do so ignoring the questions of God and human freedom and God and human evil. For those who face these issues, the Father-God is a dead God. Even the existentialist leap of faith cannot resurrect this dead God after Auschwitz…
>
> There remains the question of whether the religion of God as the source and ground of being, the God after the death of God, is truly a religion. Can there be a religion without a belief in a theistic, creator God[?] Pagan religions have never celebrated such a God… [I]n the time of the death of God, a mystical paganism which utilizes the historic forms of Jewish religion offers the most promising approach to religion in our times.[101]

It is this kind of paganistic God that Rubenstein insists will liberate the Jewish people and set them upon the self-made security of the nation of Israel:

---

[100] Ibid., pp. 153-154, 245 (emphasis in the original).

[101] Ibid., pp. 237-238, 240.

Death and rebirth are the great moments of religious experience. In the twentieth century the Jewish phoenix has known both: in Germany and eastern Europe, we Jews have tasted the bitterest and the most degrading of deaths. Yet death was not the last word. We do not pity ourselves. Death in Europe was followed by resurrection in our ancestral home. We are free as no men before us have ever been. Having lost everything, we have nothing further to lose and no further fear of loss. Our existence has in truth been a being-unto-death. We have passed beyond all illusion and hope. We have learned in the crisis that we were totally and nakedly alone, that we could expect neither support nor succor from God or from our fellow creatures. No men have known as we have how truly God in His holiness slays those to whom He gives life. This has been a liberating knowledge, at least for the survivors, and all Jews everywhere regard themselves as having escaped by the skin of their teeth, whether they were born in Europe or elsewhere. We have lost all hope and faith. We have also lost all possibility of disappointment. Expecting absolutely nothing from God or man, we rejoice in whatever we receive. We have learned the nakedness of every human pretense. No people has come to know as we have how deeply man is an insubstantial nothingness before the awesome and terrible majesty of the Lord. We accept our nothingness—nay, we even rejoice in it—for in finding our nothingness we have found both ourselves and the God who alone is true substance. We did not ask to be born; we did not ask for our absurd existence in the world; nor have we asked for the fated destiny which has hung above us as Jews. Yet we would not exchange it, nor would we deny it, for when nothing is asked for, nothing is hoped for, nothing is expected; all that we receive is truly grace.[102]

It is obvious that Rubenstein has thrown off all forms of historic and traditional Judaism. He appears to have been emotionally

---

[102] Ibid., pp. 128-129.

traumatized by the stark reality of the Holocaust: "Of one thing I am convinced: more than the bodies of my people went up in smoke at Auschwitz. The God of the covenant died there."[103]

Another spokesman for the death-of-God perspective is the previously mentioned survivor and author, Elie Wiesel. Born in a small town in Romania, he was raised in an intensely Orthodox and Hasidic environment. In 1944, the entire Jewish community was deported by the Nazis. Being but a teenager, Wiesel witnessed and experienced all the horrors of the Birkenau, Auschwitz, Buna, and Buchenwald concentration camps. He is the sole survivor of his entire family. It is not surprising, therefore, that he writes from the existential reality of total depravity and human suffering. In his autobiographical work, *Night*, he vividly describes his deepest feelings upon arriving at his first concentration camps:

> Never shall I forget that night, the first night in camp, which has turned my life into one long night, seven times cursed and seven times sealed. Never shall I forget that smoke. Never shall I forget the little faces of the children, whose bodies I saw turned into wreaths of smoke beneath a silent blue sky.
>
> Never shall I forget those flames which consumed my faith forever.
>
> Never shall I forget that nocturnal silence which deprived me, for all eternity, of the desire to live. Never shall I forget those moments which murdered my God and my soul and turned my dreams to dust. Never shall I forget these things, even if I am condemned to live as long as God Himself. Never.[104]

Later on in *Night*, Wiesel describes the hanging of a young boy in the camp, with its emotional impact upon his life:

---

[103] Richard L. Rubenstein, "Auschwitz and Covenant Theology," *The Christian Century* 86 (May 21, 1969): 718.

[104] Elie Wiesel, *Night*, translated by Stella Rodway (New York, NY: Avon Books, 1960), p. 45.

One day when we came back from work, we saw three gallows rearing up in the assembly place, three black crows. Roll call. SS all round us, machine guns trained: the traditional ceremony. Three victims in chain—and one of them, the little servant, the sad-eyed angel.

The SS seemed more preoccupied, more disturbed than usual. To hang a young boy in front of thousands of spectators was no light matter. The head of the camp read the verdict. All eyes were on the child. He was lividly pale, almost calm, biting his lips. The gallows threw its shadow over him…

The three victims mounted together onto the chairs.

The three necks were placed at the same moments within the nooses.

"Long live liberty!" cried the two adults.

But the child was silent.

"Where is God? Where is He?" someone behind me asked.

At a sign from the head of the camp, the three chairs tipped over.

Total silence throughout the camp. On the horizon, the sun was setting.

"Bare your heads!" yelled the head of the camp. His voice was raucous. We were weeping.

"Cover your heads!"

Gallows in Auschwitz; photo: © AdobeStock.

Then the march past began. The two adults were no longer alive. Their tongues hung swollen, blue-tinged. But the third rope was still moving; being so light, the child was still alive…

For more than half an hour he stayed there, struggling between life and death, dying in slow agony under our eyes. And we had to look him full in the face. He was still alive when I passed in front of him. His tongue was still red, his eyes not yet glazed.

Behind me, I heard the same man asking: "Where is God now?"

And I heard a voice within me answer him: "Where is He? Here He is—He is hanging here on this gallows…"[105]

The U.S. Holocaust scholar and rabbi Michael Berenbaum aptly summarizes the meaning of this particular scene in Wiesel's *Night* and then comments on its existential nature:

---

[105] Ibid., pp. 75-76.

The Perspective of Contemporary Judaism | 65

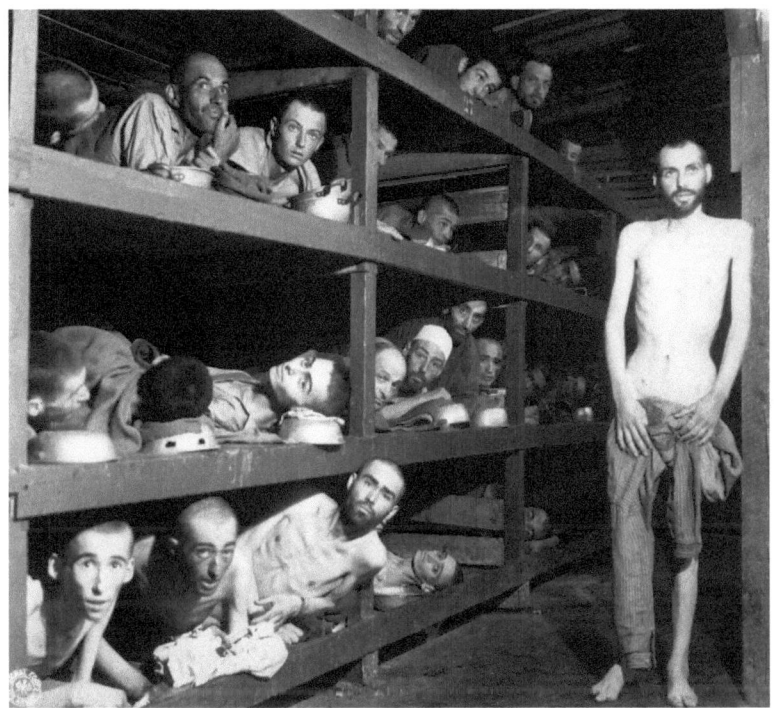

Above: Inmates of the Buchenwald Concentration Camp inside their barracks, a few days after the liberation of the camp by American troops on April 16, 1945. Elie Wiesel is lying in the middle row, seventh from the left (photo: en.wikipedia.org/wiki/Elie_Wiesel).

God dies when the innocent and the young die. The belief in God is killed in the human mind when the slaughter of innocence destroys the credibility of a just world. God is implicated in the death of the innocent, or perhaps God, in his omnipotent impotence, struggles between life and death. Perhaps He too can neither shout nor die. These images should not be taken literally or systematically, but they should be taken evocatively. Wiesel continues a long tradition within Jewish theology of dealing with the images of God in order to satisfy an existential need. His images are suggestive and, as his existential needs change, the character of his images changes.[106]

---

[106] Michael Berenbaum, *The Vision of the Void: Theological Reflections on the Works of Elie Wiesel* (Middletown, CT: Wesleyan University Press, 1979), p. 45.

Pulsating through the hearts and minds of many Jewish religious leaders is this existential need to know that if God hid Himself during the Holocaust, at least He is still alive. An existential alienation from God drives them to the limits of theological absurdity. This is poignantly demonstrated in the works of Arthur Waskow, author, political activist, and rabbi associated with the Jewish Renewal movement:

> So when we look within, at the spiritual heart of Jewishness itself, where God and Torah pulsed new life into the people, we find that empty too. We look within. We find no God within. We sheathe the empty ark in might and toughness. Hitler, we whisper to ourselves—did Hitler win? He killed the whole community of Jews who loved God most. He killed our love of God. Did he kill God, too?[107]

It is no wonder that many of these Jewish leaders have forsaken the biblical view of God and, in His place, have substituted some form of no-God, a non-theistic God, a force rather than a Person. Reform rabbi Harold M. Schulweis is one of many examples of Jewish scholars who represent this line of thinking:

> In our view, no segregated area exists where divinity may not be found. Moral evil and moral good are not supernaturalized. They are both in the same world, where men may be blameworthy or praiseworthy, but divinity is blameless. For divinity is neither person nor omnipotent will. Divinity, by our meaning, designates those energies and activities which sustain and elevate our lives. Such an understanding of divinity requires no justification in the presence of evil.[108]

---

[107] Arthur I. Waskow, *Godwrestling* (New York, NY: Schocken Books, 1978), p. 138.

[108] Harold M. Schulweis, "Suffering and Evil," in Abraham Ezra Millgram, ed., *Great Jewish Ideas*, B'nai B'rith Great Books Series, Vol. 5, p. 218.

Summary of the Radical Perspective

The following table summarizes views found within the radical position.

The Radical Perspective	The traditional religious response will not suffice for such a devastating blow as the Holocaust. New and radical approaches must be found.
The Impotence of God's Omnipotence	In the face of the radical evil of the Holocaust, either an omnipotent God was unloving or a loving God was not omnipotent. God as an all-powerful Being is rejected. God is a God of potentiality, not actuality.
The Breaking of the Covenant	God promised that if the Jews would keep their part of the covenant, He would keep His. He would protect them from their enemies. This certainly was not true during the Holocaust. Hence, God turned His back on His covenant people.
The Death of God	God died during the Holocaust. He can no longer be believed.

The Moderate Perspective

In the vast spectrum between the traditional perspective and the radical perspective fall many other Jewish responses to the Holocaust. These moderate contributions emerge from all three major divisions of Judaism (i.e., Orthodox, Conservative, and Reform).

The following perspectives represent a sample of the cross-section of thought falling within this broad spectrum. In summary form, they are the unanswerable mystery; God suffering with Israel; contending with God; the presence of two histories; dialectical faith; human freedom—human depravity; and Israel must live—the 614th commandment.

The Unanswerable Mystery

The first perspective from the moderate spectrum is that the Holocaust is inexplicable in this life. Like many other severe persecutions of the Jews, the Holocaust cannot be harmonized with a just and loving concept of God, at least by mere human theodicy. Therefore, one must submit to its mystery and respond in faith and silence.

Philosopher Frederick Sontag addresses himself to this Holocaust "mystery":

> Any God who survives the holocaust remains largely unseen on the face of history. If we continue to insist on seeing him there, it can only be during times of triumph, not destruction. A holocaust returns a never to be dispelled sense of mystery to life. And we must be careful about thinking that the depth of mystery in our experience of God "explains" anything. At best it postpones understanding, and at worst it destroys it. The rationalist impulse is to get rid of mystery. But such an attempt assumes that all phenomena have an overt and rational explanation… Of course, "mystery" simply means that a final explanation now exceeds our powers, whereas the rationalist posture is that nothing exceeds the grasp of a modern scientifically based reason. After the holocaust, we are forced to assert in opposition: To understand how God operates is something one must be God to fathom fully.[109]

---

[109] Frederick Sontag, "The Holocaust God," *Encounter* 42 (2) (Spring 1981): 165-166.

Once again, Wiesel has some pertinent words on the Holocaust as an unanswerable mystery. He says that only the survivors themselves can really enter into the meaning of the Holocaust—and even then, partially: "The survivors, more realistic if not more honest, are aware of the fact that God's presence at [the extermination camps] Treblinka or Maidanek—or, for that matter, his absence—poses a problem which will remain forever insoluble… The holocaust defies reference, analogy."[110]

Another forceful voice on the mystery of God's silence is the Austrian-Israeli philosopher Martin Buber. He speaks of the "eclipse" of God as something that has stepped between God and man. The Holocaust has eclipsed the God of heaven. He is still there, but He is mysteriously unseen:

> What is it that we mean when we speak of an eclipse of God which is even now taking place? Through this metaphor we make the tremendous assumption that we can glance up to God with our "mind's eye," or rather being's eye, as with our bodily eye to the sun, and that something can step between our existence and His as between the earth and the sun. That this glance of the being exists, wholly unillusory, yielding no images yet first making possible all images, no other court in the world attests than that of faith. It is not

Above: Stamp from 1978 with the image of the Jewish philosopher Martin Buber (photo: german-stamps.org).

---

[110] Elie Wiesel, *Legends of Our Time* (New York, NY: Avon Books, 1968), pp. 19-20; cf. 217-224.

to be proved; it is only to be experienced; man has experienced it. And that other, that which steps in between, one also experiences, to-day... Something is taking place in the depths that as yet needs no name. Tomorrow even it may happen that it will be beckoned to from the heights, across the heads of the earthy archons. The eclipse of the light of God is no extinction; even tomorrow that which has stepped in between may give way.[111]

This concept of the mysterious eclipse of God certainly does not remove all of the questions or solve all of the problems. But, as Rabbi Byron L. Sherwin reiterates, it does point to a future explanation from God:

> The eclipse of God idea is a response but is not a solution to Auschwitz and the theological problems it engenders. The ways of God remain unjustified. There is no theodicy. God remains in darkness, in hiding, eclipsed. However, as the Baal Shem [Israel ben Eliezer Baal Shem Tov, founder and first leader of Hasidism] taught, once man begins to apprehend that God is in hiding, He is no longer truly eclipsed.
>
> We still await God's explanation of why even one innocent child had to perish at Auschwitz. What is often forgotten, however, is that God may be asking man the identical question and awaiting his response.[112]

God Suffering with Israel

The second perspective from the moderate spectrum is that the Holocaust is only fathomable when one sees God Himself suffering for and with the nation of Israel. The aforementioned Rabbi Heschel aptly summarizes the biblical data on this theme:

---

[111] Martin Buber, *Eclipse of God: Studies in the Relation between Religion and Philosophy*, (New York, NY: Harper & Row, 1952), pp. 127, 129.

[112] Byron L. Sherwin, "The Impotence of Explanation and the European Holocaust," *Tradition: A Journal of Orthodox Thought* 12 (Winter – Spring 1972): 106.

> The central problem in the Bible is not God, but man. The Bible is a book about man. Rather than man's book about God. And the great problem is how to answer, to respond to the human situation.
>
> God is the meaning beyond absurdity. Wherever I go, I encounter absurdity.
>
> You see, there is an old idea in Judaism found in the Bible, strongly developed by the rabbis and very little known. And that is that God suffers when man suffers.[113]

Rabbi Arthur Lelyveld identifies a significant distinction between the Babylonian Exile and the Holocaust: "While I cannot say that God 'willed' Auschwitz, I can say that God 'wept' over Auschwitz."[114] It is the tears of God that demonstrate His suffering with the Jewish people.

Heschel maintains that this notion of God's suffering alongside Israel is common among the Jewish prophets, who perceived God's overwhelming presence in the suffering of their beloved nation. The fact that they knew of God's intimate relationship with Israel, as well as the world, gave them their prophetic consciousness:

> To the prophet... God does not reveal himself in an abstract absoluteness, but in a specific and unique way—in a personal and *intimate* relation to the world. God does not simply command and expect obedience; he is also moved and affected by what happens in the world and he *reacts* accordingly. Events and human actions arouse in Him joy or sorrow, pleasure or wrath. He is not conceived as judging facts so to speak "objectively," in detached impassivity. He reacts in an intimate and subjective manner, and

---

[113] Abraham Joshua Heschel, "Reflections on Being a Jew," in Nahum N. Glatzer, ed., *Modern Jewish Thoughts: A Source Reader* (New York, NY: Schocken Books, 1977), pp. 204-205.

[114] Arthur J. Lelyveld, *Atheism Is Dead* (Cleveland, Ohio: World Publishing Co., 1958), p. 181.

thus determines the value of events. Quite obviously in the biblical view man's deeds can move Him, affect Him, grieve Him, or, on the other hand, gladden and please Him. This notion that God can be intimately affected, that he possesses not merely intelligence and will, but also feeling and *pathos*, basically defines the prophetic consciousness of God.[115]

Elsewhere, Heschel attributes the suffering of Israel and the grieving of God to the fact that history is the place where God and His purpose are defied:

> Israel's suffering is God's grief ... It is God's involvement in the suffering of man... that explains this particular concern for the downtrodden and contrite (cf. [Isaiah] 57:15) ... The prophets never taught that God and history are one, or that whatever happens below reflects the will of God above. Their vision is of man defying God, and God seeking man to reconcile with Him.
>
> History is where God is defied, where justice suffers defeats. God's purpose is neither clearly apparent nor translatable into rational categories of order and design. There are only moments in which it is revealed.
>
> God's power in history does not endure as a process; it occurs at extraordinary events. There is a divine involvement and concern, involvement in what is done, for that which is. Even where His power is absent, His concern is present.
>
> There was a moment when God looked at the universe made by Him and said: "It is good." But there was no moment in which God could have looked at history made by man and said: "It is good."[116]

This concept has a direct bearing on the suffering of the Holocaust. Either God was there or He was not there; either He was

---

[115] Abraham J. Heschel, "The Divine Pathos: The Basic Category of Prophetic Theology," *Judaism* 2 (January 1953): 61.

[116] Abraham Joshua Heschel, *The Prophets*, 2 vols. (New York, NY: Farrar, Straus and Giroux, 1973), Vol. 1, pp. 151, 168.

present or He was absent. That God was there in the camps, suffering with the sufferers, is graphically espoused by Rabbi Reuven (Robert Alan) Hammer, former dean of the Jerusalem branch of the Jewish Theological Seminary of America:

> Evil drives God from the world. The suffering of the enslaved causes Him to suffer with them and to be with them... If one could speak of God in Egyptian slavery and Babylonian exile, one can also speak of Him—indeed one *must* speak of Him—in the agony of the Holocaust. He is in the camps, He is with the skeletons behind the barbed wire, He is in the selection at the train siding, He is in the gas chambers, the cold showers of death. He is herded with the naked into those bleak rooms and is there amid the shrieks of death and the clawing fingers. And He is in the ovens and the smoke of the chimneys. He is with His people and not with their tormentors. And only when they were liberated was He liberated. The mystery remains a mystery, but the place of God with the sufferers is clear and established.[117]

Contending with God

The third perspective from the moderate spectrum is that, in the midst of the deepest suffering, the Jew is to contend with God. It is his responsibility to argue his case with the Almighty. The Jewish sufferer is never to be a passive participant in his plight. He must be an active agent with the God who has brought such suffering into his life. Rabbi Morris Shapiro, a Holocaust survivor, maintains that "to challenge God is within our tradition."[118] This idea is certainly true, as can be seen in the examples of the following biblical characters who challenged God over differing but important matters: Abraham (Gen. 18), Moses (Exod. 5; 32), Moses

---

[117] Robert Alan Hammer, "The God of Suffering," *Conservative Judaism* 31 (Fall–Winter 1976/77): 40-41.

[118] Morris Shapiro, "For Yom Hashoah," *Conservative Judaism* 28 (Spring 1974): 57-58.

and Aaron together (Num. 16), Job (Job 13), David (Ps. 10; 13), the sons of Korah (Ps. 42; 44), Ethan the Ezrahite (Ps. 89), Jeremiah (Jer. 12; Lam. 3), and Habakkuk (Hab. 1). In fact, the innocent suffering of Job has become one of the favorite biblical paradigms of the Holocaust. It is no wonder that the rabbis followed the biblical pattern as well.

To contend with God is to blast away all personal indifference. Arguing with God is permitted, but apathy never is. Wiesel notes:

Above: *Job en Prierè* ("Job Praying"), 1960; painting by Marc Chagall (1887–1985). Chagall was a pioneer of modernism and one of the most famous Jewish artists in history. He took up many biblical themes in his paintings, but also dealt with the evil of the Holocaust (photo: originalgrafik.de).

> For a Jew to believe in God is good. For a Jew to protest against God is still good. But simply to ignore God, that is not good. Anger, yes. Protest, yes. Affirmation, yes. But indifference to God, no. You can be a Jew with God; you can be a Jew against God; but not without God.[119]

Wiesel also affirms that any genuine protest against God must come from within the covenant, not from without: "I believe that God *is* part of our experience. The Jew, in my view, may rise

---

[119] As quoted in Alice L. Eckardt, "Rebel Against God," *Face to Face: An Interreligious Bulletin [Special Issue: "Building a Moral Society: Aspects of Elie Wiesel's Work"]* 6 (Spring 1979): 18.

against God, provided he remains within God."[120] In giving a young Jew his personal counsel, Wiesel maintains this same posture:

> The agony of the believer equals the bewilderment of the non-believer. If God is an answer, it must be the wrong answer. There is no answer. If with the holocaust God has chosen to question man, man is left to answer with a quest having God as object. The interrogation is two-fold, and it is up to you to claim it as your own and link it to the actions it calls forth.
>
> But I repeat: we are talking about a double, a two-way, interrogation. It must not be divided. The question man poses to God may be the same God poses to man. Nevertheless, it is man who must live—and formulate—it. In so doing, he challenges God, which is permissible, indeed required. He who says no to God is not necessarily a renegade[;] everything depends on the way he says it, and why. One can say anything as long as it is for man, not against him, as long as one remains inside the covenant; only if you repudiate and judge your people from the outside, will you become a renegade.[121]

Wiesel insists that, after the Holocaust, the Jew must go on as a Jew, no matter the difficulty or the pain: "To be a Jew is to have all the reasons in the world not to have faith in language, in singing, in prayers, and in God, but *to go on telling the tale, to go on carrying on the dialogue*, and to have my own silent prayers and quarrels with God."[122]

---

[120] As quoted in Fackenheim, "Jewish Values in the post-Holocaust Future: A Symposium," pp. 298-299.

[121] Elie Wiesel, *One Generation After*, translated by Lily Edelman and Elie Wiesel (New York, NY: Random House, 1965), pp. 166-167.

[122] Elie Wiesel, "Talking and Writing and Keeping Silent," in Franklin H. Littell and Hubert G. Locke, eds., *The German Church Struggle and the Holocaust* (Detroit, MI: Wayne State University Press, 1974), p. 277 (emphasis in the original).

In summary, the Holocaust requires all faithful Jews to follow in the steps of their forefathers—to question, to contend with, to challenge the God of suffering, even as Fackenheim insists, "the Jew of the generation of Auschwitz [is] required to do what, since Abraham, Jeremiah, and Job, Jews have always done in times of darkness—contend with the silent God, and bear witness to Him by this very contention."[123]

The Presence of Two Histories

The fourth perspective from the moderate spectrum is that Jewish suffering in general and the Holocaust in particular demonstrate the presence of two histories. These histories develop side by side and are in conflict through the ages. One is the history of the nations, the other of Israel. Berkovits maintains that this is the only way to understand the Holocaust, by setting it in its historical dilemma:

> It would seem to us that there are two histories: one, that of the nations and the other, that of Israel. The history of the nations is self-explanatory. It is naturalistic history, explainable in terms of power and economics. It is exactly on those terms that the history of Israel remains a sealed secret: it defies that kind of interpretation. The history of Israel alone is not self-explanatory; it testifies to a supra-natural dimension jutting into history. Now, if the two could have been neatly divided and separated from each other, things might have worked out quite nicely. There would not have been either antisemitism or pogroms, either ghettos or crematoria. But unavoidably, both histories take place in the same time dimension and occupy the same space; together they form the history of mankind. Of necessity, the two histories interpenetrate. Thus, in the naturalistic realm occasionally the Voice is heard and

---

[123] Emil L. Fackenheim, *Quest for Past and Future: Essays in Jewish Theology* (Boston, MA: Beacon Press, 1970), p. 315.

a glimpse is gained of the presence of the supra-natural in this world. On the other hand, the wild unbridled forces of the naturalistic realm ever so often invade—and wreak havoc in—the this-worldly domain in which sustenance of meaning and purpose is drawn from the supra-natural dimension.[124]

This contrast between secular history (i.e., of the nations) and sacred history (i.e., of Israel) has proven to be a baffling puzzle to most historians. The Finnish American Jewish historian Max Isaac Dimont satirically comments on this phenomenon:

> Since the history of the Jews did not fit into either Spengler's or Toynbee's system, Spengler ignored them and Toynbee reduced them to an occasional footnote, describing the Jews as fossils of history. Yet, if both Spengler and Toynbee had been less blinded by prejudice and misconceptions about Jewish history, they could well have fitted it within the framework of their philosophies.[125]

Sociologist Carl Mayer is forced to draw the same conclusion. The people of Israel do not fit into any of the normal canons of historiography:

> The Jewish people represent a sociologically unique phenomenon and defy all attempts at general definition… [T]he phenomenon [of Jewish existence] does not fit into any of the usual patterns—idealistic or positivistic—by which we try to read the pages of history.[126]

The philosopher Nicholas Berdyaev, who at one point adhered to a Marxist philosophy of history, echoes the same idea:

---

[124] Berkovits, *Faith after the Holocaust*, pp. 111-112.

[125] Max I. Dimont, *Jews, God and History* (New York, NY: The New American Library, 1962), p. 20.

[126] Carl Mayer, "Religious and Political Aspects of Anti-Semitism," in Isacque Graeber and Steuart Henderson Britt, eds., *Jews in a Gentile World: The Problem of Anti-Semitism* (New York, NY: The Macmillan Company, 1942), pp. 312, 316.

> I remember how the materialist[ic] interpretation of history, when I attempted in my youth to verify it by applying it to the destinies of peoples, broke down in the case of the Jews, where destiny seemed absolutely inexplicable from the materialistic standpoint. And, indeed, according to the materialistic and positivist criterion, this people ought long ago to have perished. Its survival is a mysterious and wonderful phenomenon demonstrating that the life of this people is governed by a special predetermination, transcending the processes of adaptation expounded by the materialistic interpretation of history. The survival of the Jews, their resistance to destruction, their endurance under absolutely peculiar conditions and the fateful role played by them in history; all these point to the particular and mysterious foundations of their destiny.[127]

Berkovits goes on to explain that since most Jews are not fully aware of these two histories and the conflict that ensues between them, there is much confusion on the role of the Holocaust:

> Jews are confused in our times because they imagine that the problem of Jewish faith arises from the conflict between Jewish teaching and Jewish or general historical experience. In fact, the conflict takes place between two histories. There are two realms: the realm of the Is and that of the Ought. The history of the nations is enacted mainly in the realm of the Is. It is naturalistic history, essentially power history. The history of Israel belongs chiefly into the realm of the Ought, it is faith history, faith that what ought to be, what ought to determine and guide human life, should be and will be. Faith history is at cross-purposes with the power history, but history it is. As long as Israel lives the Ought holds on to reality be it only by the skin of its teeth. As long as this is the case, the Ought has proved its vitality as a this-worldly possibility; it has found admittance into the realm of the Is. As

---

[127] Nicolas A. Berdyaev, *The Meaning of History*, trans. by Goerge Reavey (London, England: Centenary Press, 1936), pp. 86-87.

long as Israel is, the Ought to [*sic*], is; the Supernatural has acquired a footing in the Natural. As long as this is so there is hope for both—for there is hope for the ultimate merger of the two realms, when the Ought will be fully real and the real will be convincingly identified as the life which is the Good. In the meantime the conflict obtains, not between ideas and philosophies, which is easily bearable, but between fact and fact; between the powerful reality of the Is and the meaningful and mysterious reality of the Ought. Since it is a conflict between fact and fact, history and history, reality and reality, the conflict is clash, a battle accompanied by untold human suffering.[128]

Rabbi Ignaz Maybaum, speaking out of the Reform tradition, maintains that this concept of two histories must be taken a step further. It is not only that these histories develop side by side but also that Israel's innocent suffering at the hands of the nations is God's way of driving the Gentile world to repentance—their obvious guilt is made manifest through the innocent suffering of Israel. In other words, each holocaust of the Jews brings progress into the world, a progress that leads men back to God:

> Jews are non-Christians; in this gentile world in which they are bidden by God to live as a dispersed people, Jews have a history to which the Servant-of-God texts of the Book of Isaiah provide the pattern. In Auschwitz, ... Jews suffered vicarious death for the sins of mankind. It says in the liturgy of the Synagogue in reference to the first and second *churban* ["destruction," referring to the destruction of the First Temple in 586 B.C. and of the Second Temple in A.D. 70], albeit centuries after the event: "because of our sins." After Auschwitz Jews need not say so. Can any martyr be a more innocent sin-offering than those murdered in Auschwitz! The millions who died in Auschwitz died "because of the

---

[128] Berkovits, *Faith after the Holocaust*, p. 112.

Above: Ignaz Maybaum's *Stolperstein* ("stumbling stone") can be found in Frankfurt, Germany, where Maybaum served as a rabbi from 1928 to 1936. According to the inscription on the *Stolperstein*, Maybaum fled to England in 1939. The German term "überlebt" refers to his survival of the Holocaust (photo: commons.wikimedia.org).

sins of others." Jews and non-Jews died in Auschwitz, but the Jew hatred which Hitler inherited from the medieval Church made Auschwitz the twentieth century Calvary of the Jewish people… The Golgotha of modern mankind is Auschwitz. The cross, the Roman gallows, was replaced by the gas chamber. The gentiles, it seems, must first be terrified by the blood of the sacrificed scapegoat to have the mercy of God revealed to them and become converted, become baptized gentiles, become Christians.[129]

---

[129] Ignaz Maybaum, *The Face of God after Auschwitz* (Amsterdam, Netherlands: Polak & Van Gennep Ltd. Publishers, 1965), pp. 35-36.

In other words, the catastrophe of the Holocaust is progress through sacrifice—the sacrifice of the innocent scapegoat of Israel brought the anti-Semitism of the Middle Ages to a close.[130] The Jew now lives in a purified world, not perfect yet but still progressing, even at the awesome cost of his own precious life and that of his children.

Dialectical Faith

The fifth perspective from the moderate spectrum is that Judaism must now learn to live within a dialectical faith, a faith that is stretched into theological tension. The Holocaust has cast all of Judaism into monumental tension, a tension caused by the God of the covenant, who supposedly did not keep His part of the covenant. This is a tension that most Jewish religious leaders cannot tolerate. They, therefore, try to alleviate the tension, either by affirming the God of the covenant or by denying Him in some way or another. However, some recognize the tension as a valid religious stress in contemporary Judaism. They feel that, in all theological integrity, the tension cannot be cut. There must remain an alternating rhythm between light and darkness, nihilism and redemption. After Auschwitz, an untroubled, serene faith in God as the Lord of history no longer seems possible. Jews today must live with a troubled theism.

Rabbi Greenberg affirms this dialectic of the Holocaust by speaking of "moment faiths":

> Faith is living life in the presence of the Redeemer, even when the world is unredeemed. After Auschwitz, faith means there are times when faith is overcome… We now have to speak of "moment faiths," moments when Redeemer and vision of redemption

---

[130] Ibid., pp. 32-35, 62-63.

are present, interspersed with times when the flames and smoke of the burning children blot out faith—though it flickers again…

This ends the easy dichotomy of atheist/theist, the confusion of faith with doctrine or demonstration. It makes clear that faith is a life response of the whole person to the Presence in life and history. Like life, this response ebbs and flows. The difference between the skeptic and the believer is frequency of faith, and not of certitude of position. The rejection of the unbeliever by the believer is literally the denial or attempted suppression of what is within oneself. The ability to live with moment faith is the ability to live with pluralism and without the self-flattering, ethnocentric solutions which warp religion, or make it a source of hatred for the other.[131]

Greenberg maintains that even though the establishment of the State of Israel is a redeeming act of God (perhaps *the* redeeming act of modern Judaism), the dialectic must still remain:

But if Israel is so redeeming, why then must faith be "moment faith," and why should the experience of nothingness ever dominate?

The answer is that faith is living in the presence of the Redeemer, and in the moment of utter chaos, of genocide, one does not live in His presence. One must be faithful to the reality of the nothingness. Faith is a moment truth, but there are moments when it is not true. This is certainly demonstrable in dialectical truths, when invoking the truth at the wrong moment is a lie. To let Auschwitz overwhelm Jerusalem is to lie (i.e., to speak a truth out of its appropriate moment); and to let Jerusalem deny Auschwitz is to lie for the same reason.[132]

The American philosopher and leader in Reform Judaism, Eugene Borowitz, takes this Holocaust dialectic a step further and

---

[131] Greenberg, "Cloud of Smoke, Pillar of Fire," p. 27.

[132] Ibid., p. 33.

speaks of a "covenant dialectic." God is active in history in general and in Israel's history in particular because of His covenant with the Jewish people. In this covenant relationship, God takes the responsibility, among other things, to save His people. He will act in history on their behalf. Yet this does not mean that history is without a dialectic sense of action. Borowitz explains that although God has His part in the covenant, so does Israel:

> What is critical from the point of view of the modern theological problematic [i.e., how man, in particular Judaism, can still maintain hope after the Holocaust] is the dialectic sense of action under the Covenant. Because God is expected to act does not mean that man may now do nothing and simply wait. The Hebrews must walk themselves out of Egypt, though they know they were borne on eagles' wings. The Hebrew Judges and kings must lead their armies into battle, even though they have been told that the Lord will fight for them. To be sure, God occasionally takes quite independent action in the form of a miracle. That is his free right as sovereign Lord. Yet the law forbids testing him in this regard, and waiting for his help therefore does not mean giving up trust in what men must yet do. Only when everything has been done does one wait for a miracle.[133]

In other words, Israel must never just wait passively on the Lord, as did the religious Jews slaughtered in the Holocaust. Instead, the nation must actively fight, resist, and endure—and then trust in God. This is the only guarantee of Jewish survival in the post-Holocaust era. It is the only assurance that another Holocaust will never devour the Jews again.

---

[133] Eugene B. Borowitz, *How Can a Jew Speak of Faith Today?* (Philadelphia, PA: The Westminster Press, 1969), p. 43.

Human Freedom—Human Depravity

The sixth perspective from the moderate spectrum is both a reaffirmation and a reappraisal. After the Holocaust, Judaism reaffirms its belief in the moral freedom of man, a freedom that gives man the choice of committing such an evil as the slaughter of six million Jews. Rabbi Jack Bemporad states this quite clearly: "Judaism affirms that man has a real choice and is responsible for that choice; it affirms that his choice makes a difference for good or for ill to man himself and to the universe in which man lives."[134] Rabbi Joseph Telushkin and the Jewish radio host and political commentator Dennis Prager affirm the same concept and place it within the context of the Holocaust:

> God did not build Auschwitz and its crematoria. Men did. Man, not God, is responsible for the Holocaust. Judaism posits that people have freedom of choice. Perhaps we would prefer that people had been created as robots who could do only good rather than as human beings who can also choose evil. But this is impossible; only where there exists the possibility of evil does there exist the possibility of good.[135]

However, with this reaffirmation of man's moral freedom has also come a reappraisal of the degree of evil to which man can go in his moral choices. Judaism has traditionally rejected the concept of original sin and total depravity. The conservative rabbi Robert Gordis makes this point quite clear:

> At the very outset, it must be emphasized that normative Judaism never maintained the view that man's nature is innately evil. Nor

---

[134] Jack Bemporad, "Toward a New Jewish Theology," *American Judaism* 14 (Winter 1964–65): 9, 50.

[135] Dennis Prager and Joseph Telushkin, *Nine Questions People Ask About Judaism* (New York, NY: Touchstone Edition published by Simon & Schuster, 1986), p. 35.

did it seek to buttress it by the teaching that Adam's sin of disobedience in the Garden of Eden placed a hereditary and unavoidable taint upon all his descendants. No such idea is expressed or implied anywhere in the Hebrew Bible. Thus the sin of Cain, like Lamech's exploits (Gen. 4:23) or the building of the Tower of Babel is not attributed to Adam's Fall in the Garden of Eden. On the contrary, the basic Hebrew standpoint is expressed in the admonition to Cain that sin always lies in wait for man, but that he can rule over it (Gen. 4:7).[136]

Although Judaism has traditionally rejected the doctrines of original sin and total depravity, the Jewish sages have traditionally held that man is born with two impulses or inclinations: a good impulse (*yetzer hatov*) and an evil impulse (*yetzer hara*). The direction of a man's life is determined by which impulse he chooses to obey. However, while not denying this basic twofold impulse, Judaism has become much more skeptical of man's so-called goodness. The Holocaust has driven a deep wedge into the Jews' post-Enlightenment optimism. Following the great "Age of Reason," Judaism blossomed forth into its own form of Enlightenment, called the *Haskalah* (Hebrew for "Enlightenment"). This movement originated in central Europe in the 18th century. It basically encouraged Jews steeped in exclusively religious studies to broaden their knowledge of the world through secular studies. It opposed the exclusive dependence on the Talmud and the Bible as suitable subjects for study and sought to bring the fruits of the new European emancipation to the Jewish masses. Its proudest flower was the Reform movement within Judaism, which sprang up in Germany in the early 19th century. Man in general, and Judaism in particular, had come of age. The dark ages had happily passed—

---

[136] Robert Gordis, "The Nature of Man in the Judeo-Christian Tradition," *Judaism: A Quarterly Journal of Jewish Life and Thought* 2 (April 1953): 103.

or so they thought. The Holocaust proved to be the downfall of this kind of enthusiasm, at least for many Jewish religious leaders.

Rabbi Daniel Polish aptly summarizes the death of such optimism:

> As a result of the *Shoah*, some ideas of recent generations have been repudiated altogether. Jewish thought since the emancipation reflected the optimism of the general intellectual climate. A mood prevailed which affirmed human nobility. Reason was celebrated, and with it a sense that human moderation and understanding would carry the day for the cause of virtue. Mankind, it was felt, had virtually approached the limits of its perfectibility. Pockets of corruption may have persisted, it was believed, but they would be quickly overcome by the forces of right. Humanity shines less radiant now than to those teachers of hope, many of whom, themselves, perished in the cataclysm. Our eyes have been seared by the flames of hell. Whether they see more clearly for that, or suffer a painful stigmatism, we cannot say. But to us, humanity appears less noble and less the proper object of veneration. We see the human spirit as capable of base depravity as of elevation. We see human actions as readily responsive to the impulse for evil as to the good.[137]

Borowitz says that "it was no longer possible to make the goodness of man the cornerstone of Jewish faith."[138]

In light of the Holocaust, Sontag insists:

> We must abandon any idea of "progress," or notion of the gradual uplift of humanity in modern times, that moves along a scale of increased sophistication. We now realize that horror comes from

---

[137] Daniel F. Polish, "Witnessing God after Auschwitz," in Helga Croner and Leon Klenicki, eds., *Issues in the Jewish-Christian Dialogue: Jewish Perspectives on Covenant, Mission and Witness* (New York, NY: Paulist Press, 1979), p. 136.

[138] Borowitz, *How Can a Jew Speak of Faith Today?*, p. 51.

the intellectually advanced as well as from the primitive. Destruction knows no time or place. It is as much at home in universities as in primitive villages.[139]

Shapiro insists that the Holocaust has taught mankind one lesson: "Every member of *homo sapiens*, if not humanized, is a potential Eichmann."[140] Prager and Telushkin claim that the millions of murdered victims of modern-day Nazis and Communists make belief in man and his goodness impossible:

> *The Holocaust may make faith in God difficult; but it makes faith in man impossible.* Along with the six million Jews, and tens of millions of others murdered by the Nazis and Communists, we must bury the doctrine which enabled Communism and Nazism to rise: the belief that man is the highest being. After Auschwitz…, we have two choices: belief in man under God or belief in nothing.[141]

One of the most sobering realizations in contemporary Judaism has been the knowledge that the nation that perpetrated the murder of six million Jews was the most enlightened country of its day. How could Germany, with all of its intellectual heritage and prestige, commit so heinous a crime? Berenbaum laments this terrible, but nevertheless true, fact:

> Why is the Holocaust an unrelenting event? The Holocaust, by its scope, nature, and magnitude transforms our understanding of human culture and human existence. An unspoken premise of the advocates of culture and education is that the refinements of culture and learning somehow make us into better people and intensify our moral worth. Yet the Holocaust was perpetrated not by the least cultured and least sophisticated of nations but by the

---

[139] Sontag, "The Holocaust God," p. 163.

[140] Shapiro, "For Yom Hashoah," p. 59.

[141] Prager and Telushkin, *The Nine Questions People Ask About Judaism*, p. 35 (emphasis in the original).

most cultured and most advanced of societies. Furthermore, the elements within that society that proved capable of perpetrating the evils were not the least cultured, but came from all spectrums of society including philosophers and scientists, musicians and engineers, lawyers and ministers, artists and intellectuals. No segment of German society proved immune... We see that people could love good music and kill young children. They could be admirable husbands and concerned fathers yet spend their days in constant contact with death and destruction. Human society can be organized and given meaning in such a way that the enterprise of death becomes triumphant. All this is possible in the twentieth century with technology facilitating the process.[142]

Wiesel also finds it almost unbelievable that German refinement could be so thoroughly mixed with such inhuman brutality:

If the Holocaust proved anything, it is that it is possible for a person both to love poems and kill children; many Germans cried when listening to Mozart, when playing Haydn, when quoting Goethe and Schiller—but remained quite unemotional and casual when torturing and shooting children. Their act had no effect on their spirit; the idea had no bearing on the source of inspiration.

Heidegger served as Chancellor of the Freiburg University under the Nazis. Karl Orff, the composer, was Goebbels' favorite musician. As for [Herbert] von Karajan, he did not lose his talent when conducting in Berlin and elsewhere, wearing a Nazi-uniform.

Something then must be wrong not only with their concept of evil, but with man's as well.[143]

This perplexing problem continues to fester in the heart of Wiesel: Something must be deeply wrong within the human

---

[142] Michael Berenbaum, "Teach It to Your Children," *Sh'ma: A Journal of Jewish Ideas* 11 (1 May 1981): 100-101.

[143] As quoted in Fackenheim, "Jewish Values in the Post-Holocaust Future: A Symposium," p. 282.

spirit. How could such a violent and brutal massacre have taken place in this modern, sophisticated age?

> How is it possible that the same civilization that produced Goethe, Bach, Voltaire, and Rousseau could also have produced such dehumanization of man. Something must be wrong with man himself and with man's vision of himself, and something must be wrong with culture if Germans could quote Schiller and Fichte at the same time they were killing Jews. Something must be wrong with books and language if people who write so impressively and who play music so artistically could become allies of non-human death. And something must be wrong with us, as well. Something must be wrong with us if during those years of the Third Reich all movements of the spirit failed. Communism failed. Rationalism failed. And religion failed. Evil's conquest was easy, too easy.[144]

The brutal suffering inflicted upon the Jewish people (as well as others) by the German Nazi party is almost beyond human language to describe. Consequently, Rabbi Bernard Bamberger insists that most theologians have grossly underestimated man's capacity for evil:

> What Auschwitz teaches, if it teaches anything, is that we have underestimated man's capacity for evil. We have too often assumed that men are guided by self-interest, and that their evil deeds are the result of a misguided urge to protect or aggrandize themselves. We have not recognized that men may be attracted to evil because it is evil, may even embrace it in a mad ecstasy. But our failure to take this fact into account does not mean that it never had been known. An attentive reading of the Bible makes

---

[144] Elie Wiesel, "Telling the Tale," *Dimensions in American Judaism* 2 (Spring 1968): 10.

plain the truth that moral evil is sometimes more than mere deficiency; it can be a dynamic, demonic force in human life.[145]

In summary, all of the naked allusions about the refined nature of man have been stripped away by the Holocaust. As the Israeli diplomat and scholar of the Arabic and Hebrew languages Abba Eban reiterates, all of the bright assumptions about man are gone: "Until the Nazi Holocaust there was an innocent assumption that no man, however depraved, can stand unmoved before the innocence and fragility of childhood. The human race can no longer allow itself even this consolation."[146]

Once again, it is Wiesel who dramatically points out that since the Holocaust, all of humanity has been changed:

> After Auschwitz, the human condition is no longer the same. After Treblinka, nothing will ever be the same. The Event has altered man's perception and changed his relationship to God, to his fellow man and to himself. The unthinkable has become real. After Belsen everything seems possible.[147]

The last voice to be heard in this section on human freedom and human depravity is that of Israeli psychologist and genocide scholar Israel Charny. Charny focuses on the one vital lesson of the Holocaust, a lesson aimed at every living "modern" Jew: "We ourselves must come to terms with the horrible violence that has been done to us as a mirror of the violence that lurks within us too."[148]

---

[145] Bernard J. Bamberger, *The Search for Jewish Theology* (New York, NY: Behrman House, 1978), p. 35.

[146] Abba Eban, *My People: The Story of the Jews* (New York, NY: Behrman House, 1968), p. 415.

[147] Elie Wiesel, *Report to the President – President's Commission on the Holocaust* (Washington, D.C.: U.S. Govt. Print. Off., 1979), p. 31.

[148] Israel W. Charny, "Teaching the Violence of the Holocaust," *Jewish Education* 38 (March 1968): 65.

Israel Must Live

The seventh and final perspective from the moderate spectrum involves the reestablishment of the State of Israel. If the Holocaust was the death of Israel, then the reestablishment of the nation was its resurrection. Out of the ashes of the death camps has arisen a living and viable expression of the Jewish people, and its battle cry is *Am Yisrael Chai* ("the people of Israel lives").

As Rabbi Abraham Besdin notes,

> Matching the holocaust in power and mystery is the reconstitution of the State of Israel in May of 1948. Only a dogmatic agnostic would fail to see the transcendental overtones of this sudden transformation of Jewish dignity and hope.[149]

Rabinovitch maintains that the establishment of the State restores God's sovereignty:

Above: On May 14, 1948, David Ben-Gurion announced the formation of the State of Israel, the first independent Jewish state in nineteen centuries of history (photo: www.wikipedia.org).

---

[149] Abraham R. Besdin, "Reflections on the Agony and the Ecstasy," *Tradition: A Journal of Orthodox Thought* 11, No. 4 (Spring 1971): 65.

There is one simple basic fact which is there for all the world to see. It is so utterly simple and so totally obvious that thousands of millions of people all over the globe know it and see it. Israel *is*, and it bears God's Name, and it has restored God's crown![150]

Rabbi Mark Samuels relates what the State of Israel has done for modern Jewish history:

The Holocaust has, indeed, made it very difficult to believe in a God of love, a God of justice and goodness. It has also made it difficult to believe sincerely in a God of history. Until 1948, history, and especially Jewish history, became practically meaningless to many Jews, but the establishment of the State of Israel in that year, and the splendid and almost supernatural victory of Israel in June 1967, have helped to make Jewish history perhaps a little more meaningful now.[151]

Perhaps the foremost spokesman for the radical imperative of Israel's survival, especially following the Holocaust, is the aforementioned Jewish philosopher and theologian Emil Fackenheim. This survival has been a major theme in many of his writings. He asserts that there is a commanding voice of Auschwitz, a voice that demands the attentive ears of both religious and secular Jews:

Most assuredly no *redeeming* Voice is heard from Auschwitz, or ever will be heard. However, a *commanding* Voice is being heard, and has, however faintly, been heard from the start. Religious Jews hear it, and they identify its source. Secularist Jews also hear it, even though perforce they leave it unidentified. At Auschwitz, Jews came face to face with absolute evil. They were and still are singled out by it, but in the midst of it they hear an absolute commandment: *Jews are forbidden to grant posthumous victories to Hitler.* They are commanded to survive as Jews, lest the Jewish people

---

[150] Rabinovitch, "The Religious Significance of Israel," p. 24.

[151] Marc E. Samuels, "In Praise of Doubt," *Judaism* 20 (Fall 1971): 458.

perish. They are commanded to remember the victims of Auschwitz, lest their memory perish. They are forbidden to despair of man and his world, and to escape into either cynicism or otherworldliness, lest they cooperate in delivering the world over to the forces of Auschwitz. Finally, they are forbidden to despair of the God of Israel, lest Judaism perish. A secularist Jew cannot make himself believe by a mere act of will, nor can he be commanded to do so; yet he can perform the commandment of Auschwitz. And a religious Jew who has stayed with his God may be forced into new, possibly revolutionary, relationships with Him. One possibility, however, is wholly unthinkable. A Jew may not respond to Hitler's attempt to destroy Judaism by himself cooperating in its destruction. In ancient times, the unthinkable Jewish sin was idolatry. Today, it is to respond to Hitler by doing his work.[152]

This radical imperative—namely, that the authentic Jew of today is forbidden to hand Hitler yet another posthumous victory—Fackenheim calls "a 614th commandment."[153] He also maintains that the Holocaust survivor is gradually becoming the paradigm for the entire Jewish people:

> Nowhere is this truth [i.e., the survivor as a paradigm for the entire Jewish people] as unmistakable as in the State of Israel. The State of Israel is collectively what the survivor is individually—testimony on behalf of all mankind to life against death, to sanity against madness, to Jewish self-affirmation against every form of flight from it, and (although this is visible only to those who break through narrow theological categories) to the God of the ancient covenant against all lapses into paganism... [T]he truth is obvious: the State of Israel is a collective testimony against the groundless hate which has erupted in this century in the heart of

---

[152] Emil L. Fackenheim, "Jewish Faith and the Holocaust: A Fragment," *Commentary* 46 (August 1968): 32-33.

[153] Fackenheim, "Jewish Values in the Post-Holocaust Future: A Symposium," p. 272.

Europe. Its watchword is *Am Yisrael Chai*—"the people of Israel lives." Without this watchword the State of Israel could not have survived for a generation. It is a watchword of defiance, hope and faith. It is a testimony to all men everywhere that man shall be, and be human—even if it should be necessary to cast Truth to the ground.[154]

In describing this collective experience of Israel, Fackenheim places Jerusalem right alongside Auschwitz:

> Jerusalem, while no "answer" to the Holocaust, is a response; and every Israeli lives that response. Israel is collectively what every survivor is individually: a No to the demons of Auschwitz, a Yes to Jewish survival and security—and thus a testimony to life against death *on behalf of all mankind*. The juxtaposition of Auschwitz and Jerusalem recalls nothing so vividly as Ezekiel's vision of the dead bones and the resurrection of the household of Israel. Every Israeli—man, woman or child—stakes his life on the truth of that vision.[155]

There are, of course, those who reject any kind of modern comparison between the destruction of the six million and the establishment of the State of Israel. For example, Rabbi Jacob Agus notes:

> We cannot be content with the old cliches, rehearsing the "sins" of our people and reveling in visions of Messianic Glory. Nor can we point to the "miracle" of Israel as the counterweight to the tragedy of the Six Million. The scales do not balance, however much you try.[156]

---

[154] Fackenheim, "The Human Condition after Auschwitz," p. 172.

[155] Emil L. Fackenheim, "The People Israel Lives," *The Christian Century* 87 (6 May 1970): 567.

[156] Jacob B. Agus, "God and the Catastrophe," *Conservative Judaism* 18 (Summer 1964): 14.

Wiesel holds the same position in regard to this kind of comparison:

> To me, the Holocaust teaches nothing. I object to Israeli politicians when they claim that "Israel is the answer to the Holocaust." It is not. It has no right to be. Sometimes I feel it is a disgrace to link these two events and thus diminish them both. They are two mysteries, both historic and Messianic. I refuse to give children in tomorrow's Israel such a burden, such guilt. I do not want them to think: If we are free and independent, it is because of the Holocaust. This would mean being, in a way, responsible for the past.[157]

Nevertheless, there is both a theological as well as an emotional tie between the Holocaust and the establishment of the State. Greenberg focuses on the theological significance when he says:

> The reborn State of Israel is this fundamental act of life and meaning of the Jewish people after Auschwitz. To fail to grasp that inextricable connection and response is to utterly fail to comprehend the theological significance of Israel. The most bitterly secular atheist involved in Israel's upbuilding is the front line of the Messianic life-force struggling to give renewed testimony to the Exodus as ultimate reality. Israel was built by rehabilitating a half-million survivors of the Holocaust. Each one of those lives had to be rebuilt, given opportunity for trust restored... The real point is that after Auschwitz, the existence of the Jew is a great affirmation and an act of faith. The re-creation of the body of the people, Israel, is renewed testimony to Exodus as ultimate reality, to God's continuing presence in history proven by the fact that his people, despite the attempt to annihilate them, still exist.[158]

---

[157] As quoted in Fackenheim, "Jewish Values in the Post-Holocaust Future: A Symposium," p. 287.

[158] Greenberg, "Cloud of Smoke, Pillar of Fire," pp. 43, 48.

Berkovits sees in the establishment of the State of Israel theological assurance that there will be a Messianic fulfillment of history. History is moving toward its Messianic goals:

> The assurance of the messianic fulfillment of history is beyond any doubt. The most convincing indication of its coming is the survival of Israel. The survival of Judaism and of the Jewish people in all ages, in conditions of utter political and material weakness, in spite of continuous discrimination and persecution, and in defiance of an endless series of the most barbarous and sadistic attempts at their extermination, baffles all explanation. It is the mystery of all ages. The return of Israel to its ancient homeland in our days, as Israel maintained for numberless generations that it would do, is the incomparable historic event of all times.[159]

The emotional tie between the Holocaust and the reborn State of Israel is probably even stronger than the theological one. A closing example from Jacob Neusner will demonstrate this point. The theological and the emotional blend together so that the heart speaks and not so much the head:

> The events of Europe from 1933 to 1945 and of the Middle East from 1948 to 1967 (and beyond) are interrelated and meaningful in a more than commonplace way. It is not just the killing of millions of people that happened in Europe, not merely the creation of another state in the Middle East. It was a holocaust and a rebirth, the fulfillment of prophecy, interpreted by prophetic teachings about dry bones, the suffering servant, and the return to Zion.
>
> And, as we saw, these same supposedly secular people see *themselves* as having been asphyxiated at Auschwitz and reborn in the state of Israel. They understand their group life in the most recent times as conforming to the paradigm of ancient prophecy. The

---

[159] Berkovits, *God, Man and History: A Jewish Interpretation*, pp. 153-154.

state is not merely another nation, but the state of Israel. Events of the day remain highly charged, full of meaning…

Let me confess at the end that I have never read the vision of the valley of the dry bones [Ezekiel 37:1-14] without tears. We Jews were the dry bones in 1945, without hope. We Jews were given sinews, flesh, the breath of life in 1948 and afterward—until, in 1967, we returned to the Old Temple wall. And all of this bore immense meaning not only for the religious sector within Jewry, but for millions of secular, assimilated individuals who long had supposed they were part of no particular group, least of all the Jewish one into which they were born.[160]

It is no wonder that the modern State of Israel lives with a Holocaust mentality. The *Shoah* is an omnipresent and foreboding shadow that casts its spell over the people's entire framework of thinking: their past, their present, and their future. With every breath they take comes the vow, "Never Again!"

Multilingual "Never Again" memorial at Treblinka extermination camp (photo: www.wikipedia.org)

---

[160] Jacob Neusner, *The Way of Torah: An Introduction to Judaism*, 2nd Edition, The Religious Life of History Series (Encino, CA: Dickenson Publishing, 1974), pp. 92-93 (emphasis in the original).

Summary of the Moderate Perspective

The following table summarizes positions that can be found in the broad spectrum of the moderate perspective.

The Moderate Perspective	In the vast spectrum between the traditional perspective and the radical perspective, there are many other Jewish responses to the Shoah.
The Unanswerable Mystery	The Holocaust is inexplicable in this life and cannot be harmonized with the concept of a just and loving God. Therefore, one must submit to its mystery and respond in faith and silence.
God Suffering with Israel	The Holocaust is only fathomable when one sees God Himself suffering for and with the nation of Israel.
Contending with God	The Holocaust requires every faithful Jew to follow in the steps of their forefathers to question, contend with, and challenge the God of suffering.
The Presence of Two Histories	Jewish suffering demonstrates the presence of two conflicting histories: the history of the nations and the history of Israel. Israel's innocent suffering at the hands of the nations is God's way of driving the Gentile world to repentance. The Holocaust is progress through sacrifice. The sacrifice of Israel brought the anti-Semitism of the Middle Ages to a close.
Dialectical Faith	Judaism must now learn to live within a dialectical faith that is stretched into theological tension caused by the God of the Covenant, who did not keep His part of the Mosaic Covenant. After Auschwitz, an untroubled, serene faith in God as the Lord of history no longer seems possible.

Human Freedom—Human Depravity	After the Holocaust, Judaism reaffirmed its belief in the moral freedom of man that gives man the choice of committing such an evil as the slaughter of six million Jews. The degree of evil to which man can go in his moral choices has been reappraised. All of the naked allusions about the refined nature of man have been stripped away by the Holocaust.
Israel Must Live	If the Holocaust was the death of Israel, then the reestablishment of the nation was its resurrection. Out of the ashes of the death camps has arisen a living and viable expression of the Jewish people, and the nation's battle cry is *Am Yisrael Chai* ("The People of Israel Lives").

Conclusion

This chapter has been a detailed survey of the major Jewish religious responses to the Holocaust. Eighteen major responses were surveyed, falling into three basic categories: the traditional, the radical, and the moderate. It has been seen that the responses come from all religious walks of life: the young and old, the philosopher and the rabbi, the layman and the theologian, the skeptic and the faithful, the simple and the complex, the introverted and the extroverted, the survivor and the observer, the atheist and the theist, and so on. All of them exhibit the same scars. The Holocaust has permanently changed the nature and character of contemporary Judaism. It will never be the same.

Three concluding remarks are in order at this point. First, the survey of Jewish responses has demonstrated that there are no adequate answers within Judaism to account for the terrible suffering of the Holocaust. There are no simple facts or formulas that can adequately describe the trauma of the Holocaust and integrate it into a meaningful religious experience. The facts will not even allow for any manipulation, let alone formulation. Even with a survey of eighteen major religious responses from within Judaism (plus innumerable more), the Holocaust still defies adequate answers and integrity. The responses, at best, only represent fragmentary solutions to this most complex event. The answers, both from the human side and the divine side, continue to evade the consciousness of contemporary Judaism.

Second, the survey has demonstrated that there are no universal answers to the Holocaust or, better yet, that there is no one universal answer that accounts for all of the data. Each response depends on the respondent's starting point. The facts and the responses to these facts are in large part determined by the presuppositions and methodologies used and applied. Different preconceptions and different beginnings produce very different conclusions. One's basic assumptions about God and man will greatly determine one's corresponding conclusions about both and their relationship with each other. Since each of the respondents has his own unique starting point, it is not surprising that no one universal answer has surfaced. Added to this is the fact that each of the responses is, at best, fragmentary and descriptive. No one of the respondents claims to have the final answer to the trauma of the Holocaust.

Third, the survey of Jewish responses to the Holocaust has demonstrated that Judaism is without any truly authoritative answers. How can one account for the varied and often conflicting responses to such a critical event as the Holocaust? In other words, what makes it so impossible to point to any definitive, or even agreed-upon, results either with regard to a starting point or to conclusions? The answer to these questions revolves around Judaism's view of authority—in particular, biblical authority. Judaism is committed to an open system of revelation and is therefore not bound by just the biblical text and truth. The Written Law and the Oral Law hold an equal authority base in Judaism. The Written Law (i.e., the Jewish Bible or Old Testament) is not the final authority for life and practice in the Jewish religion. Rather, it is modified and interpreted by the Oral Law, which is an equal authority in the religious Jew's life. Writing from within the Orthodox tradition, Professor of Jewish Philosophy at Yeshiva University Leon Stitskin reiterates this distinction: "To the Christians, the Bible is a self-contained book expounded in accordance with its own sources. To the Jew, however, the Written and Oral Law are one."[161] Simon describes the relationship between these laws and the implications that must follow such a distinction:

> Jewish law is based on the still ongoing procedure of finding the truth in each and every debatable problem by means of free discussion which tries to arrive at a consensus of interpreting Holy Writ and the Oral Tradition. Everyone who has acquired the necessary knowledge is not only permitted but obliged to take part in these discussions, whatever his occupation or social status.[162]

In other words, instead of coming to a completed and written text from God, which therefore carries its own unique and final authority, Judaism comes to the oral tradition about the written truth and must come to its own conclusions about life and truth, about God and man. This is not the case for conservative evangelicals. They come to a complete and final revelation from God, which, by absolute necessity, carries with it full and ultimate authority. In other words, they are bound by the text of Holy Scripture alone. That is why they alone can give an authoritative answer to the Holocaust, not necessarily a complete answer (leaving room

---

[161] Leon D. Stitskin, "A Rejoinder," *Tradition: A Journal of Orthodox Thought* 17 (Spring 1978): 91.

[162] Ernst Simon, "The Jews as God's Witness to the World," *Judaism* 15 (Summer 1966): 312.

for "mystery" within the revelation of God) but certainly an authoritative answer. The remainder of this book shall attempt to do just that.

Torah scroll (photo: www.wikipedia.org)

The Perspective of the Biblical Covenants

The Holocaust has happened. It is history. It cannot be undone or played over. From the preceding chapter, it becomes quite obvious that religious Judaism has no adequate, universal, or authoritative answers for the Holocaust. So now that Judaism's failure to meet the problem has surfaced, it is imperative to apply a truly biblical set of responses to the Holocaust. The place to begin is with the covenants established by God with the nation of Israel. These covenants lay the foundation for God's eternal relationship with Israel. This relationship is not capricious or arbitrary but is bound by a contractual agreement. In other words, Israel is secured to God by definite treaty arrangements that God Himself initiated and ratified. Israel's relationship with God, therefore, is as secure as these covenants. And these covenants are as secure as the very character of God Himself.

What then is meant when the term "covenant" is used? Charles Fred Lincoln, one of the early professors at Dallas Theological Seminary, provides the following definition:

> A definition of a divine major covenant may be expressed as follows: (1) It is a sovereign disposition of God, whereby He estab-

lishes an unconditional or declarative compact with Israel, obligating Himself, in grace, by the untrammelled formula, "I will," to bring to pass of Himself definite blessing for the covenanted ones, or (2) a proposal of God, wherein He promises, in a conditional or mutual compact with Israel, by the contingent formula "If ye will," to grant special blessings to the covenanted ones, provided they fulfill perfectly certain conditions, and to execute definite punishment in case of their failure.[1]

It is apparent, then, that there are two different types of covenants: an unconditional (or promissory) covenant and a conditional (or obligatory) covenant. This chapter will investigate how the four unconditional covenants (i.e., the Abrahamic, the Palestinian or Land, the Davidic, and the New) and the one conditional covenant (i.e., the Mosaic) bear on the nature and consequences of the Holocaust.

What is the nature of these covenants that will be investigated? The theologian J. Dwight Pentecost states, "There are certain facts which are to be observed concerning the covenants into which God has entered."[2] He then summarizes four of these crucial facts.[3] First, these covenants are *literal* covenants and are to be interpreted literally. Second, they are *eternal*, except the Mosaic Covenant. Third, they must be considered *unconditional* in character, with the exception once again of the Mosaic Covenant. And fourth, these covenants were made with *a covenant people*, Israel.[4]

---

[1] Charles Fred Lincoln, "The Biblical Covenants," *Bibliotheca Sacra* 100, Number 398 (April–June 1943), p. 316.

[2] J. Dwight Pentecost, *Things to Come: A Study in Biblical Eschatology* (Grand Rapids, MI: Dunham Publishing Company, 1958), p. 69.

[3] Ibid., pp. 69-70.

[4] For New Testament confirmation that the covenants were made solely with Israel, see: Rom. 9:4; Acts 3:25; Eph. 2:11-12; Heb. 8:6-12.

Israel's Covenants		
Name	Conditional	Unconditional
Abrahamic Covenant		✓
(Palestinian or) Land Covenant		✓
Davidic Covenant		✓
New Covenant		✓
Mosaic Covenant	✓	

The Facets of Israel's Unconditional Covenants	
Facets	✽ They are literal and must be interpreted literally. ✽ They are eternal and not limited by time. ✽ Their fulfillment is wholly dependent on God. ✽ They are made with Israel. ✽ Although the covenants are made at specific points in time, not all provisions become effective immediately. Some are immediate, some are near future, and some are distant future.

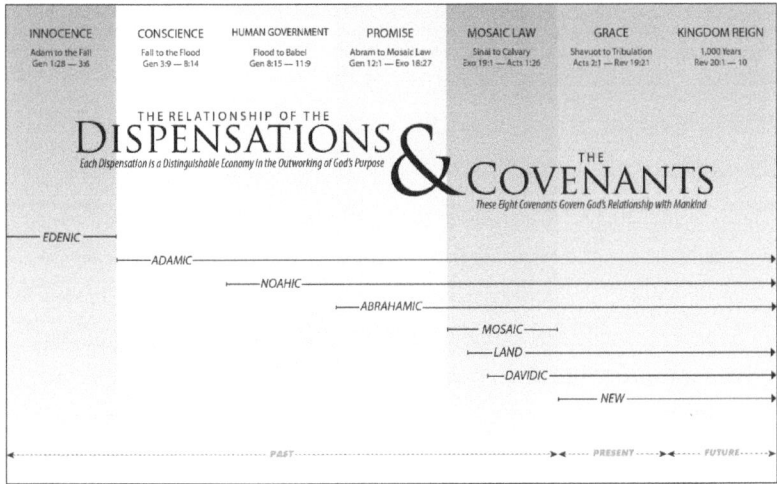

Above: This graphic, created by Mottel Baleston, is used here with permission. It illustrates the relationship between the seven dispensations and the eight covenants found in the Bible. As depicted in the chart, God made two conditional covenants that ended at specific points in human history: the Edenic Covenant (with Adam) and the Mosaic Covenant (with Israel). All other covenants are unconditional, as denoted by the solid arrows in the diagram above.

The Abrahamic Covenant

Without a doubt, the Abrahamic Covenant must be considered the most important covenant that God initiated with Israel. Its implications are not only far-reaching but also eternal. Another professor at Dallas Theological Seminary, John F. Walvoord, correctly stresses the importance of this covenant:

> It is recognized by all serious students of the Bible that the covenant of God with Abraham is one of the important and determinative revelations of Scripture. It furnishes the key to the entire Old Testament and reaches for its fulfillment into the New.[5]

This covenant, therefore, must be the place to begin when searching for biblical insight related to the Holocaust.

The Nature of the Abrahamic Covenant

In summarizing the Abrahamic Covenant, the theologian and cofounder of Dallas Theological Seminary, Lewis Sperry Chafer, describes the unconditional nature of this covenant:

> The Abrahamic covenant records Jehovah's sovereign purpose in, through, and for Abraham. The covenant is unconditional in that no obligation is imposed upon Abraham; he contributes nothing, but rather is the recipient of all that Jehovah proposed to do for him. While this covenant (cf. Gen. 12:1-3; 13:14-17; 15:4-7; 17:1-8) provided personal blessings and great honor to Abraham, its more important features reach out in two other directions, namely, that of Abraham's seed and that of the land of promise.[6]

---

[5] John F. Walvoord, *The Millennial Kingdom* (Grand Rapids, MI: Dunham Publishing Company, 1959), p. 139.

[6] Lewis Sperry Chafer, *Systematic Theology*, 8 vols. (Dallas, TX: Dallas Seminary Press, 1947-48), Vol. 5: *Christology*, p. 317.

To demonstrate the unconditional nature of the Abrahamic Covenant, Walvoord summarizes ten lines of evidence, which he feels constitute a strong line of proof:[7]

1. With the exception of the Mosaic Covenant, all of Israel's covenants are unconditional in that they are stated to be eternal (e.g., the Abrahamic in Gen. 17:7, 13, 19; 1 Chron. 16:16-17; Ps. 105:8-10; the Palestinian or Land in Ezek. 16:60; the Davidic in 2 Sam. 7:13, 16, 19; 1 Chron. 17:12; 22:10; Isa. 9:7; 55:3; Ezek. 37:25-26; and the New in Isa. 55:3; 61:8; Jer. 32:40; 50:5; Ezek. 16:60; 37:26; Heb. 13:20).
2. There are no conditions stated except for the original condition of leaving his homeland and going to the promised land (which Abraham fulfilled).
3. The covenant is confirmed on several occasions without any conditional stipulations added.
4. The covenant was confirmed by an unqualified oath of God (Gen. 15:7-21; Jer. 34:18).
5. Circumcision was never made a condition for the fulfillment of the covenant, only for the experienced blessing within the covenant (cf. Gen. 17:9-14, which came after the land promises were given).
6. When the covenant was confirmed and reconfirmed both to Isaac and to Jacob, no conditions were required of them (cf. Gen. 17:19; 26:2-5; 28:12-15).
7. The covenant was confirmed time after time, in spite of continual disobedience.
8. Even apostasy did not destroy the covenant (cf. Jer. 31:36; there are also extensive prophecies of gathering and restoration as well as Israel's continued existence as a nation in the Minor Prophets).

---

[7] Walvoord, *The Millennial Kingdom*, pp. 150-52. See also Charles Caldwell Ryrie, *The Basis of the Premillennial Faith* (Neptune, NJ: Loizeaux Brother Inc., 1953), pp. 52-61.

9. The covenant was declared immutable (Heb. 6:13-18; cf. Gen. 15:8-21).
10. Israel's revealed program confirms the unconditional nature of the Abrahamic Covenant in both the Old and New Testaments.

The Abrahamic Covenant is a foundational covenant that, as Pentecost asserts, "must be considered as the basis of the entire covenant program."[8] Pentecost therefore concludes:

> Thus it may be said that the land promises of the Abrahamic covenant are developed in the Palestinian [or Land] covenant, the seed promises are developed in the Davidic covenant, and the blessing promises are developed in the new covenant. This covenant [the Abrahamic], then, determines the whole future program for the nation Israel and is a major factor in Biblical Eschatology.[9]

The Provisions of the Abrahamic Covenant

The scope of the Abrahamic Covenant can be seen to cover three major areas (Gen. 12:1-3): first, personal promises to Abraham himself; second, national promises to the line coming through Abraham; and third, universal promises to all who come under Abraham's influence.

Regarding the third point, Abraham was called by God to receive a blessing from Him. In turn, Abraham was to become a blessing and produce a nation that would eventually bless the entire world. God's blessings and promises were not to be selfishly hoarded by Abraham or the nation that arose from him. They were meant to be extended to the whole world. God's grace and truth are for all men.

---

[8] Pentecost, *Things to Come*, p. 70.

[9] Ibid., p. 72.

The content of the Abrahamic Covenant can be divided into seven sections (Gen. 12:1-3):
1. "I will make you a great nation."
2. "And I will bless you."
3. "And make your name great."
4. "And so you shall be a blessing."
5. "And I will bless those who bless you."
6. "And the one who curses you I will curse."
7. "And in you all the families of the earth shall be blessed."

These seven points show that the content of the Abrahamic Covenant involves land, seed, and blessing. Abraham was promised a literal land (Gen. 13:14-17; 15:18-21; confirmed in the Palestinian or Land Covenant, Deut. 30:1-8), an eternal seed (Gen. 13:15-16; 15:1-6; confirmed in the Davidic Covenant, 2 Sam. 7:12-16), and an unconditional blessing (Gen. 15:7-17; confirmed in the New Covenant, Jer. 31:31-34)

The Abrahamic Covenant (Gen. 12:1-3)		
"Get out of your country, From your family And from your father's house, To a **land** that I will show you.	I will make you a great **nation**; I will bless you And make your name great; And you shall be a blessing.	I will bless those who bless you, And I will curse him who curses you; And in you all the families of the earth shall be **blessed**."
The Land	The Seed	The Blessing

The Protection in the Abrahamic Covenant

With this background to the Abrahamic Covenant in place, one particular clause must now be addressed because it has a direct bearing on the Holocaust. It is the protection clause—or, more accurately, the anti-Semitism clause—of Genesis 12:3: *And I will bless those who bless you, and the one who curses you I will curse.* God has committed Himself to the protection of His chosen people.

The way a person or a nation treats Abraham and his descendants is the same way God will treat them.

The Old Testament commentator Carl Friedrich Keil summarizes the significance of this unique anti-Semitism clause:

> Abram was not only to *receive* blessing, but to *be* a blessing; not only to be blessed by God, but to become a blessing, or the medium of blessing, to others. The blessing, as the more minute definition of the expression *"be a blessing"* in v[er]. 3 clearly shows, was henceforth to keep pace as it were with Abram himself, so that (1) the blessing and cursing of men were to depend entirely upon their attitude towards him, and (2) all the families of the earth were to be blessed in him. קָלַל [*kalal*], lit. to treat as light or little, to despise, denotes, "blasphemous cursing on the part of man;" [on the other hand,] אָרַר [*arar*] [denotes] "judicial cursing on the part of God." It appears significant, however, that the plural is used in relation to the blessing, and the singular only in relation to the cursing; grace expects that there will be many to bless, and that only an individual here and there will render not blessing for blessing, but curse for curse.[10]

George Bush, biblical scholar and pastor, also emphasizes the severity of this protection clause and points out that it goes beyond Abraham to his seed:

> This is language never used but of an object of special favour. It is declaring that he should not only be blessed himself, but that all others should be blessed or cursed as they respected or injured him and his seed. Of this the histories of Abimelech, Laban, Potiphar, Pharaoh, Balak, and Balaam furnish striking examples... But as such a contemptuous or disparaging treatment would be a direct affront to God himself, he here affirms that those who were guilty of it should incur his *curse* as a proper penalty; and the curse of

---

[10] C. F. Keil and F. Delitzsch, *The First Book of Moses*, in: Carl Friedrich Keil and Franz Delitzsch, *Commentary on the Old Testament in Ten Volumes, Volume I: The Pentateuch, Three Volumes in One* (Grand Rapids, MI: Eerdmans, 1981), p. 123-124.

heaven is but another name for the *positive infliction* of fearful judgments.[11]

It becomes apparent that the protection clause of Genesis 12:3 is closely related to the mission that God gave to Abraham and his descendants, that is, to be a "blessing" on the earth. This is brought out by Rabbi Umberto Cassuto, Professor of the Bible at the Hebrew University in Jerusalem:

> Those who bless you—that is to say, those who will show you sympathy and friendship and will seek your welfare—will also receive blessing from Me... Contrariwise, those who are opposed to you and seek to hurt you will receive My curse... Whoever is opposed to you is opposed to the mission that I gave you, and hence it is right that he should be punished.[12]

Old Testament scholar Gerhard von Rad takes this concept of a protection clause even further when he asserts that God is now beginning to bring salvation and judgment into the world in a new way:

> The promise given to Abraham has significance... far beyond Abraham and his seed. God now brings salvation and judgment into history, and man's judgment and salvation will be determined by the attitude he adopts toward the work which God intends to do in history.[13]

It is doubtful that Moses saw anything in this promise outside of Abraham and his descendants. Nor is it possible to limit this protective clause to just the times when Abraham and his descendants are involved in doing the work or mission of God. This will

---

[11] George Bush, *Notes on Genesis* (Limited Classical Reprint Library), 2 vols. (Minneapolis, MN: Klock & Klock Christian Publishers, 1981), Vol. 1, p. 196 (emphasis in the original).

[12] Umberto Cassuto, *A Commentary on the Book of Genesis*, 2 vols. (Jerusalem, Israel: Magnes Press, 1961), Vol. 2, pp. 314-315.

[13] Gerhard von Rad, *Genesis: A Commentary*, Rev. Ed., The Old Testament Library (Philadelphia, PA: The Westminster Press, 1972), p. 160.

be demonstrated below. However, it is entirely within the scope of this anti-Semitism clause to see God's universal blessing being mediated through Abraham and his descendants—in particular, how individuals and nations respond to Abraham and his descendants.[14] The question that now must be answered is how this anti-Semitism or protection clause finds its fulfillment in Scripture. Both stated and unstated fulfillments will be considered.

Stated Fulfillment

There are numerous passages that explicitly state (i.e., use the terms "bless" or "curse") that the protective clause of Genesis 12:3 is in effect. These passages reiterate that Israel's entire history is based on the protection clause in the Abrahamic Covenant. In fact, this seminal clause is part of God's philosophy of history for the nation Israel.

The passages regarding the clause demonstrate that it is at work on both the individual and national levels, in Israel's past and in her future. The two most obvious (and perhaps the most important) cases are on the individual level. In both cases, a form of the Genesis 12:3 clause is quoted and applied to the particular situation. Furthermore, it is noteworthy that in both cases, Israel (actually, Jacob in the first case) is either in some form of deception or in discipline before God. This fact reaffirms the unconditional nature of the clause itself, meaning its fulfillment does not depend

---

[14] The relationship between God's universal blessing and the protective clause can be visualized in the following diagram:

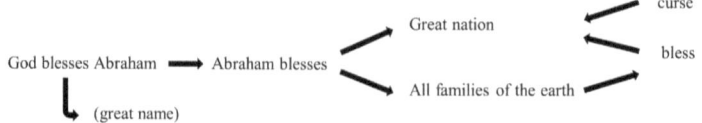

on Israel's fellowship or walk with God. Even when the nation is in disobedience, the clause is faithfully applied by the covenant God who originally gave it. All that actually matters is how the individual or nation "blesses" or "curses" Abraham and his descendants.

The first case in point is Esau's stolen blessing (Gen. 27:1-46). Jacob robbed his brother Esau of his rightful blessing through a deceptive strategy urged on by his mother, Rebekah (vv. 5-17). The lying and deceiving finally earned Jacob the blessing from his old and blind father, Isaac (vv. 18-29). The blessing included both a benediction (v. 28) and a prediction (v. 29). The prediction contains a reference to Genesis 12:3: *May peoples serve you, And nations bow down to you; Be master of your brothers, And may your mother's sons bow down to you.* ***Cursed be those who curse you, And blessed be those who bless you*** (emphasis added). Isaac thought that he was passing on the blessing to his oldest son, Esau, who was the legitimate heir to the blessing by tradition. Yet, in reality, the blessing was passed on to Jacob. Despite Esau's pleading (vv. 30-38), it remained in Jacob's possession. This means that the protective clause of the Abrahamic Covenant was passed on to Jacob in the midst of lies and deceit, yet it remained steadfast because it was not dependent upon Jacob's faithfulness but upon God's sovereign grace (cf. Rom. 9:10-13; Mal. 1:2-4). The Abrahamic Covenant itself was initiated on the basis of God's sovereign grace (e.g., Deut. 7:6-11; Josh. 24:2-3), and the protective clause, a part of that covenant, is continually enforced on the same basis. The clause was passed on from Abraham through Isaac to Jacob and is still in force. Old Testament scholar Frank Derek Kidner concludes this episode by stating: "Finally the protective curse and blessing are made to speak of what will hinge on the attitude of *every one* ([Gen. 27:]29b) to the true Israel."[15]

The second case in point, in which a form of the Genesis 12:3 protective clause is quoted on an individual level, is the failed cursing attempt by Balaam (Num. 22:1–24:25). Although this was actually a national-level attempt to curse Israel (i.e., by Moab), it was initiated by an individual, a pseudo-prophet. Nevertheless, this particular incident will forever bar any Moabite male from the congregation of Israel. Throughout Israel's long history, this one incident was paraded in front of the nation as a reminder of the danger of tampering with the anti-Semitism clause in the Abrahamic Covenant. Moses reminded the people about it (Deut. 23:3-6), as did Joshua (Josh. 24:9-10) and, finally, Nehemiah in the post-captivity community (Neh. 13:1-3). Throughout Israel's history, the Moabites remained a thorn in the side of the Jewish people (cf. Isa. 15-16; Jer. 9:25-26; 25:15-21; 27:2-3; 48:1-47; Ezek. 25:8-11; Zeph. 2:8-11).[16] Yet, when they hired Balaam to curse Israel, the Moabites sealed their own doom.

The incident occurred in the Balaam oracle (Num. 24:3-9). The setting is crucial. The Israelites were wandering in the wilderness following their disobedience to enter the promised land (Num. 13:1–20:13). They were under the just discipline and judgment of God. Almost all of the Exodus generation would die off in the wilderness; nevertheless, the protective covenant was still in force, for it did not depend upon Israel's faithfulness but upon the other nations (or individuals) and their attitude toward Abraham and his descendants. It is noteworthy that this incident did not involve the Patriarchs but only the nation as a whole; i.e., the protective clause had already been passed down to Moses and his generation,

---

[15] Frank Derek Kidner, *Genesis: An Introduction and Commentary*, The Tyndale Old Testament Commentaries (Chicago, IL: Inter-Varsity Press, 1967), p. 156.

[16] See also: Jdgs. 3:12-15; 2 Kgs. 13:20; 24:2; 2 Chron. 20:1; Ps. 83:4-8; Isa. 25:10-11.

the descendants of Abraham. Balaam closed this third oracle by referring to Israel in the following words: *He couches, he lies down as a lion, And like a lioness, who dares rouse him? Blessed is everyone who blesses you, And cursed is everyone who curses you* (Num. 24:9; emphasis added). Keil summarizes this closing portion of Balaam's third oracle by stating:

> Balaam closes this utterance, as he had done the previous one, with a quotation from Jacob's blessing, which he introduces to show to Balak, that, according to words addressed by Jehovah to the Israelites through their own tribe-father, they were to overcome their foes so thoroughly, that none of them should venture to rise up against them again. To this he also links on the words with which Isaac had transferred to Jacob in Gen. 27:29 the blessing of Abraham in Gen. 12:3, for the purpose of warning Balak to desist from his enmity against *the chosen people* of God (italics added).[17]

When God chose Abraham and his descendants to be His people, He did it on an unconditional basis and bound Himself to their eternal protection (even when they are in disobedience).

Numerous other stated fulfillments could be listed where the terms "bless" and "curse" are applied to the individual level, and the following are just a few examples:

- Laban was blessed by God because of the presence of Jacob in his household (Gen. 30:25-30).
- Potiphar was blessed by God because Joseph was present in his household (Gen. 39:1-5).
- The town of Meroz was cursed for not aiding Israel in the battle against Sisera (Judg. 5:23).
- Goliath was defeated because he cursed the God of Israel and His people (e.g., 1 Sam. 17:4, 22-23, 34-36, 43-47).

---

[17] C. F. Keil and F. Delitzsch, *Commentary on the Old Testament,* Volume 1 – The Pentateuch (Peabody, MA: Hendrickson Publishers, 2006, second printing), p. 781.

✡ David's enemies were cursed because they were opposing God's theocratic king (Ps. 37:20-22; 109:26-31).

On the national level, the following examples are noted:

✡ The Gibeonites were cursed for deceiving the Israelites (Josh. 9:22-23).

✡ The Edomites were cursed for opposing Israel (Jer. 49:13; cf. Num. 20:14-21; Jdgs. 11:17; 2 Chron. 28:17; Ps. 83:1-6; 137:17; Lam. 4:21-22; Ezek. 25:12-14; 35:12-15; 36:5; Joel 3:19; Amos 1:11; Obad. 8-14).

✡ The Babylonians were cursed because of their savage onslaught against Israel (Lam. 3:55-66, esp. v. 65). Note that even though God raised them up for Israel's judgment (Hab. 1:1–2:20), He still destroyed them for violating the Gen. 12:3 protective clause.

Two more stated fulfillments are important to mention, for they are both future events in Israel's history. The first future fulfillment is seen in Deuteronomy 30:7, *The LORD your God will inflict all these curses on your enemies and on those who hate you, who persecuted you* (emphasis added). This statement comes in the midst of the regathering of Israel from all the nations to which she has been scattered (Deut. 30:1-10). This is the great assurance of the Palestinian (or Land) Covenant: Israel, who has been scattered throughout the earth because of her disobedience and who has herself suffered the detailed curses enumerated in Deuteronomy 28:15-68, will not only be returned to her homeland but will also see these very same curses imposed upon all of her enemies (Deut. 30:1-10). Again, it should be noted that the unconditional nature of Genesis 12:3 comes to the forefront. Israel, who has been under a judicial, worldwide scattering and under the curses of the nations in which she dwells, nevertheless sees these very nations cursed by God because they violated the protective clauses of Genesis 12:3.

> וַאֲבָרֲכָה מְבָרְכֶיךָ וּמְקַלֶּלְךָ אָאֹר

Above: Genesis 12:3a in Hebrew

The second future stated fulfillment is found in Matthew 25:31-46. This passage refers to the future judgment of the Gentile nations at the close of the tribulation period.[18] Chafer summarizes this judgment and the basis for its severity:

> The period designated as "the times of the Gentiles," which times but for the intercalary age of the Church extend from the Babylonian captivity to the close of the great tribulation, ends in judgment upon the nations. Unlike other judgments which reach backward to include past generations, this judgment falls only upon the then-existing generation of Gentiles upon the earth. This is an equitable arrangement since those involved are to be judged for their treatment of Israel during the seven years of the tribulation. But one generation is thus involved. God has judged individual nations in the past because of their treatment of Israel and it has never failed to be true that a curse has rested upon those nations which have cursed Israel, and a blessing has rested upon those nations which have blessed Israel (cf. Gen. 12:3); but a specific curse and a specific blessing await the nations who in the great tribulation have either cursed or blessed Israel…
>
> The basis of the judgment of the nations will be recognized only as it is seen that the one nation Israel is chosen of God above all the nations of the earth. For this elect people God has an unchangeable and imperishable love and purpose. No right approach will be made to an understanding of the divine program for the earth unless the sovereign, divine favor toward Israel is

---

[18] For support of the position that this judgment is of the Gentile nations at the close of the tribulation period, see: Pentecost, *Things to Come*, pp. 343-348; Arnold G. Fruchtenbaum, *The Footsteps of the Messiah: A Study of the Sequence of Prophetic Events* (San Antonio, TX: Ariel Ministries, 2021, 4th Ed.), pp. 359, 627, 647-648.

acknowledged. If that sovereign favor is acknowledged, little difficulty will arise respecting the issue upon which the nations are judged at the end of the tribulation.[19]

As Chafer noted, the very words of Genesis 12:3 are used in Matthew 25:34 ("blessed") and 25:41 ("accursed"). Once again, the anti-Semitism clause will be enforced, the final time in all of history, for the Messianic kingdom follows this particular judgment. This is the kingdom in which all of the promised blessings of the Abrahamic Covenant will come to fruition for the nation Israel. In a profound editorial just following the close of World War II, Chafer applied this same passage to Hitler and all of the other Hitler-like nations. It is still a solemn warning against anyone who would seek, either on an individual or a national level, to violate the protection clause of Genesis 12:3.

> One more nation has gone to confusion having persecuted the Jew. How little this Christ-rejecting world believes in or gives attention to the Word of God! They imagine that because of vast numbers and mighty armament God is left far behind if He exists at all, and what He has said weighs not at all. It would have been difficult indeed to have made Hitler believe that his cause and his nation would certainly come to grief if they attacked and destroyed the Jew. It is difficult to make modern Gentiles—even many nominal Christians—recognize the order of cause and effect which God unfailingly imposes when the Jew is attacked. Did God not say to Abraham when promising his vast posterity, "I will bless them that bless thee, and curse him that curseth thee" (Gen. 12:3)? This purpose of God has been in force since Abraham's day. History faithfully records Jehovah's faithfulness to His word respecting Abraham's seed.

---

[19] Lewis Sperry Chafer, *Systematic Theology*, Vol. 4, *Ecclesiology, Eschatology* (Dallas, TX: Dallas Seminary Press, 1976), pp. 409-410.

The root trouble is that men do not believe that God has an elect nation, a chosen people, a sacred purpose in Israel. It is not to be taken seriously when God says of Israel, "I have chosen thee above all the nations of the earth for my glory," and "I have loved thee with an everlasting love." Just because the Jew is out of his land and away from his covenant blessings under Jehovah's chastisement, shortsighted and unbelieving men assume that if God ever had a specific purpose for Israel, it is outgrown now and only ancient history. The nations have yet to learn that God's gifts and calling respecting Israel are without repentance. His purpose is never changed.

What confusion has been wrought among so-called Christian nations by the all but universal theological notion that God is done with the Jew or that the promises to Israel are realized in the Church can never be estimated. People thus indoctrinated look with little sorrow on the massacre of five[20] million Jews and with no sense of the direct challenge to God which such a massacre really is. Hating the Jew is not the only sin nations commit; but an attack on the Jew is, according to Jehovah's covenant, to invite a curse.

When the nations have run their course in this age of utter repudiation of God, they are seen to stand for judgment before the throne of Christ's glory here on the earth and are divided on His right hand and on His left. Their judgment then is of their treatment of the Jew during the Tribulation (Mt. 25:31-46, where Christ styles the Jewish nation "my brethren"). It is not accidental that Christ should use the same words as so long ago were employed in the Abrahamic Covenant: "Come ye blessed" and "Depart ye cursed."

We… [wish] that the real cause of the curse which has fallen upon Hitler and the German people might be recognized and

---

[20] Chafer wrote the editorial before the war was over, and the exact numbers of victims had not been revealed.

proclaimed, that anti-Semitism might be checked in this and other lands.[21]

Pastor and author Walter Price reflects on the apathy of the Gentile world toward the Jews during the Holocaust and predicts the same response during the period just prior to the judgment mentioned in Matthew 25:31-46:

> The nations will be judged at the second coming of Christ according to the way that they deal with Israel during this time when she is fleeing from the wrath of the Antichrist. During the Nazi Holocaust, the world conveniently ignored the plight of the Jew. Much of the world may do so again during the great tribulation. However, for those nations who do provide protection and sustenance for fleeing Israel, there is promised a special blessing.[22]

Unstated Fulfillment

Not only are there numerous passages that explicitly state (i.e., in the terms "bless" or "curse") that the protective clause of Genesis 12:3 was (and still is) in effect, but there are also many passages that, while not specifically using these terms, still demonstrate the ongoing dynamic of the clause itself. Again, this can be seen both on an individual level and a national level, as well as in Israel's past and in her future.

The following summary of the unstated fulfillment of the protective clause relates to the individual level:

✡ The pharaoh and his house were cursed for taking in Abram's wife, Sarai, even though Abram instigated the incident through his deceit. The event proves the outworking

---

[21] Lewis Sperry Chafer, "Editorials: The Jew – A World Issue," *Bibliotheca Sacra: A Theological Quarterly* 102, Number 406 (April–June 1945):129-130.

[22] Walter K. Price, *Next Year In Jerusalem* (Chicago, IL: Moody Press, 1974), p. 132.

of the unconditional nature of the Abrahamic Covenant (Gen. 12:10-20).

✡ Abimelech and his house were cursed for also taking in Sarah, once again at the deceitful instigation of Abraham (Gen. 20:1-18).

✡ The Hebrew midwives were blessed by God because of their protection of the Jewish firstborn males (Exod. 1:15-21).

✡ Rahab was blessed by God because she protected the Hebrew spies (Josh. 2:1-21; 6:22-25; Mt. 1:5; Heb. 11:31; Jas. 2:25).

✡ The Persian politicians who sought to destroy Daniel were cursed, along with their families (Dan. 6:19-24).

The following summary of the unstated fulfillment of the protective clause relates to the national level:

✡ The Egyptians were cursed by God because they instituted a national anti-Semitic policy (Exod. 1:8-14; 4:22-23; 5:1–14:31; cf. Isa. 19:1–20:4; Joel 3:19).

✡ The Amalekites were cursed for declaring war on Israel (Exod. 17:8-16; Num. 24:20; Deut. 25:17-19; 1 Sam. 15:1-5, 7-8).

✡ The Kenites, who were descendants of Jethro the Midianite, were blessed because they aided Israel during the Exodus period (Exod. 2:16-22; 18:1-27; Num. 10:29-32; 24:21; Judg. 1:16; 4:11; 1 Sam. 15:6).

✡ The Moabites and the Ammonites were cursed because they persecuted the Israelites (e.g., Ezek. 25:1-7; Zeph. 2:8-11).

✡ The Assyrians were cursed for their brutal treatment of Israel, even though they were raised up by God as His rod (Isa. 10:5-14, 24-27; 14:24-27; 37: 21-38; 52:3-6).

- ✡ The Babylonians were cursed for their devastating abuse of Israel, although they were God's means of punishment (Isa. 13:1–14:23; Jer. 51:34-64; Hab. 1:1–2:20).
- ✡ Haman and the Persians were cursed by God for their attempted extermination of the Jewish people, even when the Jews were out of God's will by not returning to Israel along with the rest of the post-captivity community (Esth. 3:1-15; 4:7-8; 5:9-14; 6:12-13; 7:3-6).

The following summary of the unstated fulfillment of the protective clause relates to Israel's future:

- ✡ The great future conclave of nations from the uttermost part of the north of Israel and in league with some nations to the south will be utterly cursed and destroyed because of their attack on Israel in the latter days (Ezek. 38:1–39:29).
- ✡ All of Israel's oppressors will be cursed and punished at the beginning of the Messianic Age (Joel 3:1-3; Zeph. 3:8; Mt. 25:31-33, 41-46).
- ✡ The final battle of the age, which will center around Israel with all of the nations seeking to destroy her, will bring Israel's enemies to an end in a final curse and judgment (Zech. 2:8-9; 12:2-4, 9; 14:1-4, 12-13; cf. Jer. 30:16).

Jewish commentators recognize the eternal validity of the unconditional protective clause of Genesis 12:3. It was in effect throughout Israel's biblical history, and it is still true in her post-biblical history. Wyschogrod rightly concludes, "He who strikes Israel, therefore, engages himself in battle with God, and it is for this reason that the history of Israel is the fulcrum of human history."[23] Commenting on Genesis 12:3, the official edition of *The Pentateuch and Haftorahs* echoes this statement and applies it to modern European history:

---

[23] Wyschogrod, "Faith and the Holocaust," p. 293.

The story of European history during the past centuries teaches one uniform lesson: that the nations which have received and in any way dealt fairly and mercifully with the Jew have prospered—and that the nations that have tortured and oppressed him have written out their own curse.[24]

Christian commentators who have taken the biblical test seriously have come to the same conclusion. Robert L. Evans, in commenting on America's prominence in the world, states the matter plainly:

> If she desires to hold her leading place among the nations, let her people never foster or encourage the evil of anti-Semitism in her midst. The laws that govern the relationship of nations to the Jew were fixed by God four thousand years ago in the assurances and covenant promises made unto Abraham, the progenitor of the Hebrew race. The statement "I will bless them that bless thee, and curse him that curseth thee" (Genesis 12:3) has never been abrogated and applies today to this nation as it did in ancient times to Egypt, Assyria, and Babylon, who went down under the divine curse…
>
> It was only recently that Hitler boasted to his followers that he would establish a German empire that would last a thousand years. Ignoring God's ancient covenant with the Jew, he planned to place as the cornerstone of his future empire the entire extermination of the Jew. No wonder that he met with utter defeat and destruction. Moved by such an incentive his movement could not possibly have resulted otherwise.[25]

Likewise, in commenting on Genesis 12:3, theologian and pastor Donald Grey Barnhouse asserts the same assurance of the eternal validity of the anti-Semitism clause:

---

[24] J. H. Hertz, ed., *The Pentateuch and Haftorahs: Hebrew Text, English Translation and Commentary*, 2nd ed. (London, UK: Soncino Press, 1981), p. 45.

[25] Robert L. Evans, *The Jew in the Plan of God* (Neptune, NJ: Loizeaux Brothers, 1950), pp. 126-127.

Only eternity will reveal how true this ["I will bless them that bless thee"] has been in the history of the nations. Only the Gibeonites were spared when Israel entered the land of Canaan, for they sought to make a covenant with God's people. I believe that the Lord has blessed the United States because this nation is a haven for the persecuted Jews.

In the future, at the judgment of the nations, it is written that the Lord Jesus Christ will say to the nations on His right hand, "As you did it to one of the least of these my brethren, you did it to me" (Matthew 25:40). His brethren, of course, are the children of Abraham living at that day; and the passage takes on its real meaning when seen in this light.

When a man dies, a physician has to write on the death certificate the cause of death. When a nation dies, more often than not, the cause of death is that the nation has mistreated the Jews ["I will curse him that curseth thee"]. When Ham rebelled against Shem, one by one, the tribes of Ham were destroyed or reduced to a minor state: Egypt, Canaan and the Hittites. When the Greeks overran Palestine and desecrated the altar in the Jewish temple, they were soon conquered by Rome. When Rome killed Paul and many others and destroyed Jerusalem under Titus, Rome soon fell. Spain was reduced to a fifth-rate nation after the Inquisition against the Jews; Poland fell after the pogroms; Hitler's Germany went down after its orgies of anti-Semitism; Britain lost her empire when she broke her faith with Israel.[26]

The Unity of the Abrahamic Covenant

The second part of Genesis 12:3 is generally considered the universal aspect of the Abrahamic Covenant. It states: *And in you all the families of the earth will be blessed.* Some have concluded that since only this universal aspect is quoted in the New Testament

---

[26] Donald Grey Barnhouse, *Genesis: A Devotional Exposition* (Grand Rapids, MI: Zondervan Publishing House, 1973), pp. 76-77.

(Acts 3:25; Gal. 3:8), the anti-Semitism clause is no longer in effect. This position must be rejected for at least six reasons.

First, it ignores the plain facts of history. No nation, to this very day, has survived while maintaining an anti-Semitic posture. To call this a mere coincidence begs the imagination.

Second, it is an argument from silence. Just because the New Testament states that the universal aspect of the Abrahamic Covenant *is* in effect does not necessarily mean that the protective aspect of the covenant *is not* in effect. They are both in effect at the same time. Nowhere in either testament does it say that the anti-Semitism clause of Genesis 12:3 has become obsolete.

Third, the position ignores the progressive revelation of the Abrahamic Covenant itself. In no single passage are all of the details of this covenant either initially presented or later reaffirmed. Instead, they are presented and reaffirmed progressively, with only certain specific clauses detailed when God found it necessary to address them (cf. Gen. 12:1-3, 7; 13:14-17; 15:1-21; 17:1-21; 22:15-18; 26:2-5, 24; 27:27-29; 28:3-4, 13-15).[27] To assume that only one clause is in effect because the other clauses are not mentioned in that same passage is to overlook the progressive revealing and reaffirming nature of the covenant.

Fourth, the position ignores the unconditional nature of the Abrahamic Covenant (cf. Gen. 15:1-21; 27:18-33; Num. 24:2, 8-9; Hab. 1:1–2:20; Lam. 3:64-66).[28] The anti-Semitism clause never depended on Israel's faithfulness but rather on the responsiveness of the Gentile nations to Israel. The clause was in effect most of the time when Israel was actually disobedient to God. This would also include her rejection of Messiah.

---

[27] See also: Gen. 18:17-18; 35:11-12; Exod. 32;13; Deut. 34:4; Ps. 105:7-10; Mic. 5:7; Zech. 8:13; Acts 3:25; 7:2-5; Gal. 3:8-9; Heb. 6:13-14; 11:8-10.

[28] See also : Exod. 6:2-6; Deut. 33:27-29; Rom. 4; Gal. 4:28.

Fifth, the view ignores the eternal nature of the Abrahamic Covenant (Gen. 17:7, 13, 19; 1 Chron. 16:16-18; Ps. 105:8-11).

Sixth, it ignores the unity of the covenant. This point is the cumulative effect of the five reasons above. Although the covenant was initially given and later confirmed and reconfirmed in progressive stages, it nevertheless remained one, unified covenant. All of the parts of the covenant, adding up to the total covenant, were sovereignly bestowed by God in His grace. In particular, the protective clause was in effect and to this day remains in effect because of the response of individuals and nations to Israel, not because of Israel's response to them or, for that matter, even to God.

In concluding this discussion of the Abrahamic Covenant and in particular the Genesis 12:3 protective clause with its bearing on the Holocaust, it is fitting to quote the author Samuel Langhorne Clemens (Pseudonym: Mark Twain, 1835–1910) and his immortal question on the Jew:

> If the statistics are right, the Jews constitute but *one percent* of the human race. It suggests a nebulous dim puff of star dust lost in the blaze of the Milky Way. Properly the Jew ought hardly to be heard of; but he is heard of, has always been heard of. He is as prominent on the planet as any other people, and his commercial importance is extravagantly out of proportion to the smallness of his bulk. His contributions to the world's list of great names in literature, science, art, music, finance, medicine, and abstruse learning are also away out of proportion to the weakness of his numbers. He has made a marvelous fight in this world, in all the ages; and has done it with his hands tied behind him. He could be vain of himself, and be excused for it. The Egyptian, the Babylonian, and the Persian rose, filled the planet with sound and splendor, then faded to dream-stuff and passed away; the Greek and the Roman followed, and made a vast noise, and they are gone; other peoples have sprung up and help their torch high for a time, but it burned out, and they sit in twilight now, or have

vanished. The Jew saw them all, beat them all, and is now what he always was, exhibiting no decadence, no infirmities of age, no weakening of his parts, no slowing of his energies, no dulling of his alert and aggressive mind. All things are mortal but the Jew; all other forces pass, but he remains. What is the secret of his immortality?[29]

The answer to Clemens' question is simple: the Abrahamic Covenant in general and the anti-Semitism (or protection) clause in particular (Gen. 12:3).

David L. Cooper, a Christian scholar of the Hebrew Bible, almost played the role of a prophet during the height of World War II. Being fully convinced of the anti-Semitism clause of Genesis 12:3, Cooper knew what Clemens did not. In 1943, he penned the following words concerning God's commitment to the protective clause of Genesis 12:3:

A special blessing is promised to the one who sincerely, and not for material considerations, blesses Abraham and his seed. Those who have followed the spirit and the letter of this condition testify that God has made good on this promise to them. He has likewise cursed those nations and individuals who have persecuted the Jew. Egypt became one of the basest kingdoms of the world… Assyria and Babylon likewise fell under the judgment of God because of ill-treatment of the Jews. The same thing is true of ancient Rome and medieval Spain. *This special curse will likewise fall upon the Nazi regime and all supporting it who have as their objective the persecution of the seed of Abraham* (italics added).[30]

---

[29] Samuel Langhorne Clemens (Pseudonym: Mark Twain), "Concerning the Jews," in Janet Smith, ed., *Mark Twain on the Damned Human Race*, American Century Series (New York, NY: Hill and Wang, 1962), pp. 176-177.

[30] David L. Cooper, *What Men Must Believe or God's Gracious Provision for Man* (Los Angeles, CA: Biblical Research Society, 1963), p. 306.

The Land Covenant

The second unconditional covenant that God initiated with Israel was once called the Palestinian Covenant. Since the reestablishment of Israel in 1948, it is accurately known as the Land Covenant.

The parameters of this strategic covenant are given in Deuteronomy 30:1-10. Pentecost summarizes its setting:

> In the closing chapters of the book of Deuteronomy, the children of Israel, the physical seed of Abraham, are facing a crisis in their national existence. They are about to pass from the proved leadership of Moses into the unproven leadership of Joshua. They are standing at the entrance to the land that was promised to them by God in such terms as:
>
> Unto thy seed will I give this land (Gen. 12:7).
>
> For all the land which thou seest, to thee will I give it, and to thy seed for ever (Gen. 13:15).
>
> And I will establish my covenant between me and thee and thy seed after thee in their generations for an everlasting covenant, to be a God unto thee, and to thy seed after thee. And I will give unto thee, and to thy seed after thee, the land wherein thou art a stranger, all the land of Canaan, for an everlasting possession; and I will be their God (Gen. 17:7-8).
>
> But this land is possessed by Israel's enemies, who have shown they will resist any attempt by Israel to enter the land promised them. It is impossible for them to return to their former status as a slave nation and the land to which they were journeying as "strangers and pilgrims" seemed shut before them. As a result, certain important considerations must be faced by the nation. Is the land of Palestine still their possession? Did the inauguration of the Mosaic Covenant, which all agree was conditional, set aside the unconditional Abrahamic covenant? Could Israel hope to en-

ter into permanent possession of their land in the face of such opposition? To answer these important questions God stated again His covenant promise concerning Israel's possession of and inheritance in the land in Deuteronomy 30:1-10, which statement we call the Palestinian covenant, because it answers the question of Israel's relation to the land promises of the Abrahamic covenant.[31]

The Provisions of the Land Covenant

The provisions of the Land Covenant can be divided into seven major features:
1. The nation will be plucked off the land for its unfaithfulness (Deut. 28: 63-68; 30:1-3).
2. There will be a future repentance of Israel (Lev. 26:40-42; Deut. 30:1-3).
3. Israel's Messiah will return (Deut. 30:3-6).
4. Israel will be restored to the land (Deut. 30:5).
5. Israel will be converted as a nation (Deut. 30:4-8; cf. Rom. 11:26-27).
6. Israel's enemies will be judged (Deut. 30:7).
7. The nation will then receive her full blessing (Deut. 30:9).

Pentecost maintains that the Land Covenant was confirmed later in Israel's history by the prophet Ezekiel:

> This same covenant is confirmed at a later time in Israel's history. It becomes a subject of Ezekiel's prophecy. God affirms His love for Israel in the time of her infancy (Ezek. 16:1-7); He reminds her that she was chosen and related to Jehovah by marriage (vv. 8-14); but she played the harlot (vv. 15-34); therefore, the punishment of dispersion was meted out to her (vv. 35-52); but this is not a final setting aside of Israel, for there will be a restoration (vv. 53-63). This restoration is based on the promise:

---

[31] Pentecost, *Things to Come*, p. 91 (italics added).

> Nevertheless I will remember my covenant with thee in the days of thy youth, and I will establish unto thee an everlasting covenant. Then thou shalt remember thy ways, and be ashamed, when thou shalt receive thy sisters, thine elder and thy younger; and I will give them unto thee for daughters, but not by thy covenant. And I will establish my covenant with thee; and thou shalt know that I am the Lord (Ezek. 16:60-62).

Thus the Lord reaffirms the Palestinian covenant and calls it an eternal covenant by which He is bound.[32]

The Character of the Land Covenant

Pentecost lists four major reasons in support of the assertion that the Land Covenant is unconditional in nature.[33] First, in Ezekiel 16:60, God refers to it as *an everlasting covenant*. It could only be everlasting if its fulfillment was independent of human responsibility and grounded in the Word of the Eternal One.

Second, it is merely an amplification and expansion of portions of the Abrahamic Covenant, which is itself an unconditional covenant. Therefore, this expansion must also be eternal and unconditional.

Third, God guarantees that He will effect the necessary conversion that is required for the fulfillment of the Land Covenant. This is made clear in Romans 11:26-27, Hosea 2:14-23, Deuteronomy 30:6, and Ezekiel 11:16-21. This conversion is viewed as a sovereign act of God in Scripture and must be acknowledged to be certain because of His integrity.

Fourth, parts of this covenant have already been literally fulfilled. Israel has experienced dispersion as a judgment for unfaithfulness. Israel has also seen restorations to the land and now awaits

---

[32] Pentecost, *Things to Come*, p. 92-93.

[33] See: ibid., p. 93.

the final restoration. There are numerous examples in history of Israel's enemies being judged. These literal partial fulfillments all point to a future fulfillment of the unfulfilled portions in the same way.

After listing these reasons, Pentecost concludes:

> It may be argued by some that this covenant is conditional because of the statements of Deuteronomy 30:1-3: "when. . . then." It should be observed that the only conditional element here is the time element. The program is certain; the time when this program will be fulfilled depends upon the conversion of the nation. Conditional time elements do not make the whole program conditional, however.[34]

Moses had earlier stated the seriousness of violating the covenant that God had made with Israel, a violation that would eventually scatter the nation throughout the world, forcing them into repentance "in the latter days." He made this clear in Deuteronomy 4:23-31:

> *²³So watch yourselves, that you do not forget the covenant of the Lord your God which He made with you, and make for yourselves a carved image in the form of anything against which the Lord your God has commanded you. ²⁴For the Lord your God is a consuming fire, a jealous God. ²⁵"When you become the father of children and children's children and have remained long in the land, and act corruptly, and make an idol in the form of any-thing, and do that which is evil in the sight of the Lord your God so as to provoke Him to anger, ²⁶I call heaven and earth to witness against you today, that you will surely perish quickly from the land where you are going over the Jordan to possess it. You shall not live long on it, but will be utterly **destroyed**. ²⁷The Lord will **scatter** you among the peoples, and you will be left few in number among the nations where the Lord*

---

[34] Ibid.

*drives you. ²⁸There you will serve gods, the work of man's hands, wood and stone, which neither see nor hear nor eat nor smell. ²⁹But from there you will **seek** the Lord your God, and you will **find** Him if you search for Him with all your heart and all your soul. ³⁰When you are in distress and all these things have come upon you, **in the latter days** you will **return** to the Lord your God and **listen** to His voice. ³¹For the Lord your God is a compassionate God; He will not fail you nor destroy you nor forget **the covenant with your fathers which He swore to them*** (emphasis added).

The British rabbi and biblical scholar Joseph Hertz, in *The Pentateuch and Haftorahs*, reaffirms the words of Moses in Deuteronomy 30:1-10 (which he maintains is a fuller restatement of the vital lesson taught in Deut. 4:29-31) when he says: "Punishment is not God's last word unto Israel. If Israel seeks God, Israel will find mercy at the hands of the LORD, and be brought back to the land of his fathers."[35]

The Outworking of the Land Covenant

The outworking of the Land Covenant takes place through three dispossessions of the promised land and three restorations back to the land. Chafer summarizes this particular outworking of the covenant:

> Prophecy respecting Israel's tenure of the land anticipates three distinct dispossessions of the land (cf. Gen. 15:13-14, 16; Jer. 25:11-12; Deut. 28:63-68 with 30:1-3) and three restorations (cf. Gen. 15:14 with Josh. 1:2-7; Dan. 9:2 with Jer. 25:11-12; Deut. 30:3; Jer. 23:5-8; Ezek. 37:21-25; Acts 15:14-17). The three dis-

---

[35] Hertz, *The Pentateuch and Haftorahs*, p. 880. On the "latter days," see also Deut. 31:29; Jer. 30:24.

possessions have been fulfilled, so also the first and second restorations. The final restoration for which the nation waits is yet future.[36]

And again, Chafer states:

The Palestinian covenant conveys the land to Abraham and his earthly seed through Isaac and Jacob for an everlasting possession. Added predictions modify the covenant only with respect to the time of its final tenure. Three dispossessions were anticipated and three restorations... All three of the dispossessions are now fulfilled and two restorations. Thus the nation is out of her land for the third and last time. When restored again, as predicted, that people will go out no more forever.[37]

The Dispossessions

Three times, the Jews have been expelled from the land of Israel due to disobedience to God. The first dispossession occurred in the era of the Patriarchs and led the Israelites into Egypt (Gen. 15:13-16; chapters 37–38; cf. Gen. 43:32; 46:31-34; Exod. 8:25-26).[38] The second dispossession occurred in two phases: (1) the captivity to Assyria in 722 B.C. (2 Kgs. 17:7-23)[39]; and (2) the captivity to Babylon in 586 B.C. (2 Chron. 36:11-21; Ezek. 20:23-24).[40] The third dispossession caused the dispersion of the Jews into the Roman Empire in A.D. 70 and has lasted until 1948 (Mt. 23:37-39; Lk. 19:37-44; 21:20-24).[41] That particular year marks the beginning of the end of the final expulsion from the

---

[36] Chafer, *Systematic Theology*, 8 vols., vol. 4: *Ecclesiology – Eschatology*, p. 317.

[37] Ibid., vol. 5: *Christology*, pp. 320-321.

[38] See also: Gen. 34; 46:3-4; Exod. 12:40-41.

[39] Cf. 2 Kgs. 15:29; 1 Chron. 5:25-26; Hos. 8-10; Amos 7:16-17; 9:8-10; Mic. 1:1-7.

[40] Cf. 2 Kgs. 21:10-16; 24:1-4; 25:8-12; Jer. 15:4; 25:1-12; 29:10.

[41] Cf. Jer. 9:13-16; 24:9-10; Dan. 9:26.

promised land. However, it must be recognized that this dispossession will last until the end of the tribulation period, when Messiah returns, i.e., the entirety of "the times of the Gentiles" (cf. Dan. 2:11; 7:13; 9:27; 12:1, 11; Joel 3:1-3; Zech. 14:4; Mt. 24:15-22, 29-31; 25:31-46).

During these dispossessions or dispersions, Israel suffers at the hands of Gentile nations, and the intensity of this suffering is unprecedented in human history. The biblical scholar and professor of Semitics and Old Testament Charles Feinberg summarizes the fate of dispersed Israel:

> During the time of Israel's rejection she is scattered, persecuted, and blind. The scattering of Israel had been the subject of Moses' prophecy in the Book of Deuteronomy. He foretold: "The LORD shall scatter you among the nations"; "The LORD shall scatter thee among the people, from one end of the earth even unto the other"; "I said, I would scatter them into corners" (Deuteronomy 4:27; 28:64; 32:26, KJV). Before His crucifixion Christ, predicting the destruction of Jerusalem, said of Israel that "they shall fall by the edge of the sword, and shall be led away captive into all nations" (Luke 21:24, KJV). Blessing for Israel has been linked with dwelling in the land. How literally the words of Christ and the prophets have been fulfilled in this instance! The Jew has been the man without a country, the wandering Jew. They are to be found in every country of the world. There are white Jews and black Jews, Indian Jews, French Jews, German Jews, English Jews, American Jews, and so on. But always they are Jews, for God in His scattering of them has preserved their national existence for His yet future purposes.
>
> Israel scattered has not meant Israel blessed. Far from it, for she has been hounded and persecuted to this day. To read the tale of Israel's woes is to learn of a people which has been the object of

the hatred of all nations. But so it is always: the world hates that which God has loved.[42]

J. Palmer Muntz, who at one time in his fruitful life served as the Vice President of the American Association for Jewish Evangelism, shares Feinberg's view:

> This dispersion of Israel is one of the great tragedies of history. How bitterly and relentlessly have the Jews been persecuted! They have been banned and banished from almost every nation. They have been shamefully treated and downtrodden, ruthlessly plundered, abominably abused, diabolically tortured and barbarously martyred. But Israel, dispersed and persecuted is also the miracle of history in her preservation. No other people could have survived such treatment without extermination or utter degradation.[43]

David Baron, a committed Zionist and the co-founder of the Hebrew Christian Testimony to Israel missionary organization, also reiterates this point but adds divine causation to it when he says:

> The history of the Jews since the destruction of the second Temple is one long martyrology, the record of an almost unbroken chain of unparalleled suffering—a chronicle of massacres, oppressions, banishments, fiendish tortures, spoliations, and degradations which have been inflicted upon them for the most part by so-called Christian nations...
>
> At the cost of repetition, it must be emphasized that the calamities and sufferings of Israel are due in the first instance to God's retributive anger against His people on account of their sins and

---

[42] Charles L. Feinberg, *Israel at the Center of History & Revelation* (Portland, OR: Multnomah Press, 1980), pp. 129-30.

[43] J. Palmer Muntz, "The Jew in History and Destiny," in John W. Bradbury, ed., *The Sure Word of Prophecy* (New York, NY: Fleming H. Revell Company, 1944), p. 228.

apostasies, and are in fulfillment of prophetic forecasts, predictions, and warnings, some of which were uttered at the very beginning of their national history.⁴⁴

The Holocaust historian Raul Hilberg maintains that the Nazi annihilation of six million Jews was the natural result of three consecutive policies against Jewry during its dispersion in Western civilization:

> Anti-Jewish policies and anti-Jewish actions did not have their beginning in 1933. For many centuries, and in many countries, the Jews have been victims of destructive action. What was the object of these activities? What were the aims of those who persisted in anti-Jewish deeds? Throughout Western history [since the fourth century], three consecutive policies have been applied against Jewry in its dispersion…: conversion, expulsion, and annihilation. The second appeared as an alternative to the first, and the third emerged as an alternative to the second…
>
> The missionaries of Christianity had said in effect: You have no right to live among us as Jews. The secular rulers who followed had proclaimed: You have no right to live among us. The German Nazis at last decreed: You have no right to live.
>
> These progressively more drastic goals brought in their wake a slow and steady growth of anti-Jewish thinking. The process began with the attempt to drive the Jews into Christianity. The development was continued in order to force the victims into exile. It was finished when the Jews were driven to their deaths. The German Nazis, then, did not discard the past; they built upon it. They did not begin a development; they completed it.⁴⁵

---

⁴⁴ David Baron, *The History of Israel: Its Spiritual Significance* (London, England: Morgan & Scott, Ltd., n. d.), pp. 76, 79.

⁴⁵ Raul Hilberg, *The Destruction of the European Jews* (New York, NY: Harper Colophon Books, 1961), pp. 1, 3-4.

It is no wonder that leading Jewish Orthodox theologian Joseph Soloveitchik proclaims that the Holocaust is a decisive moment of "suffering unparalleled in the history of exilic millennia."[46]

The Restorations

The Jews have experienced two restorations to the promised land, both within the sovereign grace and purpose of God. The first was under Moses and Joshua, when God restored the Jewish people from under the Pharaoh and Egyptian bondage after four hundred years of slavery (Gen. 15:13-16; Exod.; Josh.). The second was under Nehemiah, Ezra, Zerubbabel, Haggai, and Zachariah, when God restored the Jewish people from under Cyrus and the Persians, following seventy years of captivity first to the Babylonians and then the Medo-Persian Empire (2 Chron. 36:22-23; Ezra 1:1-7; 5:1-2; 6:14; Neh. 1:17-20; 7:5-6; Isa. 44:28; Jer. 25:1-11; 29:1-14). There yet remains one more restoration to the promised land—the final return. This return will be permanent and take place in two different phases: (1) the Jews will be brought back in partial restoration to the land in unbelief, in preparation for judgment—the judgment of the tribulation period (Isa. 28:14-22; Jer. 30:1-24; Ezek. 20:33-38; 22:17-22; 36:22-27; 37:1-14; 38:8, 12; 39:7, 22, 23-29; Dan. 9:24-27; Mt. 24:15-22, 29-31); and (2) the Jews will finally be brought back in total restoration to the land in faith, in preparation for blessing—the blessing of the Messianic kingdom to be established at the end of the tribulation period when Messiah returns to the earth (Deut. 27:12-13; 30:1-10; Isa. 11:11-16; 60:1-22; 61:4-9; Jer. 16:14-15; 23:1-8; 31:27-37; Dan. 12:1-3; Joel 3:18-21; Amos 9:11-12; Micah 4:11-13; 5:4-15; 7:11-20; Zech. 10:8-12; 12:1–14:21; Rom. 11:15-27).

---

[46] Joseph B. Soloveitchik, "*Kol Dodi Dofek*," in Shimon Federbush, ed., *Torah u-Melukhah* (Jerusalem, Israel: Mossad Harav Kook, 1961), p. 18.

The twentieth century marked the beginning of a phenomenon that is unparalleled in all of human history. A tiny people, dispersed throughout the entire world, has begun to return to its ancient homeland. After centuries of unmitigated humiliation and suffering, Israel is once again a nation. Scattered throughout the nations of the world, she has outlived them all. No other people has survived such a scattering. They have all been either conquered or assimilated. But God, in His wisdom and power, has kept the Jews distinct and unique, and He has kept His promises true and viable to this people of His own calling. Since 1948, Jews from all over the world have been returning to their ancient homeland. It is, for sure, a regathering in unbelief, but that is how the prophets portrayed it. This is the first phase of the final restoration to the land.

It is highly unlikely that this regathering could now be taking place without the Holocaust. From a human standpoint alone, world sympathy was directed toward the surviving Jews of Eastern Europe. Never before had such a world opinion been so favorable to the Jew and his ancient homeland. Born out of the ashes of Auschwitz and into the furnace of Arab hostility, Israel is alive and striving to be a refuge for all Jews who may have to face another possible genocide threat. This is not to say that the nation was born out of the redemption provided by the six million martyrs. Rather, it is to say that, in the providence of God, the prophetic time clock has once again begun to tick for the people of Israel.

The current regathering is only the beginning. How long it will take to accomplish the final phase of restoration remains to be seen. That particular phase will begin with the signing of the protective treaty between unbelieving Israel and the Antichrist (cf. Dan. 9:24-27; Mt. 24:15ff.; 2 Thess. 2:3-12; Rev. 12:13–13:10).[47]

---

[47] See also: Isa. 28:14-22; Dan. 7:25; 8:23-25; 11:36-39, 40-45; 12:1, 11; Rev. 12:6.

Judgment for Israel is an imminent possibility, but the blessing of God will follow. Baron affirms this order of events by stating:

> The return in unbelief is, we believe, *the necessary precursor to the resumption of God's dealing with them as a nation*; but of this we are certain, on the ground of prophetic Scripture, that the Jews will never possess the land *in blessing* until God's longstanding controversy with them is ended.[48]

The Davidic Covenant

The Davidic Covenant is the third unconditional covenant that God initiated with Israel (2 Sam. 7:1-17; 1 Chron. 17:1-15; Ps. 89:1-4, 19-37, 49; cf. 1 Kgs. 11:9-13, 29-39). This particular covenant reaffirms the seed promises that God made to Abraham. Old Testament scholar and author Walter C. Kaiser Jr. has adequately explained the relationship between the three major passages listed above concerning this covenant:

> II Samuel 7 will be treated as it purports to be: the historical record of the event itself, while I Chronicles 17 places a parallel account in a post-exilic theological context. The historical event, in turn, also became the basis for the Psalm 89 composition by one of David's contemporaries, Ethan the Ezrahite…
>
> What was given to the original "man of promise" [David] is now applied to this new historical manifestation of the "man of promise" by Ethan, under the revelation of God.[49]

---

[48] Baron, *The History of Israel*, p. 143.

[49] Walter C. Kaiser, Jr., "The Blessing of David: The Charter for Humanity," in John H. Skilton, ed., *The Law and the Prophets: Old Testament Studies Prepared in Honor of Oswald Thompson Allis* (Nutley, NJ: Presbyterian and Reformed Publishing Company, 1974), pp. 301-302.

The Provisions of the Davidic Covenant

Walvoord summarizes the provisions of the Davidic Covenant as spelled out in 2 Samuel 7:12-16 into five major categories:

> The provisions of the Davidic covenant include, then, the following items: (1) David is to have a child, yet to be born, who shall succeed him and establish his kingdom. (2) This son (Solomon) shall build the temple instead of David. (3) The throne of his kingdom shall be established forever. (4) The throne will not be taken away from him (Solomon) even though his sins justify chastisement. (5) David's house, throne, and kingdom shall be established forever.[50]

The crucial provision in regard to this study about the Holocaust is the fourth: that chastisement would be exercised within a father/son relationship and that this discipline would in no way abrogate the ultimate fulfillment of the covenant itself. It is obvious from Psalm 89 that this father/son discipline was not confined to just Solomon but indeed extended to the entire Davidic line. This is affirmed both by Jewish and Christian commentators alike.

Writing in the Soncino series, Rabbi Solomon Goldman affirms the Jewish position on this point when he summarizes the 2 Samuel passage:

> In Jewish tradition, the prophecy is interpreted as referring to Solomon, who was not yet born. So [in this manner,] David interprets it in I Chron. xxii. 9ff. and [as does] Solomon in I Kings viii. 15ff. [O]n the other hand, the view of most modern scholars is that the Davidic dynasty as a whole, not any individual member of it, is the burden of the prophecy in this and the following verses, and that the third person singular pronoun throughout refers to David's *seed* or posterity...

---

[50] Walvoord, *The Millennial Kingdom*, p. 195.

God's favour to David's line will not be unconditional. If any of his posterity sin, he will have to suffer the penalty of his wrongdoing...

The deep impression which this great promise [verse 16] made is manifest from the number of subsequent references to it. David applied it to Solomon (I Chron. xxii. 9f., xxviii. 2ff.), Solomon claimed it to himself (I Kings v. 19, viii. 17ff.), it is confirmed to Solomon (I Kings ix. 4f.)[,] and it is repeatedly affirmed that, in spite of the sins of individual kings, the kingdom shall not be withdrawn from David's house for his sake (I Kings xi. 31ff., xv. 4f.; 2 Kings viii. 19). Ps. lxxxix recapitulates the promise and pleads with God that it should not be frustrated. Moreover, this promise of an everlasting kingdom of the house of David powerfully influenced the development of the Messianic hope in Israel.[51]

Keil and Delitzsch, writing from a Christian point of view, affirm the same conclusion concerning 2 Samuel 7:

It is very obvious, from all the separate details of this promise, that it related primarily to Solomon, and had a certain fulfillment in him and his reign... At the same time, however unmistakable the allusions to Solomon are, the substance of the promise is not fully exhausted in him. The threefold repetition of the expression "for ever," the establishment of the kingdom and throne of David *for ever*, points incontrovertibly beyond the time of Solomon, and to the eternal continuance of the seed of David. The word *seed* denotes the posterity of a person, which may consist either in one son or in several children, or in a long line of successive generations. The idea of a number of persons living at the same time, is here precluded by the context of the promise, as only one of David's successors could sit upon the throne at a time. On the other hand, the idea of a number of descendants following one another

---

[51] Solomon Goldman, *Soncino Books of the Bible: Samuel* (London, England: Soncino Press, 1949), pp. 227-229.

is evidently contained in the promise, that God would not withdraw His favour from the seed, even if it went astray[,] as He had done from Saul, since this implies that even in that case the throne should be transmitted from father to son… The promise consequently refers to the posterity of David.[52]

The Character of the Davidic Covenant

The Davidic Covenant is an eternal covenant (2 Sam. 7:13, 16; 23:5; 1 Chron. 17:12, 14; 22:9-10; 2 Chron. 13:5; 21:7; Ps. 89:1-4, 28-29, 36-37; 132:11; Isa. 9:7; 55:3; Jer. 33:20-22; Ezek. 37:25; Lk. 1:32-33; Acts 13:34). Like the Abrahamic Covenant, upon which it was founded, the Davidic Covenant guarantees an eternal seed on the throne of David. This will, of course, be ultimately fulfilled by David's greatest Son, Jesus the Messiah.

Furthermore, the Davidic Covenant is an unconditional covenant. This can be seen from its eternal nature, for only an unconditional covenant can truly be an eternal covenant. Its complete fulfillment exclusively rests upon the faithfulness of God Himself. Also, the covenant has built into it a father/son clause, which guarantees discipline to David's unfaithful descendants. This presupposes its unconditional and ultimate fulfillment. Scripture reaffirms this to be so by its numerous references to this covenant, even after the many gross failures of David's seed.

The Outworking of the Davidic Covenant

The Davidic Covenant, with its disciplinary father/son clause (2 Sam. 7:14-15; Ps. 89:30-33), is worked out in two distinct ways: First, it is worked out in the Davidic line alone; and second, it is worked out in the nation as a whole.

---

[52] C. F. Keil and F. Delitzsch, *The Books of Samuel*, K & D, pp. 346-347.

Regarding the Davidic line, it is obvious from both 2 Samuel 7 and Psalm 89 that the disciplinary father/son clause found its primary fulfillment in David's descendants. It began in the life of Solomon (1 Kgs. 11:9-13) and continued down through both houses of Israel (cf. the books of Kings and Chronicles). With rare exceptions, the kings of Israel and Judah were continually exposed to the *rod of men and the strokes of sons of men* (2 Sam. 7:14b). The continual discipline they experienced is a profound testimony both to the depravity of the Davidic line and to the faithfulness of God to the Davidic Covenant. He continually chastised the line but never cut it off.

Regarding the nation as a whole, although the Davidic line experienced continual discipline in accordance with the Davidic Covenant, the chastisement was not confined merely to that line. It extended to the entire nation. The reason is, in one sense, the kingly line always represented the people as a whole, and when the king defected from the ways of God, he not only brought judgment upon himself but also upon his people as well. When the king was conquered with *the rod of men*, his people also suffered the same *strokes of the sons of men*.

Given the disciplinary father/son clause of the Davidic Covenant, it is not surprising that the Bible describes Gentile nations as being used by God as His instruments of divine chastisement upon the covenanted nation of Israel as a whole. Five specific nations are so described:

1. Egypt (Isa. 10:24-27; cf. Gen. 15:13-16)
2. Assyria (2 Kgs. 17:1-41; Isa. 10:5-19, 24-27, esp. v. 5 where the phrase "the rod of My anger" is used; 14:24-27; 30:30-32; 37:21-29)
3. Babylon (2 Chron. 36:17-21; Isa. 13:1–14:23; 42:23-25; Jer. 25:8-14; 27:4-11, 16-22; 29:10; 43:8-13; 50:1–51:64; Lam. 3:1, where the phrase "the rod of His wrath" is used; Ezek.

21:8-17, where Babylon is described as "a sword"; Mic. 5:1; Hab. 1:1–2:20; Zech. 1:12-15)
4. Syria (Dan. 8:9-14, 23-25; 11:15-35)
5. Rome (Dan. 9:26; Mt. 23:37-39; Lk. 19:41-44; 21:20-24; Jn. 11:47-52)

In His sovereignty, God is not only the Lord of His covenant people Israel but also the Lord of the pagan nations, directing them (albeit, without their knowledge) to accomplish His perfect will (cf. Hab. 2:20).

The fifth nation in particular is pertinent to the discussion of the Holocaust. Rome came to destroy Jerusalem because of the Jewish rejection of the Messiahship of Jesus. The destruction was total and cast the Jews into worldwide dispersion. Historian Max Dimont describes the A.D. 70 devastation in the following words:

> The end was inevitable. With battering rams and portable bridges, the Romans stormed the walls of Jerusalem. Like termites they spilled into the city, slaughtering a populace reduced to helplessness by starvation. Four years of bitter defeats at the hands of the Jews had made mockery of the vaunted invincibility of the Roman legions, and only killing could now soothe their bruised vanity. The Temple was put to the torch, infants thrown into the flames, women raped, priests massacred, Zealots thrown from the wall. Survivors of the carnage were earmarked for the triumphal procession to be held in Rome, sold as slaves, held for the wild beasts in the arenas, or saved to be thrown off the Tarpeian Rock in Rome for amusement. At no time did the Romans more justly earn the grim words of their own historian, Tacitus, who said, "They make a desolation and call it peace." Altogether, Tacitus estimates 600,000 defenseless Jewish civilians were slain in the aftermath of the siege.[53]

---

[53] Dimont, *Jews, God and History*, pp. 105-06. For a detailed description of the destruction, see Flavius Josephus, *The Wars of the Jews*, Books V–VII.

Although the rabbis refused to see the destruction as a punishment for the national rejection of Jesus' Messiahship, they nevertheless sought to explain it through different national sins. The Babylonian Talmud lists eight reasons for the destruction of the Temple:

1. The Sabbath was desecrated.
2. The reading of the *Shema* in the morning and evening was neglected.
3. The education of schoolchildren was neglected.
4. The inhabitants of Jerusalem were not ashamed of each other.
5. The small and the great were made equal.
6. The inhabitants of Jerusalem did not rebuke each other.
7. Scholars were despised in the city.
8. Truthful men ceased to exist in the city.[54]

Tractate *Yoma* 9b lists three additional reasons for the Temple's destruction:

> Due to what reason was the First Temple destroyed? It was destroyed due to the fact that there were three matters that existed in the First Temple: Idol worship, forbidden sexual relations, and bloodshed.
>
> … considering that the people during the Second Temple period were engaged in Torah study, observance of mitzvot, and acts of kindness, and that they did not perform the sinful acts that were performed in the First Temple, why was the Second Temple destroyed? It was destroyed due to the fact that there was wanton hatred during that period. This comes to teach you that the sin of wanton hatred is equivalent to the three severe transgressions: Idol worship, forbidden sexual relations and bloodshed.[55]

---

[54] *b. Shabbat* 119b, accessible at www.sefaria.org/shabbat.119b:6-11.

[55] *b. Yoma* 9b:3, 8; retrieved from www.sefaria.org, where the English translation from The William Davidson digital edition of the *Koren Noé Talmud* is used.

While Rabbinic Judaism recognized idolatry, fornication, the shedding of blood, and wanton hatred as the main reasons for the destruction of the First and Second Temple, it is not possible to claim that God's use of *the rod of men* ended with the A.D. 70 destruction. The eternality of the Davidic Covenant guarantees the continuation of the disciplinary father/son clause in 2 Samuel 7:13-14. Until the ultimate Messianic fulfillment of the Davidic Covenant in the millennial kingdom, the nation of Israel as a whole (including the Davidic line, which is known only to God) is subject to "the rod of God's anger" (Isa. 10:5). The covenant nation is in disobedience to the covenant God, but He has not rejected her. Nevertheless, He continues to raise up pagan nations as His instruments of chastisement during her years of dispersion (cf. Lev. 26:33, 36-45; Deut. 28:64-68; 30:1-10). It is with tremendous difficulty that those committed to biblical truth must affirm that Nazi Germany was one of those pagan nations.

For the Jewish theologian, this truth is an impossibility. Rubenstein graphically illustrates the general response to it among Jewish religious leaders:

> Traditional Jewish theology maintains that God is the ultimate, omnipotent actor in the historical drama. It has interpreted every major catastrophe in Jewish history as God's punishment of a sinful Israel. I fail to see how this position can be maintained without regarding Hitler and the SS as instruments of God's will. The agony of European Jewry cannot be likened to the testing of Job. To see any purpose in the death camps, the traditional believer is forced to regard the most demonic, antihuman explosion in all history as a meaningful expression of God's purposes. The idea is simply too obscene for me to accept.[56]

It is the emotional trauma of the Holocaust destruction that has paralyzed contemporary religious Judaism. But is the trauma that

---

[56] Rubenstein, *After Auschwitz*, p. 153.

was inflicted upon the Jewish people by the Germans any worse than that by the Assyrians in 722 B.C., the Babylonians in 586 B.C., or the Romans in A.D. 70? Thousands of men, women, and children suffered and died horrible deaths in all of these catastrophes, and yet the Holocaust is seen as unique. Perhaps in degree it is, but certainly not in kind. In fact, a probable case could be made for the fact that the Holocaust was not even unique in degree. This is maintained by biblical scholar and professor H. L. Ellison:

> Let us look at the tragedy of the destruction of Jerusalem and the Second Commonwealth in A.D. 70 and the time of trouble that reached its climax in the crushing of Bar Cochba's uprising in 135. The figures in Josephus are unfortunately so unreliable that we cannot make any certain calculation of casualties. The most likely estimate of the number of Jews in the Roman empire in the 1st Century A.D. is just under seven million, i.e. not that far short of the number within Hitler's reach. Of these about two and a half million will have lived in Judea. This number will have reduced to about 800,000 at the end of the Bar Cochba rising. But in the interval between A.D. 70 and 135 there was a tremendous loss of Jewish lives in Egypt, Cyrenaica, Cyprus and other parts of the Roman world. In other words the loss of life must have been comparable with those who perished under the Nazis.[57]

These comparisons are certainly not meant to minimize the horrendous guilt and responsibility of the Nazis. Like the nations of old that God raised up, the Nazis ended where all the other anti-Semitic peoples have ended: in total judgment (cf. Gen. 12:3). God's ways are indeed mysterious, in particular with His covenant nation Israel, and yet His Word remains true: David's eternal kingdom will be established under the Messiah, but it will

---

[57] H. L. Ellison, "The Impact of Auschwitz on Theology Today," *The Hebrew Christian* 54 (Autumn 1981): 89.

only arrive after the Messiah's nation is disciplined into submission and obedience. *The rod of men* (2 Sam. 7:14) is yet to strike again, one final time—the worst time in Israel's history (cf. Zech. 13:7-9; Mt. 24:15-22; Rev. 12:1-17).[58] In fact, each of the above holocausts is like another wave, each building in intensity and violence and finally spilling into the final time of *Jacob's trouble*, i.e., the tribulation (Jer. 30:1-24; Ezek. 20:33-44).

The New Covenant

The New Covenant is the fourth and final unconditional covenant that God initiated with Israel (Jer. 31:31-34).[59] This particular covenant reaffirms the blessing promises that God made with Abraham. The Abrahamic Covenant included certain personal promises to Abraham, certain national promises to Israel, and certain universal promises to the Gentiles (cf. Gen. 12:1-3).[60] The New Covenant spells out the detailed blessings that God has committed to the nation Israel.

The Provisions of the New Covenant

In an excellent summary of the provisions of the New Covenant, Ryrie emphasizes that Israel is the people of this covenant. Furthermore, he notes that the covenant will be fulfilled in the millennium, which is the period of the New Covenant. Then he lists several provisions for Israel as they are found in the Hebrew Bible:

> (1) The new covenant is an unconditional, grace covenant resting on the "I will" of God. The frequency of the use of the phrase in Jeremiah 31:31-34 is striking. Cf. Ezekiel 16:60-62.

---

[58] See also: Isa. 13:9; Ezek. 7:2-13; Dan. 9:24, 27; 12:1, 11; Joel 1:15; 2:1-3; Amos 5:18-20; Zeph. 1:14-18.

[59] Cf. Lk. 22:20; 1 Cor. 11:25; 2 Cor. 3:6; Heb. 8:8-13; 9:15; 12:24

[60] Cf. Gen. 17:5; Exod. 23:22; Zech. 8:13; Acts 3:25; Gal. 3:8.

(2) The new covenant is an everlasting covenant. This is closely related to the fact that it is unconditional and made in grace... (Isa. 61:8; cf. Ezek. 37:26; Jer. 31:35-37).

(3) The new covenant also promises the impartation of a renewed mind and heart which we may call regeneration... (Jer. 31:33, cf. Isa. 59:21).

(4) The new covenant provides for restoration to the favor and blessing of God... (Hos. 2:19-20, cf. Isa. 61:9).

(5) Forgiveness of sin is also included in the covenant, "for I will remove their iniquity, and I will remember their sin no more" (Jer. 31:34b).

(6) The indwelling of the Holy Spirit is also included. This is seen by comparing Jeremiah 31:33 with Ezekiel 36:27.

(7) The teaching ministry of the Holy Spirit will be manifested, and the will of God will be known by obedient hearts... (Jer. 31:34).

(8) As is always the case when Israel is in the land, she will be blessed materially in accordance with the provisions of the new covenant... (Jer. 32:41) ... (Isa. 61:8) ... (Ezek. 34:25-27).

(9) The sanctuary will be rebuilt in Jerusalem, for it is written, "I... will set my sanctuary in the midst of them for evermore. My Tabernacle also shall be with them" (Ezek. 37:26-27a).

(10) War shall cease, and peace shall reign, according to Hosea 2:18. The fact that this is also a definite characteristic of the millennium (Isa. 2:4) further supports the fact that the new covenant is millennial in its fulfillment.

(11) The blood of the Lord Jesus Christ is the foundation of all the blessings of the new covenant, for "by the blood of thy covenant I have sent forth thy prisoners out of the pit wherein is no water" (Zech. 9:11).

By way of summary, it may be said that, as far as the Old Testament teaching on the new covenant is concerned, the covenant was made with the Jewish people. Its period of fulfillment is yet future, beginning when the Deliverer shall come and continuing throughout all eternity. Its provisions for the nation Israel are glorious, and they all rest and depend on the very word of God.[61]

The Character of the New Covenant

As stated, the New Covenant is an eternal covenant (Isa. 55:3; 61:8; Jer. 31:35-37, 40; 32:40; 50:5; Ezek. 16:60-63; 37:26-28). Like the Abrahamic Covenant, upon which it is founded, the New Covenant guarantees an eternal blessing for the nation of Israel, which will ultimately be fulfilled in the Messianic kingdom.

Furthermore, the New Covenant is an unconditional covenant. This fact can be seen from its eternal nature, for only an unconditional covenant can truly be an eternal covenant. Its ultimate fulfillment must rest on the faithfulness of God Himself. Since this covenant is based on the Abrahamic Covenant, which is an unconditional covenant, it must also be unconditional. The strong emphasis on God's "I will" promise in Jeremiah 31:33 guarantees its unconditional and final fulfillment.

The Outworking of the New Covenant

As stated, Israel is the people of the New Covenant, and the millennium is its fulfillment. Nevertheless, the New Testament contains five explicit references to the New Covenant: Luke 22:20; 1 Corinthians 11:25; 2 Corinthians 3:6; Hebrews 8:8; and 9:15. In addition, it also contains six less specific references: Matthew 26:28; Mark 14:24; Romans 11:27; Hebrews 8:10-13; and 12:24. These references demonstrate that some aspects of the covenant are now in effect. Five points should not be missed in this context.

First, since all post-Noahic biblical covenants were made with the nation of Israel (Rom. 9:4; Eph. 2:11-12), it follows that the New Covenant was also made with Israel (Jer. 31:31).

---

[61] Ryrie, *The Basis of the Premillennial Faith*, pp. 112-14.

Second, when Jesus the Messiah instituted the Lord's Supper, He made reference to the New Covenant (Lk. 22:20). It can hardly be supposed that His disciples did not understand His reference to be anything other than the New Covenant mentioned by the prophet Jeremiah. Given that the Lord did not explain it as anything else, the Lord's Supper must in some way relate to the New Covenant in Jeremiah.

Third, when the Lord instituted the Lord's Supper, He did not apply all of the provisions in the New Covenant. He only applied the single provision of the forgiveness of sins (Mt. 26:27-28). All of the other various provisions remain in abeyance, awaiting their ultimate fulfillment in Israel's Messianic kingdom.

Fourth, Jesus Himself ratified the New Covenant by His sacrificial death (1 Cor. 11:25) and, therefore, became the Mediator of the covenant (Heb. 8:6; 9:15-17; 12:24). Sacrificial ratification was required to institute a covenant, as Pentecost explains: "According to the Old Testament principle that such a conversion [of Israel referred to in Jer. 31] cannot be effected permanently without the shedding of blood, this covenant necessitates a sacrifice, acceptable to God, as the foundation on which it is instituted."[62]

Fifth, the Gentiles have been *brought near by the blood* of the Messiah, the Mediator of the New Covenant (Eph. 2:13, 19). This "mystery" has been revealed through the apostolic ministry (Eph. 3:1-12) and qualifies all who share in the New Covenant to be *servants* of the New Covenant (2 Cor. 3:6). In other words, the Gentiles share in the spiritual aspect of the New Covenant (i.e., the forgiveness of sins) because God foresaw their inclusion in the universal provision of the Abrahamic Covenant (Gen. 12:3; Gal. 3:7-8, 13-14). However, the remainder of the provisions of the New Covenant are still valid for Israel and are currently held in abeyance until the second advent (Rom. 11:25-27).

---

[62] Pentecost, *Things to Come*, p. 116.

In relation to Israel, the New Covenant has two basic points of application: national blessing in the future and personal blessing in the present.

Regarding the national blessing, Israel as a whole awaits its future fulfillment in the New Covenant (Rom. 11:25-27). The context of the Jeremiah 31 exposition of the New Covenant is quite clear on the timing of this future national blessing. First, there will be "the time of Jacob's trouble," meaning the tribulation (Jer. 30:1-17). Second, following this terrible time period will come Israel's restoration to kingdom glory (Jer. 30:18-24). Third, Israel will experience her national homecoming and salvation (Jer. 31:1-26). Fourth, the cause of this salvation will be God's New Covenant with the nation, which will render it an everlasting nation to the glory of God (Jer. 31:27-40). The covenant nation, which has been at odds with its covenant Lord, will finally experience its *covenant of peace* (Ezek. 34:25; 37:26). This covenant of peace will bring spiritual enablement (Jer. 31:33b), divine fellowship (Jer. 31:33c), and national redemption (Jer. 31:34).

Regarding personal blessing in the present, individuals from within the nation can experience the personal blessing of the forgiveness of sins. Each major crisis that the Jews face brings a renewed Messianic expectation. In a real sense, the crisis itself turns individual Jews back toward God and His plan for the nation. God uses tragic events to reach *a remnant according to* His *gracious choice* (Rom. 11:5). The remnant, those from within the nation who are His *chosen* (Rom. 11:7), often comes to Him through great personal tragedy. The Holocaust was just such a tragedy.

Prior to the Holocaust, there were numerous communities throughout eastern Europe that were populated by Messianic Jews, the *remnant according to God's choice*. Most of these believers found themselves herded into Nazi ghettos and eventually shipped off to Nazi extermination camps.⁶³ Although most of them perished in the flames of the Holocaust, they did not die in vain, for they maintained a vibrant testimony for their Messiah, thus echoing in their lives the words of Paul in Romans 11:13-14:

¹³But I am speaking to you who are Gentiles. Inasmuch then as I am an apostle of Gentiles, I magnify my ministry ¹⁴if somehow I might move to jealousy my fellow countrymen and save some of them.

In addition to these godly ones from the remnant of Israel, there were a number of godly Gentiles who also found themselves in concentration camps because they refused to capitulate to Hitler's atrocities.⁶⁴ They also maintained a vital ministry to those suffering in the camps and thus likewise modeled in their lives the words of

---

⁶³ For two sources on Jewish believers living in pre-war eastern Europe, see: Celia S. Heller, *On the Edge of Destruction: Jews of Poland Between the Two World Wars* (New York, NY: Schocken Books, 1977), pp. 183-209; Rachmiel Frydland, *When Being Jewish Was A Crime* (Nashville, TN: Thomas Nelson Publishers, 1978). For a source on Jewish believers in the ghettos and the camps, see: Donat, *The Holocaust Kingdom*, pp. 28-31; Joanna-Ruth Dobschiner, *Selected to Live* (Old Tappan, NJ: Fleming H. Revell Company, 1973); Myrna Grant, *The Journey: The Story of Rose Warmer's Triumphant Discovery* (Wheaton, IL: Tyndale House Publishers, 1978); Jan Markell, *Angels in the Camp: A Remarkable Story of Peace in the Midst of the Holocaust* (Wheaton, IL: Tyndale House Publishers, 1979); Elwood McQuaid, *Zvi* (West Collingwood, NJ: The Spearhead Press, 1978); Ulrich Simon, *A Theology of Auschwitz: The Christian Faith and the Problem of Evil* (Atlanta, GA: John Knox Press, 1967); and A. M. Weinberger, *I Escaped the Holocaust* (Alberta, Canada: Horizon House Publishers, 1978).

⁶⁴ For examples of godly Gentiles ministering in the camps, see: Dietrich Bonhoeffer, *Letters and Papers from Prison* (New York, NY: Macmillan Publishing Co., 1971); Maria Anne Hirschmann, *Hansi: The Girl Who Left the Swastika* (Wheaton, IL: Tyndale House Publishers, 1973); Linette Martin, *Hans Rookmaaker: A Biography* (Downers Grove, IL: Inter-Varsity Press, 1979); Basil Miller, *Martin Niemoeller: Hero of the Concentration Camp* (Grand Rapids, MI: Zondervan, 1942); Jack Overduin, *Faith and Victory in Dachau* (Ontario, Canada: Paideia Press, 1978); Corrie ten Boom, *The Hiding Place: The Triumphant True Story of Corrie ten Boom* (New York, NY: Bantam Books, 1974); Corrie ten Boom, *A Prisoner and Yet...* (Fort Washington, PA: CLC Publications, 1954).

the apostle Paul, *But by their transgression* [Israel's national rejection of Jesus' Messiahship] *salvation has come to the Gentiles, to make them* [the Jews] *jealous* (Rom. 11:11).

During this present age, God is drawing both Jews and Gentiles to Himself that, as individuals, they might experience certain aspects of the blessings of the New Covenant (Rom. 3:21-30; 10:11-13). Heaven alone knows the number of Jews who met their Messiah as they marched slowly toward some foreboding gas chamber. How beautiful are the feet of those who brought them glad tidings of good things (Rom. 10:14-15; cf. Isa. 52:7)![65]

The Mosaic Covenant

Unlike the previous four covenants God made with Israel, the Mosaic Covenant was a conditional covenant, meaning that it was not based on the unconditional "I will" promises of God but on the conditional "if you" obedience of Israel (cf. Exod. 19:5).[66]

Ryrie summarizes the content of the Mosaic Covenant in the following manner:

> The law which is involved… is the Mosaic Law. Although the word "torah" was used quite widely in Judaism, it especially referred to the code that was given at Sinai…
>
> The law is generally divided into three parts—the moral, the ceremonial, and the judicial. The moral part is termed "the words of the covenant, the ten words" (Ex. 34:28)—from which Greek equivalent we derive the label *decalogue*. The judgments begin at Exodus 21:2 and determine the rights between man and man with attendant judgments on offenders. The ceremonial part,

---

[65] For a summary of the provisions of the Abrahamic Covenant and a demonstration of how these provisions developed in the other unconditional covenants that God made with Israel, see: Arnold G. Fruchtenbaum, *What the Bible Teaches about Israel: Past, Present, and Future*, 2nd Edition (San Antonio, TX: Ariel Ministries, 2022), p. 69.

[66] See also: Lev. 26:3-6; 14-18; Deut. 28:1-2, 9, 13, 15.

which commences at Exodus 25:1, regulated the worship life of Israel.

Although this threefold division of the law is quite popularly accepted in Christian theology, the Jews either did not acknowledge it or at least did not insist on it. They first counted all the particular precepts; then divided them into families of commandments. By this method they counted 613 total laws and twelve families of commandments…

These 613 individual laws were further divided into negative and positive commands, and it was said that there were 365 negative ones and 248 positive ones.[67]

The specifics of the Mosaic Covenant are found in Exodus and Leviticus, having been given by Moses to the generation coming out of Egypt in the Exodus. These particulars were reaffirmed and supplemented by Moses in Deuteronomy for the next generation, which would enter the promised land under the leadership of Joshua.

The Provisions of the Mosaic Covenant

The provisions of the Mosaic Law may be summarized under two broad categories: that which was revelatory and that which was regulatory. Under that which was revelatory are four purposes that abide eternally:[68]

1. To reveal the holiness of God
2. To expose the sinfulness of man

---

[67] Charles C. Ryrie, "The End of the Law," *Bibliotheca Sacra* 124 (July–September 1967): 239-240.

[68] The summary of the provisions is based on: J. Dwight Pentecost, "The Purpose of the Law," *Bibliotheca Sacra* 128 (July–September 1971): 229-230. See also: Arnold G. Fruchtenbaum, *What the Bible Teaches About Israel: Past, Present, and Future* (San Antonio, TX: Ariel Ministries, 2022, 2nd ed.), pp. 54-56; Arnold G. Fruchtenbaum, *The Word of God – Its Nature and Content* (San Antonio, TX: Ariel Ministries, 2019, 3rd ed.), pp. 85-87.

3. To reveal the standard of holiness required of those who are in fellowship with a holy God
4. To function as a pedagogue, leading one to Messiah as Savior

These purposes reflect the lawful use of the Mosaic Law (cf. 1 Tim. 1:8-11) as well as the abiding holy, just, and good character of the law (cf. Ps. 19:8; Rom. 7:12).

Under that which was regulatory are six purposes that have a temporary function:

1. To be the unifying principle that made possible the establishment of the nation of Israel
2. To separate Israel from the nations in order that she might become a kingdom of priests
3. To provide forgiveness and restoration to fellowship for the redeemed people of Israel
4. To provide a system of worship for the redeemed nation
5. To provide a test as to whether one was in the kingdom or the theocracy over which God ruled
6. To reveal Jesus as the Messiah and Savior

It can be seen, therefore, that the Mosaic Covenant (i.e., the Mosaic Law) was given to Israel with certain particulars that only related to her as a theocratic nation, while certain other aspects of the covenant relate to all individuals living at any specific time (cf. Mt. 5:17-20; Rom. 7:12-16; Gal. 3:10-13, 23-25; 1 Tim. 1:8-11; James 2:8-13; 1 Pet. 1:14-16).

The Character of the Mosaic Covenant

The Mosaic Covenant was an additional covenant. It was added to the Abrahamic Covenant some 430 years after the ratification of that covenant without nullifying any of the provisions or promises that God made to Abraham (Gal. 3:15-18; cf. Gen. 22:17-18). It was added because of transgressions so that men might be made ready for the coming of the Messiah and Savior (Gal. 3:19-22). That is why Israel might experience all of the curses of the Mosaic Covenant without ultimately being cut off from the eternal purpose of God (Lev. 26:40-45; Deut. 4:30-31; cf. Lk. 1:72-73; Rom. 11:2, 26). Theologian Louis Goldberg explains the relationship between the Abrahamic Covenant and the provisions of the Mosaic Covenant in Leviticus 26:

> The terms of the Abrahamic covenant preclude any disappearance of the sons of Israel from the pages of history (Gen. 17:7). If the people will confess their iniquity, if they will acknowledge their unfaithfulness before the God of Israel, and if they will humble their uncircumcised hearts (vv. 40-41), God will take note of the covenant He made with Jacob, Isaac, and Abraham and will "remember the land" (v. 42). The Abrahamic covenant is an unconditional covenant, which guarantees the perpetuity of the line of Jacob and allots the land of Israel to Jacob's descendants for as long as there is a history of the human race. The restoration to favor with God and the blessings upon the land are all intertwined with a good spiritual relationship between God and His people.[69]

As mentioned, the Mosaic Covenant was a conditional covenant. The Abrahamic Covenant, with all of its supplemental covenants (i.e., Davidic, Palestinian or Land, and New Covenants), unconditionally established the eternal relationship between the people of Israel and their God. The Mosaic Covenant established the conditions upon which that eternal relationship might be enjoyed and blessed or distressed and cursed within time and space.

Again, Goldberg affirms the conditional nature of the Mosaic Covenant in Leviticus 26:

---

[69] Louis Goldberg, *Leviticus: A Study Guide Commentary* (Grand Rapids, MI: Zondervan Publishing House, 1980), pp. 141-142.

The distinction between the Abrahamic covenant and the Mosaic constitution is clear. The conditional aspect of the Mosaic covenant is seen again in the possibility of blessings for the sons of Israel: "If you follow my decrees and are careful to obey my commands, I will send you…" (vv. 3-4). The Abrahamic covenant established the relationship between the people of Israel and their God.[70]

The New Testament does not disavow this relationship between the unconditional Abrahamic Covenant and the conditional Mosaic Covenant. Indeed, it reaffirms it. The British Old Testament scholar Gordon J. Wenham asserts this fact when he comments on Leviticus 26:

> The NT does consider that the nation of Israel is still God's covenant people and subject, therefore, to the blessings and curses entailed in this chapter [Leviticus 26]. Christ's warnings to his fellow countrymen presuppose that they are God's covenant people, liable to God's judgment if they do not listen to his word. Some of the curses in Lev. 26 have their counterparts in Christ's teaching about wars and famines and the destruction of the temple (Mark 13//Luke 19–21).
>
> Paul categorically asserts that the covenant with the Israelites has not been invalidated by their unbelief. "The gifts and call of God are irrevocable" (Rom. 11:29) simply means that they must suffer the covenant curses rather than enjoy its blessings. But one day he expects them to be saved (Rom. 11:26), just as Lev. 26 and Deut. 30 do. There seems to be a hint of this in Jesus' own teaching as well, when he speaks of Jerusalem being "trodden down by the Gentiles until the times of the Gentiles are fulfilled" (Luke 21:24; cf. Rom. 11:25).[71]

---

[70] Ibid., pp. 138-139.

[71] Gordon J. Wenham, *The Book of Leviticus* (Grand Rapids, MI: William B. Eerdmans Publishing Company, 1979) p. 333.

The Outworking of the Mosaic Covenant

The Mosaic Covenant, as a conditional covenant, is worked out in two specific ways: First, it is worked out in a temporary dispensational sense; and second, it is worked out in a permanent condemnatory sense.

Temporary in a dispensational sense: It is clear from specific New Testament passages that the Mosaic Covenant or Law, in some sense, has passed away as a rule of law for the Jewish people.[72] For example, Jesus declared all foods clean (Mk. 7:18-19; Lk. 11:37-41; cf. Acts 10:9-16; 11:5-10), as did the apostle Paul (Rom. 14:1-12; Col. 2:16-17; 1 Tim. 4:1-5). Paul refused to have Titus circumcised according to the Mosaic Law (Gal. 2:3; cf. 5:1-6). The early church, made up primarily of Jewish believers in Messiah, did not observe the Sabbath but rather worshipped on the first day of the week (Acts 20:7; 1 Cor. 16:2). It would appear, therefore, that Jewish believers today operate under a different code than those who lived before the coming of the Messiah. As Ryrie insists, one must distinguish "between a code and the commandments contained therein."[73] He goes on to explain:

> The Mosaic law has been done away in its entirety as a code. God is no longer guiding the life of man by this particular code. In its place He has introduced the law of Christ [Gal. 6:2; cf. Rom. 8:2]. Many of the individual commands within that law are new, but some are not. Some of the ones which are old were also found in the Mosaic law and they are now incorporated into the law of

---

[72] As the Messianic Jewish scholar Arnold G. Fruchtenbaum points out, "The covenant was not made with the Gentiles or the church but with Israel only, a point... made in [Exodus 19:3-8,] Deuteronomy 4:7-8, Psalm 147:19-20, and Malachi 4:4." (Fruchtenbaum, Arnold G. *The Word of God: Its Nature and Content*. San Antonio, TX: Ariel Ministries, 3rd ed. 2019. P. 90.)

[73] Ryrie, "The End of the Law," p. 246.

Christ. As a part of the Mosaic law they are completely and forever done away. As a part of the law of Christ they are binding on the believer today.[74]

Still, there are other New Testament passages that would indicate that the Mosaic Covenant has passed away in another sense as well. Jesus instituted a New Covenant (Mt. 26:26-29; Lk. 22:19-20; cf. 1 Cor. 11:23-25). He is said to be the Mediator of this new covenant (Heb. 9:15; 12:24), which is better than the Mosaic Covenant (Heb. 8:6). His death has brought a new priesthood, which, by the very nature of the case, must also bring a change of law as well (Heb. 7:11-28). Since coming to faith in the Messiah, the Jewish believer is no longer under the Mosaic Law as a pedagogue (Gal. 3:23-26). Messiah is said to be *the end of the law for righteousness to everyone who believes* (Rom. 10:4), and believers are said to be *servants of a new covenant* (2 Cor. 3:6). It would appear again that believers today are not under the law as a curse (cf. Gal. 3:10-14). Since the Mosaic Law was the rule of life for the Jewish people only, what rule of life existed for the Gentiles? The Messianic Jewish scholar Arnold G. Fruchtenbaum explains:

> Jews and Gentiles are judged on the same basis: the law that they possess, whether it be the Mosaic Law or the principle of law. The principle of law is the presence of conscience within man... [the] "instinctive sense of right and wrong" ... The pagan world knew nothing about the Mosaic Law, and they had not been touched by biblical culture as today's western world has been. Yet, there is a common element in the pagan world that the majority agrees upon. For instance, it is generally understood that murder and stealing from one's neighbor is wrong.... These rules are found in most codices of law around the world. They are also often the

---

[74] Ibid.

guiding principles of unwritten law, and they are part of the Mosaic Law. The reason is that in the conscience of man, which operates as a principle of law, certain behaviors and actions are judged as being wrong, which in turn teaches that there is a standard of right and wrong that is somehow written in the heart of man. The conscience of man sits as judge, either accusing or excusing the person, declaring him guilty or innocent. Hence, Gentiles, who did not possess the Mosaic Law, are still a law unto themselves.

[So,] … although the Gentiles did not possess the Mosaic Law, they acted according to some kind of legal standard. There is evidence in the pagan world that there is a law of God written in the conscience of man, and it is this law or principle of law that accuses them of wrongdoing or excuses their behavior…. While the principle of law written on the heart of man is not the basis of salvation, it is the basis of judgment.[75]

The curse of the law, under which all men are born, requires death, temporal and eternal. Messiah has borne that curse of death for all men, and those who have believed on Him have received salvation from the curse of the law. Therefore, for Jewish believers today, the Mosaic Law has passed away both as a code for daily life and as a curse requiring death.

Permanent in a condemnatory sense: From what has been said above, it is obvious that the Mosaic Covenant must still be in effect for those outside of Messiah. Jewish unbelievers reside under the just condemnation of the Mosaic Law. For those who believe, Messiah is *the end of the law for righteousness* (Rom. 10:4). In his commentary on Romans, the Swedish theologian Anders Nygren explains:

---

[75] Arnold G. Fruchtenbaum, *Ariel Bible Commentary: The Book of Romans* (San Antonio, TX: Ariel Ministries, 2022), pp. 69-70.

Christ is the end of the law, the terminus of the law, the law's τέλος. And yet this must not be construed as an ordinary historical judgment, to the effect that the law ceased to function at a given point in time. The statement about the τέλος of the law applies only to those who have through Christ been made sharers in the righteousness of the law. Otherwise, outside of the realm of faith, the law still rules.[76]

The Bible expositor William Newell, likewise, graphically portrays the significance of Romans 10:4 when he states:

To him that believeth, therefore, Jew or Gentile, *Christ*, dead, buried, and risen, is the end of the law for righteousness—in the sense of *law's disappearance from the scene*! Law does not know or take cognizance of believers! We read in Chapter Seven (verse 6) that those who had been under the Law were discharged from the Law, brought to nought, put out of business (*katargeo*), with respect to the Law! The Law has nothing to do with them, as regards righteousness.[77]

Fruchtenbaum brings in the Messianic Jewish perspective when he notes:

The Mosaic Law had never pertained to the Gentiles, yet Gentiles were not without law. They possessed the principle of law and will be judged according to its standards. Hence, ignorance of the Mosaic Law did not save them because the principle of law had always been available to them. Living according to this principle was not sufficient to save the Gentiles either, but it was sufficient to condemn them if they broke it...

In [Romans 10] verse 4, Paul explained the reason for the statement he had made in verse 3: *For Messiah is the end of the law unto righteousness to every one that believes*. Again, the apostle used the

---

[76] Anders Nygren, *Commentary of Romans* (Philadelphia, PA: Fortress Press, 1949), p. 380.

[77] William R. Newell, *Romans: Verse by Verse* (Chicago, IL: Moody Press, 1938), p. 391.

Greek conjunction *gar* ("for") to indicate that he was now providing more details regarding Israel's failure to submit to God's righteousness. He showed why the pursuance of righteousness on the basis of law is wrong: The Messiah is the end of the law. Of interest is the order of words in the beginning of the verse. In the Greek, the first word is *telos*, translated as "end." The order of words puts the focus on this term. *Telos* can mean two things. First, it can mean "termination": Messiah is the termination of the law; He brought the end of the law. This is the primary meaning of the term. Second, *telos* can also mean "goal": The goal of the law was the Messiah; the law was not an end in itself, but it was intended to bring one to faith in the Messiah. From other passages, it is clear that both of these meanings apply in this verse. The Messiah was the goal of the law, to bring one to faith (Gal. 3:10–4:7). The death of Yeshua also brought the law to an end (Rom. 7:1-6; Heb. 7:11-19; II Cor. 3:1-18). In either case, Israel as a whole failed on both counts. The nation failed to realize that the goal of the law was faith in the Messiah and that the law had ended as a rule of life. Israel also failed to understand that the law was never a means of salvation but a rule of life for those who were already saved. The law was rendered inoperative because Messiah was to be seen as the One through whom man attains righteousness. He brought a new law, the Law of Messiah (Gal. 6:2; Rom. 8:1-2), which is now the rule of life for those who believe.

In summary of verse 4, Paul stated that Israel was ignorant of two things. First, the Law of Moses was never a means of earning salvation but only a mandatory rule of life for those already saved. Second, with the Messiah's death, the law has also ceased to be a rule of life. The new rule of life for believers is the law of Messiah.[78]

The Mosaic Law, which reflects the very character of God Himself, demands perfect righteousness in thought, word, and

---

[78] Fruchtenbaum, *Ariel Bible Commentary: The Book of Romans*, pp. 67, pp. 200-201.

deed. To fail to measure up to such a holy standard leaves the Jew under the just condemnation of the law (cf. Rom. 3:21-31; 10:1-3).[79] The "curse" of the law rests on all who reject Messiah's death as God's perfect solution for that curse (Gal. 3:10-14). That is why the Law is rightly called "the ministry of death" (2 Cor. 3:7) and "the ministry of condemnation" (2 Cor. 3:9).

In Galatians 2:19, the apostle Paul further describes his condition in relation to the Mosaic Law since his salvation: *For through the Law I died to the Law, so that I might live to God.* Luther put his own unique stamp of approval on this verse when he said:

> And here Paul speaketh not of the ceremonial law only (as before we have declared more at large,) but of the whole law, whether it be ceremonial or moral, which to a Christian is utterly abrogate, for he is dead unto it: not that the law is utterly taken away: nay, it remaineth, liveth and reigneth still in the wicked. But a godly man is dead unto the law, like as he is dead unto sin, the devil, death, and hell: which notwithstanding do still remain, and the world with all the wicked shall still abide in them.[80]

This principle of the believer's death to the Law of God (or, more specifically, to the Law of Moses) is probably Paul's idea in 2 Corinthians 3:11 as well. The glory of the Old Covenant is fading away with the preaching of the gospel (cf. Heb. 8:13).[81]

Paul also made it clear in Romans 2:12 that the Law of God would be the final point of judgment in every man's life, be he Jew or Gentile: *For all who have sinned without the Law will also perish without the Law; and all who have sinned under the Law will be*

---

[79] See also: Ps.143:2; Acts 13:39; Rom. 3:20; Gal. 3:11, 21, 22; Philip. 3:9.

[80] Martin Luther, *A Commentary on Saint Paul's Epistle to the Galatians*, translated by Edwinus London (Philadelphia, PA: John Highlands, 1891), pp. 159-160.

[81] In commenting on the term "passeth away" (*katargoumenon*), Robertson states: "In process of disappearing before the gospel of Christ" (in: Robertson, Archibald Thomas. *Word Pictures in the New Testament: Volume 4 – The Epistles of Paul*. Nashville, TN: Broadman Press, 1930. P. 221).

judged by the Law. Each will be judged according to the light he received: the Gentile through the law written on his heart, i.e., the conscience (Rom. 2:14-16); and the Jew according to the written Law of Moses. As the biblical scholar Archibald T. Robertson explains concerning this verse, "the Jew has to stand or fall by the Mosaic law."[82] This is affirmed by the Protestant theologian Frédéric Louis Godet as well when he says, "The very thing the apostle wishes is by this antithesis to emphasize the idea that the Jews *alone* shall be, strictly speaking, subjected to a judgment, a detailed inquiry, such as arises from applying the particular articles of a code."[83]

It is not surprising, then, to discover that Israel's history is bound up with her relationship to the Mosaic Covenant. There is never a time when Israel *as a nation* is not under this covenant. From the time of its inception until the realization of the New Covenant, the Mosaic Covenant ruled over the nation of Israel. Since the New Covenant has not been accepted and therefore realized by the nation as a whole, the judgments of the Mosaic Covenant rest upon the nation (cf. Lev. 26:1-46; Deut. 28:1–30:30).

The curses that were established in the Mosaic Covenant can be traced throughout Israel's history, as the following nine examples show:

1. Even before the official establishment of the Mosaic Covenant, Simeon and Levi were cursed by dispersion and scattering because of their cruelty (Gen. 34; 49:5-7). This is almost a prototype of the nation's future.
2. The tribes of Israel bound themselves to the Mosaic Covenant through a recitation of the blessings and curses on Mount Gerizim and Mount Ebal (Deut. 11:26-32; 27:1-

---

[82] Ibid., p. 336.

[83] Frederic Louis Godet, *Commentary on St. Paul's Epistle to the Romans* (Grand Rapids, MI: Kregel Publications, 1977; reprint of the 1883 version), p. 121.

26). This covenant renewal and ratification took place again under Joshua (Josh. 8:30-35) and was repeated under Nehemiah (Neh. 10:28-39).
3. Eli and his sons brought a curse upon themselves for their wicked behavior (1 Sam. 2:12-17, 22-25, 27-36; 3:10-18).
4. The psalmist reflected on God's cursing those who wander from His commandments (Ps. 119:21).
5. God cursed the people in Josiah's day because of their evil idolatry (2 Kgs. 22:8-20; 2 Chron. 34:14-28; cf. Exod. 20:3-6; Deut. 4:23-27; 5:7-10; 7:1-11; 11:13-17, 26-28; 17:2-7; 31:14-29).
6. Jeremiah denounced Israel and predicted God's curse on her because she broke His covenant (Jer. 11:2-5; 17:5-8; 23:10; 24:8-10; 25:15-29, esp. v. 18; 26:4-6; 29:15-23; 42:18; 44:7-10, 22-23).
7. Daniel confessed the sins of Israel, acknowledging God's just curse upon her (Dan. 9:11-14).
8. Zechariah acknowledged God's just curse on the people of his day (Zech. 5:1-4).
9. Malachi also acknowledged God's just curse on the people of his day (Mal. 2:1-9, esp. 2; 3:7-12, esp. 9).

This dismal history of curses carried over into the day of Jesus' ministry as well. Just before His betrayal and arrest, He pronounced a series of curses on Israel's national leaders for leading the nation astray, a pattern that had been established in the nation's history (Mt. 23:1-39). Longtime professor at Dallas Theological Seminary Stanley Toussaint correctly emphasizes the severity of these series of curses:

> Perhaps the most outstanding element of these verses [Mt. 23:1-36] is the severity of the words and the emphasis on judgment. The Lord uses such words as "hypocrites" (seven times), "son of hell," "blind guides," "fools," "whitewashed tombs," "serpents,"

and "brood of vipers" in connection with the scribes and Pharisees. It is evident that Christ is casting them aside as hopeless and giving them up to their own desires. These leaders even bore witness to themselves that they were the descendants of those who had killed the prophets...[84]

It is no wonder that Walvoord notes, "No passage in the Bible is more biting, more pointed, or more severe than this pronouncement of Christ upon the Pharisees."[85]

While it is true that Israel's past was replete with the curses of the Mosaic Covenant, climaxing in Jesus' rejection of the nation, her future will see the removal of these curses. Isaiah predicted a day when Israel would repent of her sins and see the curse turned into kingdom blessing (Isa. 65:15-16; cf. Zech. 13:8-9). Zechariah also predicted a day when Jerusalem would no longer be a curse among the nations but a kingdom blessing (Zech. 8:11-15, esp. v. 13; 14:9-11, esp. v. 11; cf. Rev. 22:3). Malachi predicted a day when Elijah would come just prior to *the great and terrible day of the Lord* (Mal. 4:5b) in order to restore Israel's families and thus avoid a curse upon the land. This final prophecy is directly related to the Mosaic Covenant that was established *in Horeb for all Israel* (Mal. 4:4b).

This blessed future of the nation will follow the time of Jacob's trouble, i.e., the tribulation, (Jer. 30:1–31:26) and will see Israel as a whole entering into the blessings of the New Covenant (Jer. 31:27-40). Until this blessed future of the nation arrives, the nation abides under the curses of the Mosaic Covenant (cf. Jer. 31:31-32). The Mosaic Covenant or treaty was broken and, there-

---

[84] Stanley D. Toussaint, *Behold the King: A Study of Matthew* (Portland, OR: Multnomah Press, 1980), p. 264. Quotation marks were added for better reading.

[85] John F. Walvoord, *Matthew: Thy Kingdom Come* (Chicago, IL: Moody Press, 1974), pp. 171-172.

fore, is no longer in effect. In fact, with the destruction of Jerusalem and the nation's Temple, God has made the whole Mosaic system incapable of functioning according to His design (cf. Lk. 21:20-24; Deut. 28:64-68). Since the covenant has been broken, is no longer in effect, and cannot be reestablished, all that remains are the penalties for breaking it (i.e., the curses listed in Lev. 26 and Deut. 28–30). These curses relate to the nation as a whole, while individual Jews can experience the forgiveness offered in the New Covenant by personally accepting God's sacrifice for these curses—a sacrifice provided by the Messiah, who bore the curses of the Law in order to redeem all people on an individual basis (Gal. 3:10-14; cf. Lev. 18:5; Deut. 21:23; 27:26).

It was national disobedience that brought the nation under the Mosaic curses, and it must be national obedience that removes the curses. This moment will come at the end of the time of Jacob's trouble (cf. Mt. 23:37-39; Deut. 4:27-31; Zech. 12:1–14:21).[86]

The Old Testament scholar Claus Westermann summarizes the relationship between disobedience and the curses in Deuteronomy when he says:

> In Deuteronomy, however, it is characteristic of the concept of blessing that by being connected with the covenant it is tied to the obedience of the people. As a result, blessing is necessarily subject to possible limits. When the people are commanded as they enter the land (Deut. 11:29) not simply to place blessing on the land but to place blessing on Mount Gerizim and curse on Mount Ebal, a limitation of God's granting or blessing is depicted. Because blessing is tied to the people's obedience, the curse henceforth stands side by side with blessing as a possibility. These two possibilities confronting Israel are developed in chapters 27 and

---

[86] See also: Lev. 26:40-45; Ps. 79:1-13; 80:1-19; 107:13-14; Isa. 53:1-9; 64:1-12; Jer. 3:11-18; 30:7-11; Hos. 5:15; 6:1-3; Joel 2:28-32; Lk. 13:34-35; Rom. 11:25-27. For more information regarding the end of the tribulation, see: Fruchtenbaum, *The Footsteps of the Messiah*, pp. 326-333.

28. The instruction mentioned above is repeated (27:11-13), and in 28:1ff. and 28:15ff. the people are confronted in deadly earnest with the choice that will determine their future. The curse that will result from disobedience is described in terrifying terms unlike anything else in the Bible (28:15-68). It signifies disaster, terror, and destruction.[87]

To be "under the law" is to be subject to "disaster, terror, and destruction." This terrible judgment is unique to the nation Israel, as the founder and first president of Grace Theological Seminary and Grace College, Alva McClain, affirms:

> Regarded as a covenant, the blessings of the law were conditional, dependent on Israel's obedience... On the other hand, if the people of Israel find themselves groaning under the judgments of God, they must understand that all this is come upon them because "They kept not the covenant of God, and refused to walk in his law" (Ps. 78:10) ...
>
> The Israelite is "under" this Mosaic written law until he finds forgiveness and freedom in the "new covenant" under grace in Christ...
>
> It is clear that Paul regarded the unsaved Jews of his day as being under the law, for he says in Romans 3:19, "We know that what things soever the law saith, it saith to them who are under the law." The Greek verbs here indicate a present reality, not merely a relationship which once existed but is no longer in force...
>
> This view does not conflict in any way with the fact that what we call the Dispensation of Law ended at Calvary. For God may change in his way of dealing with men without totally abolishing the main feature of a former dispensation. Conscience was not abolished when human government was established. Nor were the promises abrogated when the Dispensation of Law began. So

---

[87] Claus Westermann, *Blessing: In the Bible and the Life of the Church*, translated by Keith Crim (Philadelphia, PA: Fortress Press, 1978), pp. 48-49.

today, in this Age of Grace, there is still law for those who will not come to Christ for freedom. And if when men believe, they are "made dead to the law" (Rom. 7:4 ASV) in order that they may be joined to Christ, then this dominion of the law must be very genuine and present reality.[88]

The climax of the Mosaic curses was the worldwide dispersion of the nations; this was true in the original covenant (Lev. 26:33-45), as well as in the renewed covenant (Deut. 4:27-31; 28:36-37, 41, 47-48, 64-68; 30:1-4). Deuteronomy 4:30 places the final exile in "the latter days." This corresponds with Jesus' words in Luke 21:20-24, where Jerusalem would remain trodden down until the times of the Gentiles be fulfilled. This period of dispersion began in A.D. 70 as a national judgment for the rejection of the Messiahship of Jesus. When Israel is outside the land and subject to the harassment of the nations, utter destruction is an ever-present reality. This was certainly the case with Nazi Germany. The Jews were outside of the protective care not only of the land but also of God Himself. Dispersion was the final, climactic curse laid upon them by the hand of God. This has been recognized by some Jewish scholars from the ranks of orthodoxy, but it remains a rarity within Judaism.[89]

Perhaps the most despicable aspect of the judgments found in Leviticus 26 and Deuteronomy 28–30 is the curse of cannibalism. It is found both in the original covenant (Lev. 26:29) and in the renewed covenant (Deut. 28:53-57):

---

[88] Alva J. McClain, *Law and Grace* (Chicago, IL: Moody Press, 1954), pp. 32, 34-36.

[89] For examples of Jewish religious leaders who take the Leviticus 26 and Deuteronomy 28–30 curses as present-day realities in regard to the Holocaust, see Norman M. Bronznick, "A Theological View of the Holocaust," *Jewish Education* 42 (Summer 1973): 13-20, 28; Abraham Besdin, "Reflections on the Agony and the Ecstasy," *Tradition: A Journal of Orthodox Thought* 11 (Spring 1971): 64-70; also, by the same author, *Reflections of the Rav*, pp. 31-39.

You shall eat the flesh of your sons, and you shall eat the flesh of your daughters. (Lev. 26:29)

[53]You shall eat the fruit of your own body, the flesh of your sons and your daughters whom the Lord your God has given you, in the siege and desperate straits in which your enemy shall distress you. [54]The sensitive and very refined man among you will be hostile toward his brother, toward the wife of his bosom, and toward the rest of his children whom he leaves behind, [55]so that he will not give any of them the flesh of his children whom he will eat, because he has nothing left in the siege and desperate straits in which your enemy shall distress you at all your gates. [56]The tender and delicate woman among you, who would not venture to set the sole of her foot on the ground because of her delicateness and sensitivity, will refuse to the husband of her bosom, and to her son and her daughter, [57]her placenta which comes out from between her feet and her children whom she bears; for she will eat them secretly for lack of everything in the siege and desperate straits in which your enemy shall distress you at all your gates. (Deut. 28:53-57)

The curse of cannibalism is especially repulsive in light of the God-ordained position of the family in the nation of Israel and her theocracy (cf. Gen. 1:26-28; 2:18-25; Deut. 6:4-9; Ps. 127–128). The judgment falls when Israel, in her disobedience to God, is attacked by a foreign army. The siege would be so severe that starvation would ravage the cities of Israel, and this would lead to the unthinkable act of eating one's own children.

This very curse of cannibalism has found fulfillment in Israel's past and will do so once again in her future. Jewish history records at least four major periods where it fell on the Jews:

1. The siege of Samaria by the Syrians (2 Kgs. 6:24-29)
2. The siege of Jerusalem by Nebuchadnezzar (prophesied in Jer. 19:7-9 and Ezek. 5:7-10; fulfilled in Lam. 2:19-20 and 4:8-11)

3. The siege of Jerusalem by Titus and the Roman legions in A.D. 70[90]
4. The Nazi Holocaust under Hitler and the Germans[91]

The future holocaust of the tribulation will be the worst of all and, undoubtedly, will once again bring brutal starvation and the consequent curse of cannibalism (cf. Deut. 4:30; 31:29; Zech. 13:7-9; Mt. 24:15-22; Rev. 6:3-8).[92]

One last word must be added since the curse of cannibalism has raised the issue of innocent children suffering along with their parents. During the Holocaust, more than one million children were slaughtered.[93] This tragedy is possibly the major stumbling block for most Jewish historians and theologians. How could a God of love and covenant permit such terrible infanticide? Israeli historian Jacob L. Talmon perhaps represents the vast majority of Jewish thinkers when he says, "I shall never be able to believe in a Guardian of Israel who claims the lives of a million children as the price of national revival."[94]

---

[90] See: Josephus, *Wars of the Jews*, V, 10.4; 12.4; VI, 3.3-5; cf. Mt. 27:25; Lk. 19:41-44; 21:20-24; 23:27-31.

[91] See: Jacob Robinson, Nira Feldman, and Lenii Yahill, *Israel Pocket Library: Holocaust* (Jerusalem, Israel: Keter Books, 1974), pp. 67-68, 94-95; Victor E. Frankl, *Man's Search for Meaning* (New York, NY: Pocket Books, 1984), p. 76; Gideon Hausner, *Justice in Jerusalem* (New York, NY: Holocaust Library, 1966), p. 160; Hilberg, *The Destruction of the European Jews*, p. 172; and H. J. Zimmels, *The Echo of the Nazi Holocaust in Rabbinic Literature* (New York, NY: KTAV Publishing House, 1977), p. 93. See also Otto Friedrich, "The Kingdom of Auschwitz," *The Atlantic Monthly*, September 1981, p. 33.

[92] See also: Deut. 32:5; Ps. 18:6; 59:16; 107:13; Isa. 65:8,9; Dan. 12:1; Ezek. 4:16; Hos. 13:14; Zech. 11:6-9; Rev. 3:10; 7:14.

[93] Secretary-General Ban Ki-Moon, "'One and a Half Million Jewish Children Perished in the Holocaust', Message for the International Day of Commemoration in Memory of the Victims of the Holocaust." 27 January 2012, *United Nations: Information Service Vienna*, Press release UNIS/SGSM/316, 25 Jan 2012; Eban, *My People: The Story of the Jews*, p. 430.

[94] Talmon, "European History as the Seedbed of the Holocaust," p. 430.

In a similar manner, the aforementioned Orthodox Rabbi, Irving Greenberg, states his revulsion over associating a loving God with the death of a million children when he says, "To talk of love and of a God who cares in the presence of the burning children is obscene and incredible."[95] In response to this emotional and spiritual traumatization, it must be admitted that this is no easy question for the one committed to biblical truth either. In fact, the biblical characters themselves often wrestled with the problem of innocent suffering, especially of children (e.g., Gen. 18; Job 1–3; Lam. 2–3).

The Bible treats this difficult problem on two different levels. First, it treats the suffering of children on an individual level, where each child must bear his own personal responsibility for his sins. The child will not suffer for the father's sins, nor will the father suffer for the child's sins (cf. Deut. 7:9-10; 24:16; Jer. 31:29-30; Ezek. 18:1-4, 19-23).

Second, the Bible also treats the suffering of children on a national level, where each child born into the nation must share in the corporate solidarity of the nation. By the very nature of being born into the covenant nation, they share in the corporate personality of the nation—in its past, its present, and its future.[96] It is possible that the concept of cumulative sin and its effects was in view—that is, the cumulative effect of sin could be passed down from the father to the children, to the third and fourth generations, especially with the sin of idolatry. This was uniquely related to the Mosaic Covenant (cf. Exod. 20:5-6; 34:6-7; Deut. 5:9-10;

---

[95] Greenberg, "Cloud of Smoke, Pillar of Fire," pp. 41-42.

[96] Circumcision is an example of this concept of corporate identity (cf. Gen. 17:10-14, 22-27; 21:1-5; Exod. 4:24-26; 12:43-51; Lev. 12:1-3; Josh. 5:1-9). At eight days, the child could not personally enter into the covenant, but his father, by the act of circumcision, identified the child with the nation and the covenant that God made with the nation.

Jer. 32:17-19; Mt. 23:34-36).⁹⁷ God's great desire under the Mosaic Covenant was to pour out His steadfast, loyal love to thousands of generations, but when the people forsook Him for idols, they invited the curse and judgment of that covenant down upon their own lives, including their children and grandchildren. It was almost assumed that the child would embrace the ungodly lifestyle of the parent, choosing to worship foreign gods, and when the judgment inevitably fell, it fell on parent and child alike.⁹⁸

Israel's national history is replete with examples of this concept of corporate personality. Theologian H. Wheeler Robinson summarizes the major significance of this concept in the Old Testament when he says of the nation Israel:

> The whole group, including its past, present, and future members, might function as a single individual through any one of those members conceived as representative of it. Because it was not confined to the living, but included the dead and the unborn, the

---

⁹⁷ See also: Num. 14:18; Ezek. 18:19-20; Mt. 23:31-33; Acts 7:51. For other examples of the cumulative effects of sin, see: Jer. 16:10-12; Mt. 23:29-36; and 1 Thess. 2:14-16.

⁹⁸ The concept of the child adopting the father's lifestyle of idolatry can be seen in Exodus 20:5-6: *You shall not worship them or serve them* [foreign gods or idols]*; for I, the LORD your God, am a jealous God, visiting the iniquity of the fathers on the children, on the third and the fourth generations of those who hate Me* [the children]*, but showing lovingkindness to thousands, to those who love Me and keep My commandments* [the children]. Two things must be noticed. First, the judgment fell on the children, even to the third and fourth generations, only when those children themselves chose to follow their fathers' sin of idolatry (i.e., they chose to "hate" the Lord). Second, the children were not necessarily predestined to follow their fathers into this sin. They could reject the idolatry of their parents and choose to follow God. The Old Testament theologian Edmond Jacob reiterates the point of the children's culpability when he says: "Punishment is always collective; the iniquity of the fathers extends to their children (Exod. 20:5); no one is concerned [in the Old Testament] to challenge the justice of such a principle and it is always thought that the one who is punished is really culpable" (in: Jacob, Edmond. *Theology of the Old Testament*. New York, NY: Harper & Row, 1958. P. 153). Later, Jacob makes it clear that the covenant given to the nation as a whole must be applied on an individual basis: "Even a text like the Decalogue, which belongs to the realm of election and covenant and which is addressed to the nation as a whole, sets out its commandments in such a way that their execution is only possible by individuals" (ibid., pp. 155-156).

group could be conceived as living forever... The individual could not come into existence at all without some form of society and depends upon it for his growth and development. The society finds articulate expression only through the individuals who constitute it. Human personality is in itself as truly social as individual.[99]

Theologian Hans Walter Wolff emphasizes the same principle when he states, "In the different epochs of Israel's history—in the great revolutionary changes from the days before she became a nation to the period of the kings, and then to the Babylonian exile and to the post-exilic period—the fate of the individual in Israel was largely the fate of his people."[100]

This concept of Israel's corporate personality worked itself out in both a positive sense and a negative sense. In a positive sense, obedience to the Mosaic Covenant always extended the covenant blessings to the children (cf. Deut. 4:40; 5:29; 12:23-25, 28; Mt. 23:37; Lk. 13:34).[101] Numerous specific examples abound in the Hebrew Bible, but none are more obvious than those relating to the Day of Atonement (Lev. 16). On this annual and solemn day, the high priest alone entered the holy of holies to offer the prescribed sacrifice and confession for the entire nation, adults and children alike. Pulitzer Prize-winning author Herman Wouk captures the immense significance of this corporate confession on the Day of Atonement when he says:

> But in a sweeping paradox, this same confession that seals the individual in his privacy with God draws him into an ancient communal bond. All the prophecy of Israel turns on one simple but

---

[99] H. Wheeler Robinson, *Corporate Personality in Ancient Israel* (Philadelphia, PA: Fortress Press, 1980, rev. ed.), pp. 25, 45.

[100] Hans Walter Wolff, *Anthropology of the Old Testament* (Philadelphia, PA: Fortress Press, 1974), p. 216.

[101] For New Testament examples of this principle, see: 1 Cor. 7:12-16; Heb. 7:4-10; Rom. 5:12-21.

extremely difficult idea: namely, that *all Israel, living and dead, from Sinai to the present hour, stands in its relation to God as a single immortal individual.* The mass confession stamps that idea at the heart of Yom Kippur [the Day of Atonement].[102]

Another obvious example of the principle that the Mosaic Covenant always extended the covenant blessings to the children is seen in the sacrifice of the Suffering Servant for the entire nation, again for adults and children alike (Isa. 52:13–53:12).

In a negative sense, disobedience to the Mosaic Covenant also extended the covenant curses to the children as well (cf. Lev. 26:22, 39; Deut. 4:23-31; 28:32, 41, 58-59). Four nations in Israel's past brought these covenant curses not only upon the parents but also upon their children:

1. Syria (2 Kgs. 8:12)
2. Assyria (2 Kgs. 15:16; 17:1-41, esp. 41; Hos. 10:14; 13:16)
3. Babylon (2 Chron. 36:15-17; Jer. 6:11-12; 31:15-17; 44:1-10, esp. 7; Lam. 1:5, 16; 2:11-12, 19, 21-22; 4:4;[103] Ezek. 9:6)
4. Rome (Mt. 2:13-18; 27:25; Lk. 19:41-44; 21:23-24; 23:27-31)

Once again, numerous individual examples could be cited. Children in the wilderness wanderings suffered because of the sins of their parents (Num. 14:31-33). Achan's deception and sin were reckoned to the whole nation, and his entire family was judged

---

[102] Herman Wouk, *This is My God: The Jewish Way of Life* (New York, NY: Pocket Books, 1974, rev. ed.), p. 66. For a complete description of this idea, see: ibid., pp. 65-68.

[103] It is to be noticed that the Lord Himself is the ultimate cause behind such a judgment (Lam. 1:5, 12, 14-15, 17-18; 2:1-2, 5-9, 17, 20; 3:1, 18, 32, 43-45; 4:11, 16; 5:22) and that the reason for the judgment is the nation's own sins (Lam. 1:18; 3:39-42; 4:13, 22; 5:7, 16-18).

along with him, children and all (Josh. 7:1-26).[104] This phenomenon was not just unique to Israel, either. Babylon was overrun by the Medes, bringing cruel punishment upon the children as well as the adults (Isa. 13:16-18; 14:21). It was also true of No-amon (Thebes), the capital of Upper Egypt, when it was ransacked by the Assyrians in 663 B.C. (Nah. 3:8-10).

Another striking example affecting the nations surrounding Israel was the concept of *herem* or *cherem*.[105] This Hebrew term means "to ban," "to destroy," or "to devote" and "refers to something that was totally set apart, either for God or for destruction."[106] When the iniquity of the Amorites was complete (Gen. 15:16), God commanded the Israelites to destroy the entire civilization, including men, women, and children (cf. Lev. 18:24-28; 20:23; 27:28-29; Deut. 7:1-6; 12:2-3; 20:16-18). This command was in just accord with the righteousness and holiness of God. To fail to obey this judicial *herem* ban and judgment upon these foreign nations was to invite God's consuming punishment.[107] Added to the example of the Amorites is the further example of the imprecatory psalms that call down destruction upon God's unrighteous enemies, including the children (cf. Ps. 109:9-10, 12-13; 137:8-9). Professor of Biblical Literature at Western Seminary J. Carl Laney (b. 1948) relates these imprecatory curses directly to the protection clause of the Abrahamic Covenant (Gen. 12:3):

---

[104] Other examples of the broader principle of corporate identity can be seen in the songs of Moses (Exod. 15:1-21) and Deborah (Judg. 5:1-21), the confessions of the people bringing their first fruits before the Lord (Deut. 26:5-9), and the confessional prayers of Moses (Exod. 32:1-14, 30-32), Jeremiah (Jer. 14:17-22; Lam. 3:19-54; 5:1-22), Daniel (Dan. 9:1-21), and Nehemiah (Neh. 1:4-11). The principle can be further demonstrated in the "individual lament" and the corporate "I" of the psalms.

[105] Hebrew: חרם, *ḥērem*

[106] Fruchtenbaum, *Ariel Bible Commentary: The Book of Romans*, p. 177.

[107] Cf. the example of Amalek, Exod. 17:8-13; Num. 24:20; Deut. 25:19; 1 Sam. 15:1-35; and the example of Achan, Josh. 6:17, 21; 7:1-26.

> The fundamental ground on which one may justify the imprecations… in the Psalms is the covenantal basis for a curse on Israel's enemies. The Abrahamic covenant (Gen. 12:1-3) promised blessings on those who blessed Abraham's posterity, and cursing… on those who would curse… Abraham's posterity. Because of the unconditional nature of the covenant, its promises and provisions remain in force throughout Israel's existence as a nation. Balaam is an example of one who received judgment for cursing Israel (Num. 22–24; 31:16). Actually Balaam was unable to curse Israel, and he fell under God's judgment because of his attack on Israel by undermining the spiritual life of the nation (31:8). All the Midianites except for the little ones and the virgin girls were slain because of their part in the attack against the spiritual life of Israel (31:1-18). Truly those who had cursed were cursed!
>
> On the basis of the unconditional Abrahamic covenant, David had a perfect right, as the representative of the nation, to pray that God would effect what He had promised—cursing on those who cursed or attacked Israel. David's enemies were a great threat to the well-being of Israel! The cries for judgment in the imprecatory psalms are appeals for Yahweh to carry out His judgment against those who would curse the nation—judgment in accordance with the provisions of the Abrahamic covenant.[108]

Not only was Israel's past replete with examples of judgments falling alike on parent and child, but so will be her future. She is yet to face another tempestuous judgment, which will fall on parent and child alike. It will be the terrible time of Jacob's trouble, falling just prior to the Messianic return of Jesus (Jer. 30:10, 20; 46:27-28; Joel 2:16; 3:3; Zech. 13:2-3, 7-9; Mt. 24:19; Mk. 13:17; Lk. 23:29). The Holocaust may have inflicted upon the children a

---

[108] J. Carl Laney, "A Fresh Look at the Imprecatory Psalms," *Bibliotheca Sacra* 138 (January–March 1981): 41-42.

unique suffering in degree but surely not in kind, for Israel's history and destiny both testify to the nation's sins, bringing upon her the heartrending grief of infanticide.

Conclusion

In concluding this chapter on the perspective of the biblical covenants, two important points must be made in reference to the Holocaust: the security of the covenants and the sensitivity of the covenants.

The Security of the Covenants

There is nothing more secure in Israel's relationship with God than the four unconditional covenants, as well as the one conditional covenant, that He has established with the nation. Israel's past, present, and future are securely locked into the purpose and plan of God, and His purpose and plan for the nation are bound

Above: This seal was designed by Jesse and Josh Gonzales for the cover of Dr. Paul Wilkinson's important book *Israel – The Inheritance of God* (San Antonio, TX: Ariel Ministries, 2020). It represents the fact that God's covenants with Israel are unbreakable.

up in the manifold details of these covenants. Chafer has summarized the seven major features provided in the four unconditional and eternal covenants that God sovereignly and graciously established with Israel: "(1) a nation forever, (2) a land forever, (3) a King forever, (4) a throne forever, (5) a kingdom forever, (6) a new covenant, and (7) abiding blessings."[109]

Whatever else the Holocaust signifies, it certainly does not point to God's rejection of His chosen nation. Quite the contrary, it points to God's faithfulness to the nation, for while one-third of the Jews were slaughtered by the Nazis, two-thirds were preserved and spared by God. Hitler's ultimate goal was the complete extermination of the Jewish race. In faithfulness to the secure covenants that He graciously established with Israel, God stopped the Nazi hordes far short of their demonic aspirations, and no other nation shall ever be able to eliminate the Jews from the face of the earth either, for the Jews *must* continue and flourish until they experience the total fulfillment of all the covenant promises. God has established it. The Jew shall experience it (Rom. 11:25-36).

The Sensitivity of the Covenants

While there is nothing more secure than Israel's covenants with God, there is certainly nothing more sensitive in her relationship with God than these covenants. If these covenants bind God to the Jew, they also bind the Jew to God, and His hand will always be upon the Jew, either for blessing or for cursing. The nation's posture toward God determines His posture toward her. While the covenants guarantee Israel's eternal destiny, her obedience or disobedience to these covenants governs God's blessing or cursing in time, space, and history.

---

[109] Chafer, *Systematic Theology*, Vol. 4: *Ecclesiology – Eschatology*, p. 315. Chafer develops these seven features on pp. 315-328.

Once again, whatever else the Holocaust means, it certainly does not mean that God broke His covenants with Israel, thus proving Himself unfaithful in their worst hour of crisis and peril. Quite the contrary, the Holocaust demonstrated not only the faithfulness of God to His covenants but also the accuracy of the Word of God. What He said would occur to the nation when she forsook Him happened in frightening detail.

In commenting on the appalling curses listed in Deuteronomy 27:11–28:68, the conservative Anglican Bible scholar John Wenham makes the following insightful statement:

> Such a passage can be matched by only one thing: that is by a historical recital of the actual sufferings of the Jewish people. It takes an Eichmann trial to equal the horror of the divine warnings in Deuteronomy. Yet God's people were bidden to pray for such curses of God upon themselves, if they forsook him. The 'jealous' God of the Old Testament is every bit as severe on his own covenant people when they are unfaithful to him, as he is on the nations who have always served other gods.[110]

God is a jealous God. What He has called to Himself, He guards with a sensitive eye. The Jew may wish that God would drop him from His eternal plan, but God cannot. He has bound Himself by sacred oath and national covenants, which He must fulfill to the letter both in time and eternity. To do anything less would mean He must deny Himself.[111] The blessings and the curses will always remain the Jew's eternal choice (cf. Deut. 30:19-20; Rom. 11:11-24).

---

[110] John William Wenham, *The Enigma of Evil: Can We Believe in the Goodness of God?* (Grand Rapids, MI: Zondervan Publishing House, Academie Books, 1985), p. 155. For the New Testament parallel of the principle that God will not excuse in the believer what He condemns in the unbeliever, see: Heb. 10:26-31; 13:3; Jas. 4:1–5:12; 1 Pet. 4:12-19; 1 Jn. 2:28–3:3.

[111] For the New Testament parallel of the principle that God cannot ultimately reject a believer without denying Himself, see: 2 Tim. 2:11-13, 19.

Auschwitz (photo: © AdobeStock)

The Perspective of the Nation Israel

The biblical covenants establish the broad parameters of Israel's eternal relationship with God, but there are many other scriptures that set out the particulars of Israel's unique nationhood. This nation stands alone both in its inferno of suffering and its abiding survival. Secular theories abound for Israel's enigma in history, but they all fall short, for they are derived from a worldview that totally ignores the intervention of the divine. Evans comments on this unique perplexity of history when he says:

> That the Jews still survive is a marvel of history, for by every known law they should have disappeared long ago. Nineteen centuries have passed since they were driven out of their land and scattered by the wind of hate as chaff among the nations. Other nations have risen, and by the sword have won for themselves a place in the world, only to decay and disappear and be forgotten; but the Jews are still here, showing no marks of decay. It presents an unsolved problem to the skeptic and the unbeliever.[1]

Hatred, persecution, and suffering continue to be Israel's lot in this world. But for a brief respite here and there, the pattern re-

---

[1] Evans, *The Jew in the Plan of God*, p. 135.

Above: Alfred Edersheim (1825–1889) was a Messianic Jewish believer and a biblical scholar known especially for his book *The Life and Times of Jesus the Messiah* (1883; photo: www.wikipedia.org).

mains the same in country after country. Like Evans, the Messianic Jewish scholar Alfred Edersheim traces this phenomenon back to the destruction of Jerusalem in A.D. 70. Following his description of the nation's rejection of Jesus' Messiahship and the ensuing siege by Titus and the Romans, Edersheim offers the following summary of Israel's plight since A. D. 70:

Thus perished the proud and beautiful city, which "would not have this man reign over it." With it perished the last remainder of the typical dispensation, and of the Jewish state. A new era now commences. Israel is again cast forth as a wanderer, but this time without a home in view—without a tabernacle in which to worship—and without the cloud by day, or the guiding pillar of fire by night. Yet can we learn many a lesson as we trace the footmarks in the sand of time. And these footmarks they have left on *every* shore, as they have inscribed their name on *every* page of history. A nation without a country—a religion which, historically speaking, belongs to the past, and has become impossible in the present—a people persecuted yet not exterminated, driven from every place yet always reappearing, and who, without having a present, bear in their past the seed of future greatness—such is the picture now presented to us. Israel can be neither transformed nor subdued by the hand of *man*. *They belong to God*. Since the destruction of Jerusalem, a continual miracle, kept as a testimony to the God of the Bible before the eyes of an unbelieving world, and as the harbinger of future blessings in the prayers of an expectant Church, both they and their history are unaccountable by an ordinary mode of reasoning, and can only be understood when viewed in the light of scriptural statement and prediction.[2]

This chapter will attempt to bring the light of Scripture to bear on the sufferings of Israel, in particular the suffering of the Holocaust. Three major aspects of the nation will be surveyed: First, Israel's election will be studied; second, Israel's remnant will be defined; and third, Israel's adversary will be exposed. In other words, God has eternally elected or chosen Israel as a unique nation in the world. Apart from a faithful remnant within that nation's past, present, and future, Israel has brought itself into the immense suffering that it has experienced. The ultimate cause behind these sufferings has always been and always will be the arch enemy and adversary of Israel, the preeminent anti-Semite, Satan himself.

Israel's Election

The nation Israel did not slowly evolve into a people who belonged to God. No, her origin was sudden, dramatic, and decisive. It was the electing work of God Himself. God chose one man, Abraham, in order to create a chosen people. This people became a nation blessed by God in order that He might bless the entire world through her (cf. Gen. 12:1-3; 17:5-7; 22:18; 28:14; Exod. 23:22; Num. 24:9; Acts 3:25; 7:2-3; Rom. 4:17; Gal. 3:8). It is true that, after the original calling of Abraham, Israel went through a progressive metamorphosis until she reached her fully developed nationhood at Sinai, when she received her constitution from God.

---

[2] Alfred Edersheim, *The History of the Jewish Nation: After the Destruction of Jerusalem Under Titus*, rev. by Henry A. White (Grand Rapids, MI: Baker Book House, 1979; reprint of the 1895 edition), p. 25.

However, that nationhood was secure from the moment that God laid His hand on Abraham and said, "Go forth from your country…" (Gen. 12:1). In order to see how this election of the nation Israel relates to the Holocaust, three major facts must be surveyed: the nature of the election, the purpose of the election, and the results of the election.

The Nature of the Election

The nature of Israel's election was sovereign. God did not have to choose Israel to be His people. He was not coerced into it. He simply made a decision arising out of His own sovereign will. The New Testament scholar John Gresham Machen states that "Israel was God's people, not because of anything that it had done or could do or might do, but simply because of God's sovereign choice."[3] This view is affirmed by the theologian Gustav F. Oehler, when he says: "The adoption of Israel as the covenant people is a free act of God, or in other words, *an act of divine love, and necessary only so far as God has bound Himself by His oath*—that is, as a proof of His truth and his faithfulness—but is in no way dependent on man's desert."[4]

Four distinct features must be noted in relation to this sovereign election of the nation:
1. The Scriptures directly assert that God Himself chose Israel above all the other nations (Deut. 7:6; 26:5; Isa. 51:2; Ezek. 16:1-14, 22, 43-45, 60; 20:5; Mal. 1:2-3; Rom. 9:6-13).
2. This election of Israel raised her to a unique position (albeit a position of service) among the other nations (Deut. 4:32-37; 7:6; 10:14-15; 14:2; Ps. 147:19-20).

---

[3] John Gresham Machen, *The Christian View of Man* (London, England: The Banner of Truth Trust, 1937), p. 55.

[4] Gustav Friedrich Oehler, *Theology of the Old Testament* (New York, NY: Funk & Wagnalls, Publishers, 1884), p. 176.

3. Even before Israel's election, God had already established the nations' boundaries according to their future relationship to Israel, and Israel became the navel of the nations (Deut. 32:8-9; Ezek. 5:5; 38:12).
4. The election of Israel resulted in the nation belonging totally to God by virtue of the fact that the election itself included God's forming, redeeming, and calling the nation (Isa. 43:1).

The nature of Israel's election was not only sovereign but also gracious. This means that, in its ultimate fulfillment, the election is unconditional. The Old Testament theologian Walther Eichrodt asserts this unconditional and gracious expression of God's love for electing Israel:

> For there can be no escaping the fact that in the Old Testament *divine love is absolutely free and unconditioned in its choices*; it is directed to one man out of thousands and lays hold on him with jealous exclusiveness despite all his deficiencies. What the prophets had to say about the divine love in the highest flights of their preaching is still to be found—in more simple and popular form—as the real and profound meaning at the heart of all those stories about Yahweh's favourites, and can never be separated from the interpretation of Israelite history as the history of the Chosen People.[5]

Three distinct features of God's gracious election of the nation must be noted. First, the Scriptures directly assert that God chose Israel out of His gracious love (Deut. 4:37; Jer. 31:3; Mal. 1:2; Rom. 9:13). Second, God's gracious love for Israel was in spite of her natural insignificance and unrighteousness (Deut. 7:7-8; 9:4-6). Old Testament scholar Harold Rowley rightly notes, "No-

---

[5] Walther Eichrodt, *Theology of the Old Testament*, 2 vols., translated by J. A. Baker (Philadelphia, PA: The Westminster Press, 1961–67), Vol. 1, p. 286.

where is it taught in the Old Testament that God chose Israel because of her inherent greatness; yet there are passages where it is held that Israel's greatness lies in the fact that God chose her."[6] Third, this gracious love for Israel was supremely manifested in God's supernatural deliverance at the Exodus. In fact, this becomes the supreme motive for Israel's obedience to the newly established Mosaic Covenant (Exod. 19:3-4).

If the nation's election was sovereign and gracious, it must also, by the very nature of the case, be eternal. Along with the direct statements concerning the eternal nature of Israel's four unconditional covenants[7] upon which the nation's election is founded, the Scriptures give eight guarantees that this election is eternal:

1. The unalterable character of God Himself (Mal. 3:6)
2. The inviolability of the covenant of God (Lev. 26:44-45; cf. Gal. 3:15-22; Heb. 6:13-18)
3. The irrevocability of the gifts and calling of God (Rom. 11:1-2, 25-29)
4. The immunity of the earth from another universal flood (Isa. 54:7-9; cf. Gen. 9:8-17)
5. The immobility of the mountains (Isa. 54:10)
6. The immeasurability of the heavens and the impenetrability of the earth (Jer. 31:37)
7. The regularity of the planetary and tidal motion (Jer. 31:35-36)
8. The fixity of the earth's daily motion (Jer. 33:20-21, 25-26)

---

[6] Harold Henry Rowley, *The Biblical Doctrine of Election* (London, England: Lutterworth Press, 1950), p. 19.

[7] The eternal nature of Israel's four unconditional covenants is seen in the following Scriptures: (1) the Abrahamic Covenant: Gen. 17:7, 13, 19; 1 Chron. 16:16-17; Ps. 105:8-10; (2) the Palestinian or Land Covenant: Ezek. 16:60; (3) the Davidic Covenant: 2 Sam. 7:13, 16; 23:5; Isa. 55:3; Ezek. 37:25; and (4) the New Covenant: Isa. 24:5; 61:8; Jer. 32:40; 50:5; Heb. 13:20.

The Purposes of the Election

If Israel's election was sovereign, gracious, and eternal, it certainly was not without purpose. God's call to Israel was for service, not elitism. Rowley makes this point quite clear when he says, "Election is for service. And if God chose Israel, it was not alone that He might reveal Himself to her, but that He might claim her service."[8] The theologian Carroll Stuhlmueller echoes this sentiment when he summarizes the two basic components of Israel's election: "In Israel the general idea of 'election' included two essential components: separation from other nations because of the particular love of Yahweh for Israel; and secondly, readiness for Yahweh's special task or commission."[9]

The Scriptures teach that God elected Israel for seven basic purposes. The first purpose of her election was that she would be a blessing to the entire earth. This purpose initially appeared in the patriarchal narratives, especially with Abraham (Gen. 12:1-3; 22:18), Isaac (Gen. 26:4), and Jacob (Gen. 28:14). Later, under the theocracy, Moses assured the Israelites that if they obeyed God's law, He would bless them above all the nations (Deut. 7:11-14). According to the psalmists, this blessing was to be shared with the entire earth (Ps. 67:1-7; 72:1-20). That is why God placed the nation Israel at the center or navel of the rest of the nations, who would continually have to pass through and come into contact with this blessed nation (Deut. 4:5-8; 32:8-9; Jer. 4:1-2; Lam. 1:1; Ezek. 5:5; 16:14; 38:12). The strategic location of Israel is emphasized by Evans:

---

[8] Rowley, *The Biblical Doctrine of Election*, p. 43.

[9] Carroll Stuhlmueller, "God in the Witness of Israel's Election," in Sebastian A. Matczak, ed., *God In Contemporary Thought: A Philosophical Perspective* (New York, NY: Learned Publications, 1977), p. 353.

> Canaan... was in the providence of God chosen to be the national home of the seed of Abraham because of its geographically strategic position among the nations. The great lines of world travel passed through the land. The trade route between Europe and Africa passed through... [Canaan]. Also the great road between Europe and the greater part of Asia passed through the country, as well as the trade route between Africa and Asia. Thus the people of Israel were placed where the world's great highways of travel met, that their testimony for Jehovah might readily be carried to the ends of the earth.[10]

This universal blessing ultimately found its expression in Jesus the Messiah (Gal. 3:6-9) and will only be finally fulfilled in His millennial kingdom (cf. Isa. 19:23-25; 65:15-16; Zech. 8:13; Mal. 3:12).

The second purpose for Israel's election was that she would be a special nation to God. She could only bless all the other nations if she maintained her special relationship with the God who had elected her. This special and privileged position before God is described in eight different ways in the Bible:

1. As God's first-born son (Exod. 4:22-23; cf. Isa. 63:16; 64:8; Jer. 31:9; Hos. 11:1; Rom. 9:4)
2. As a servant-nation to God (Exod. 4:22; 7:16; 8:1, 20; 9:1, 13; 10:3, 7-8, 11, 24, 26; 20:3-6; 23:25; 1 Chron. 16:13; Isa. 41:8-16; 43:1-10; 44:1-8, 21; 45:4; 48:20)
3. As a nation worshipping God (Exod. 3:12, 18; 5:1-3; Josh. 24:14-15; cf. priests "serving" in this capacity, Exod. 28:41; Lev. 7:35; Num. 3:3; Deut. 10:8; 17:12; 18:5-7; 21:5)
4. As God's own people; i.e., He would be their God and they would be His people (Exod. 6:6-7; 29:45-46; Lev. 26:11-13, 44-45; Deut. 27:9-10; 29:10-13; 32:9; 2 Sam. 7:23-24; Ps. 33:12; 100:3; Isa. 43:1; Jer. 31:1, and in particular, Isa.

---

[10] Evans, *The Jew in the Plan of God*, p. 28.

33:22, where God is called Israel's judge, lawgiver, and king, the One who will save her)

5. As a special treasure and possession of God (Exod. 19:4-6; Deut. 4:20; 7:6; 14:2; 26:18; Ps. 135:4; Mal. 3:17)
6. As a holy people, uniquely set apart to God (Exod. 19:5; Lev. 11:44-45; 19:2; 20:7, 26; Deut. 7:6; 14:2; 26:18-19; 28:9; Jer. 2:2-3)
7. As a nation covenanted to God alone (Rom. 9:4; Eph. 2:12)
8. As a nation bearing God's glory (Isa. 43:7; 44:23; 46:13; 60:1-2)

The third purpose for Israel's election was that the nation would be a kingdom of priests on God's behalf (Exod. 19:5-6). Israel was to be a nation mediating priestly access for other nations. She stood between God's holiness and the sinfulness of the nations and brought them into fellowship through her priestly service. According to Keil, Israel was to be "a kingdom or commonwealth consisting of priests, i.e., a kingdom the members and citizens of which were priests, ... possessed of royal dignity and power."[11] Keil goes on to state that "Israel was to be a regal body of priests to Jehovah, and not merely a nation of priests governed by Jehovah."[12]

The fourth purpose for Israel's election was that the nation was to be a witness to the one true God. Moses clearly understood this commission of testimony before the idol-serving nations that surrounded Israel (Exod. 3:13-15; 5:1-2; 20:2-3; Deut. 6:4ff.; 28:10), as did David (1 Chron.16:24-31), and later, the prophet Isaiah (Isa. 43:10-12; 45:5, 23). Israel was to be a light of testimony to the pagan nations that crowded in around her (Isa. 42:6; 49:6; 51:4; 60:1-3; cf. Acts 13:44-47). She was to be the one nation that continually declared God's glory and praise (Isa. 42:12; 43:21; cf. Rom. 2:28-29).

---

[11] Keil and Delitzsch, *The Pentateuch*, Vol. 2, p. 97.
[12] Ibid.

The fifth purpose for Israel's election was that the nation would demonstrate God's gracious and faithful dealing available to all men. By obeying God's law, Israel would display the wisdom and understanding that only come from God and His Word (Deut. 4:5-8). His work in their midst would proclaim His goodness for generations (Ps. 102:18-22; cf. 1 Cor. 10:6, 11; Rom. 15:4). The nation would demonstrate not only the blessing that would come to a people who loved and served God (Ps. 33:12; 144:15) but also the cursing that would come to a people who hated and reviled Him (Exod. 9:16; Josh. 2:9-11; Ezek. 5:7-8; 36:22-32; 38:16, 23). The Bible teacher Erich Sauer captures the reality of this purpose:

> On the stage of world history by the example of Israel, there should be publicly shown to the nations what sin and grace, judgment and redemption are. In Israel's conduct and fate there should be given, in as it were a paradigm, an object lesson, not to be misunderstood or ignored, such as awakens the conscience and leads the sinner to the knowledge of himself, and then, through repentance and faith, to the knowledge of God.[13]

The sixth purpose for Israel's election is that the nation was to be entrusted with *the oracles of God* (Rom. 3:2), meaning the written Word of God. In commenting on Romans 3:2, theologian Charles Cranfield notes, "The Jews have been given God's authentic self-revelation in trust to treasure it and to attest and declare it to all mankind."[14] This written record of God's authentic self-revelation contains God's words (Deut. 4:5-8, 33, 36; 6:6-7; Ps. 147:19-20), as well as His works (Rom. 15:4; 1 Cor. 10:1-13; 2 Cor. 3:4-18). God has bridged the communication gap between man and Himself (Isa. 55:8-11) through the nation of Israel. God

---

[13] Erich Sauer, *From Eternity to Eternity: An Outline of the Divine Purposes* (Grand Rapids, MI: Eerdmans Publishing Co., 1951), p. 27.

[14] Charles Ernest Burland Cranfield, *A Critical and Exegetical Commentary on the Epistle to the Romans*, 2 vols. (London; New York: T&T Clark, 1975–79), Vol. 1, p. 179.

has not revealed everything about Himself, but sufficient enough for Israel to know, love, and serve Him in each generation (Deut. 29:29). The most important aspect of Israel's oracles was the Messianic prophecy that pointed to Jesus the Messiah (Lk. 24:25-27, 44; Jn. 5:39-40). The major facets of His life, death, and resurrection were enshrined in the oracles of Israel (1 Cor. 15:3-4). God called the nation to be the recorder and preserver of His Spirit-inspired Word (cf. 2 Tim. 3:16; 2 Pet. 1:21).

The seventh and final purpose for Israel's election is for her to bring God's Messiah into the world (Rom. 9:5). This was undoubtedly her greatest calling. Jesus came into the world as God's Messiah, born of the seed of Abraham (Mt. 1:1; Gal. 3:7-16; 4:4-5) and in the line of David (Mt. 1:1; Lk. 1:26-35; Rom. 1:3). That is why the Scriptures can accurately assert that *salvation is from the Jews* (Jn. 4:22), for salvation comes only through Israel's promised Messiah (cf. Jn. 4:25-26; 14:6; Acts 4:12; 1 Tim. 2:5-6).

The Results of the Election

Since God has called Israel to these seven major purposes, two major results must logically follow: First, Israel was to respond to this divine election with loving obedience; and second, if she refused to respond to her calling, God would be forced to reciprocate with severe judgment or discipline. Jacob reiterates the relationship between these two results:

> For the people, election implies the duty of loving Yahweh with a love worthy of that with which he has loved them, otherwise election will be turned to judgment; but the insistence that the prophets place upon the continuance of a remnant proves that neither acts of disobedience nor judgment mean in their view the end of election.[15]

---

[15] Jacob, *Theology of the Old Testament*, p. 207.

The only reasonable response to God's gracious election is loving obedience. Moses made this clear in Deuteronomy 6:4-9, when he called the nation to respond to its divinely elected Lord:

> *⁴"Hear, Israel. The LORD our God, the LORD is one. ⁵And you shall love the Lord your God with all your heart and with all your soul and with all your strength. ⁶These words, which I am commanding you today, shall be on your heart. ⁷And you shall **repeat** [or "teach"] them diligently to your sons and **speak** of them when you sit in your house, when you walk on the road, when you lie down, and when you get up. ⁸You shall also **tie** [or "bind"] them as a sign to your hand, and they shall be as frontlets*[16] *on your forehead. ⁹You shall also **write** them on the doorposts of your house and on your gates* (emphasis added).

Israel's response to God was to be total in each generation, and it was to be characterized by a loving obedience to Him and His words. This attitude certainly characterized the forefather of the Israelites, Abraham (Gen. 18:19), and it was to be the distinctive mark of each generation in the newly elected nation (cf. Exod. 19:4-6; Deut. 29:29). Each generation was responsible for determining its own response to the electing Lord and His covenant. The Old Testament scholar Walther Zimmerli affirms this truth when he says, "Israel, the chosen nation, is not a passive privileged object; it is always called to act obediently as subject. The 'dialogical' nature of election is made especially clear by the possibility of speaking of a 'choice' on the part of the people."[17] This "choice" is referred to in numerous passages, such as Deuteronomy 11:26-28; 29:14-29; 30:15-20; Joshua 24:14-28; and Nehemiah 10:28-29.

---

[16] Or "frontlet bands"; literally, "between your eyes."

[17] Walther Zimmerli, *Old Testament Theology in Outline*, translated by David E. Green (Atlanta, GA: John Knox Press, 1978), p. 46.

Rowley summarizes the significance of the covenant as representative of the nation's election:

> At Sinai God's election of Israel found that response in the Covenant. Of the importance of the idea of the Covenant in the thought of the Old Testament there can be no doubt, but of its character there is often much misunderstanding. It was not a commercial bargain or a legal contract, but rather Israel's pledge of loyalty to him who had first chosen and saved her. It laid no obligations on God, who had already of his free grace both pledged himself to Israel and given the evidence of his devotion to her in the deliverance he had wrought. On Israel's side it was as unconditional as God's deliverance of her had been.[18]

God's desire for the elected and covenanted nation was not mere legalistic obedience, but rather a loving response from the heart that expressed itself in true obedience. Eichrodt clarifies the vast difference between these two kinds of obedience:

> Moreover, any legalistic misunderstanding of the command to love God [Deut. 6:5; cf. 10:12; 11:13, 22; 19:9; 30:16] is countered by the great stress laid on the demonstration of God's love for man. Long before there was any human action in response, this love chose the people for God's own possession and gave them the law as a token of their special position of favour. To obey the law thus becomes man's response of love to the divine act of election [Deut. 4:5-8, 37; 7:6ff.; 10:14ff.].[19]

God's election of Israel cannot be seen apart from the service that it demands. In the Scriptures, great privilege always brings great responsibility as well as accountability. Once God initiated Israel's election, the nation had to continually live under His stewardship and was always accountable to Him personally. In other

---

[18] Harold Henry Rowley, *The Faith of Israel: Aspects of Old Testament Thought* (London, England: SCM Press, 1956), pp. 68-69. See also p. 70.

[19] Eichrodt, *Theology of the Old Testament*, Vol. 1, p. 94.

words, God's love is a tough love—a love of conviction and discipline (cf. Prov. 3:11-12). Cranfield clearly sees the true nature of God's love and its relation to His elected nation:

> God's punishment of sin is no contradiction of his love; it was precisely because he loved that he took Israel's sin so seriously (cf. the 'therefore' in Amos 3:2). His love was love in deadly earnest and could be severe. It was willing to hurt in order to save, to shatter all false securities and strip Israel of his gifts, if so be that in the end, in nakedness and brokenness, they might learn to know their true peace. But the severity was never separated from tenderness (cf. Hos. 11:8, Isa. 63. 9, etc.).[20]

It was Moses who saw the shattering experience of the wrath of God against His people (e.g., Exod. 32:6-35; cf. 1 Cor. 10:1-13) and who later sternly warned the next generation against the danger of forgetting the goodness of God (Deut. 8:11-20). In fact, Israel's entire history, right up to the Messianic kingdom, bears testimony to the severe discipline imposed on her by the God of her election (cf. Deut. 30:1-20; Ezek. 20:33-38).

Perhaps the clearest statement in Scripture concerning the relationship between God's love and wrath for the nation of Israel is Amos 3:2: *You* [Israel] *only have **I chosen** among all the families of the earth; therefore, I will **punish** you for all your iniquities* (emphasis added). In other words, God's "choosing" is inseparably linked to God's "punishment." Von Rad brings out the sense of Amos' words in this passage:

> Israel's election, as he [Amos] states, is… in actual fact the very reason given for Jahweh's imminent act of judgment (Am. III:2)…
>
> Amos's Jahweh watches over the established orders of international law not only in Israel but also among the other nations, and

---

[20] Charles E. B. Cranfield, "Love," in Alan Richardson, ed., *A Theological Word Book of the Bible* (New York, NY: MacMillan Company, 1951), p. 132.

whenever they are broken, he imposes a historical punishment upon the culprits. Israel's breaches are, of course, immeasurably more serious, since she was the nation with whom, above all others, he had made himself intimate (Am. III. 2)...

The very saving act by which Israel was elected becomes her judgment (Am. III. 2).[21]

Rowley affirms this correlation between election and judgment as seen in Amos 3:2:

Here the discipline is the corollary of the election, and the proof of the divine love. It is not simply because God is just that He punishes Israel's sins; it is rather because He is gracious that He seeks to chasten her for her profit. It is not due to His variability, but to His unchanging love.[22]

In summary, it can be said that Israel's election guarantees her existence. Yet it is not to be an existence free from national accountability to the God of her election. Just as the Holocaust can be related to the consequences of the divine covenants, so likewise it can be related to the consequences of the divine election. In fact, the divine covenants and the divine election are inseparably connected as parts of a whole, for the covenants give the details or fine print of the election. The covenants spell out the obligations and privileges of the divinely ordained election, and since the national election is eternal, so must be the national accountability.

All of the woes of the Jewish people, including the Nazi Holocaust, do not repudiate the election of Israel. Quite the contrary, these woes reaffirm the election of the nation (Amos 3:2). As has been said before, the hand of God always remains upon the Jew, either for blessing or for cursing. Despite the Jews' attempted rejection of their own "chosenness" (Deut. 17:14-20; 1 Sam. 8:1-22;

---

[21] Gerhard von Rad, *Old Testament Theology*, 2 vols., translated by D. M. G. Stalker (New York, NY: Harper and Row, 1962–65), Vol. 2, pp. 133, 135, 397.

[22] Rowley, *The Biblical Doctrine of Election*, p. 53.

Ezek. 20:32[23]), the divinely initiated "choosing" will remain intact forever. This means that there will also be severe discipline whenever required. This unique relationship with God makes the Jew the mystery person of the ages (Rom. 11:25-36). Sauer explains:

> But also exactly at this point occurs a chief riddle of history, even the continuance of the Jewish people in spite of the numerous periods of judgment into which God caused unbelieving Israel again and again to fall. The laws which govern the existence of many other peoples are in part explicable by the philosophy of history. But Israel's development mocks at all explanation. For, in spite of everything, Israel is Jehovah's people, and the Lord its God is a God Who hides Himself (Isa. 45:15). Every Jew is a walking mystery.[24]

Israel's Remnant

If Israel's continued existence is a profound mystery, so must be the existence of a remnant within that nation, but to an even greater degree. The *Encyclopedia Judaica* defines the concept of the remnant in the following words:

> Remnant of Israel, a term denoting the belief that the future of Israel would be assured by the faithful remnant surviving the calamities that would befall the people as a result of their departing from the way of God. On the one hand the prophets foretold the forthcoming exile and destruction of Israel, and on the other they held forth the hope and promise of its survival and eternity. The doctrine of the Surviving Remnant resolved this contradiction.[25]

---

[23] See also: Exod. 14:11-12; 16:3, 8; Deut. 9: 7-29 (esp. vs. 23-24); Judg. 2:1-5, 10-14; 1 Sam. 12:14; Ps. 106:5-9, 3-15.

[24] Erich Sauer, *The Dawn of World Redemption: A Survey of Historical Revelation in the Old Testament* (Grand Rapids, MI: Eerdmans, 1951), p. 119.

[25] C. Roth and G. Wigoder, et al., eds., *Encyclopedia Judaica* (Jerusalem, Israel: Keter Pub. House, 1972), Vol. 14, p. 70.

According to Jacob, the doctrine of the remnant has two facets:

> The remnant is a concept with two facets: one catastrophic—only a remnant will survive; the other full of promise—for a remnant will escape… [H]owever small the remnant may be, it is the germ, the root from which a new plant will be able to spring, for it is in favour of this remnant that the election and consecration granted formerly to Abraham's posterity are renewed.[26]

Fruchtenbaum elaborates on the doctrine of the remnant in the following terms:

> [One of the bases] of the Messianic Jewish distinctive is described in Romans 11:1-7… The question here is whether or not God has cast off His people Israel. Paul answers in the negative. Paul's proof is he himself; he is a Jew who believes. The critic may argue that the Jews who believe are a very small minority; so does it not follow that the nation has indeed been cast off? Again, the answer is negative. What is happening now, Paul explains, is what has always happened throughout Jewish history; that is, only a remnant believes. It is always the remnant that believes. This was true in Elijah's day, and it is true today. The fact that the majority do not believe is not evidence enough that the whole nation has been cut off. The point is that in Israel—past, present, and future—it is the remnant that is faithful to the revelation of God. This is also true in this present Dispensation of Grace; the Messianic Jews are the remnant of Israel today. The remnant is always in the nation, not outside of it; the present-day remnant is part of Israel and the Jewish people. The Jewishness of the remnant is distinct.
>
> Isaiah 1:9 and 65:8 point out that it is the remnant that is keeping Israel as a whole alive…
>
> Because of the believing remnant, God did not permit the success of the many attempts throughout this age to wipe out the

---

[26] Jacob, *Theology of the Old Testament*, p. 323.

Jewish people. Again, we see position and function in this basis of the Messianic Jewish distinctive.[27]

The remnant concept has at least three major ideas in relation to the nation of Israel: (1) national apostasy; (2) national judgment; and (3) surviving remnant. In other words, the nation's sin is followed by the nation's test, out of which will come the nation's hope—the remnant. God has always had a remnant within the nation of Israel, and He always will. While the nation as a whole, for the most part, usually defected from the God of their election, the faithful remnant remained true to Him. Keil explains the tremendous importance that the remnant played in the history of the nation:

> Even in times of greatest apostasy on the part of the nation there would always be a holy seed [i.e., the remnant] which could not die out; because otherwise the nation would necessarily have been utterly and for ever rejected, whereby the promises of God would have been brought to nought—a result which was absolutely impossible.[28]

This chapter will first survey the concept of the remnant chronologically (as it is expressed in its past, present, and future manifestations) and then systematically (in terms of its universal functions). Then, it will relate the concept to the Holocaust.

---

[27] Arnold G. Fruchtenbaum, *The Remnant of Israel: The Theology, History, and Philosophy of the Messianic Jewish Community* (San Antonio, TX: Ariel Ministries, 2021, 4th Edition), pp. 39-40.

[28] C. F. Keil and F. Delitzsch, "Deuteronomy," in *Commentary on the Old Testament: The Pentateuch, Volume 1* (Grand Rapids, MI: Eerdmans, 1973; reprint edition), p. 451.

The Remnant Chronologically Developed

In order to survey the biblical concept of Israel's remnant, the following approach will be taken: First, the remnant will be considered historically (i.e., the past); second, the remnant will be considered prophetically (i.e., the future); and third, the remnant will be considered contemporarily (i.e., the present).

The Remnant Considered Historically

In order to simplify the survey of the remnant of Israel in the past, the remnant leaders will be considered first, followed by the remnant members. The remnant leaders comprise five distinct groups:

1. The theocratic founders—the patriarchs Abraham, Isaac, and Jacob, as well as Joseph
2. The theocratic legislator—Moses[29]
3. The theocratic administrators—Joshua, the judges, the kings, and the priests[30]
4. The theocratic counselors—the wisdom and poetic writers[31]
5. The theocratic advocates—the prophets[32]

---

[29] Cf. Heb. 11:23-29.

[30] Along with Joshua should be included Caleb (Num 13:30; 14:6-9, 30; Josh. 14:6-15). On Joshua, the judges, and the kings, see Hebrews 11:30-40. Of course, not all of the priests were a part of the remnant (cf. Lev. 10:1-20; 1 Sam. 2:11-36), but they were nevertheless called by God to administer in the areas of worship and teaching the law (cf. Lev. 8:1–9:24; 10:8-11; Deut. 24:8; 31:9-13; 33:8, 10; Jer. 18:18).

[31] Cf. Jer. 18:18 and Eccl. 12:9-11 on the wisdom sages or counselors. The following psalms may also refer to the remnant: Ps. 44:10-26; 55–57; 64; 79; 80.

[32] The theocratic advocates as a part of the remnant would not just include the writing prophets but also the speaking prophets, such as Samuel (1 Sam.; cf. Heb. 11:32), Elijah (1 Kgs. 17:1–2 Kgs. 2:11; cf. Jas. 5:17-18), Elisha (1 Kgs. 19:19–2 Kgs. 13:21), Obadiah and his 100 faithful prophets (1 Kgs. 18:3-16). On the prophets, see Matthew 5:10-12; 23:29-36; Mark 12:1-12; Luke 11:47-51.

The remnant members were addressed by Moses (Lev. 26:36-45) and by nine of the writing prophets. These prophets ministered to the needs of the faithful remnant of their day.

The following prophets, presented here in chronological order, ministered encouragement and hope to the remnant of their day:

1. Amos (3:11-15; 5:1-3, 14-17;[33] 7:1-6)
2. Isaiah (1:9,[34] 27-28; 6:13; 7:3; 8:17-18; 10:20-23;[35] 17:4-8; 43:3-13)
3. Zephaniah (2:6-7, 9)
4. Habakkuk (2:4)
5. Jeremiah (6:9; 40:11, 15; 41:16; 42:1-2, 15, 19; 43:5-6; 44:12, 14, 28; 50:20; Lam. 3:19-25)
6. Ezekiel (5:3, 10, 12; 6:8-10; 9:4-8; 12:15-16; 14:12-23)
7. Daniel (1:1–2:3; 8:1–12:13)[36]
8. Haggai (1:12-15; 2:1-9)
9. Malachi (3:16-18)

Two more men must be added to this list, although they were not prophets: Ezra (2:1ff.; 3:1ff.; 9:5-15) and Nehemiah (1:3; 3:1ff.; 7:5ff.; 9:1-2ff.). Both ministered in a great way to the remnant of their day. In fact, Ezra the priest and Nehemiah the governor were greatly undergirded in their work by Malachi the prophet.

---

[33] On Amos 5:15, see Genesis 45:7.

[34] On Isaiah 1:9, see Romans 9:29.

[35] On Isaiah 10:22-23, see Romans 9:27-28.

[36] Daniel 1:1–2:3 and 8:1–12:13 are the Hebrew sections of the book, written as an encouragement to the Jewish people. The remainder of the book was written in Aramaic and mainly concerns the nations of the world. It should also be noted that Daniel does write to encourage another remnant, but not of his own day. In 8:9-14 and 11:32-35, he writes prophetically, but not eschatologically, concerning the Maccabees. Also, it is well to note that Daniel himself is a part of the remnant (cf. Ezek. 14:14, 20; Mt. 24:15) but is not alone in his ministry to the remnant. He is accompanied by his three friends, themselves also a part of the remnant (1:6-7, 8-21; 2:13, 17-18, 49; 3:1-30).

The Remnant Considered Prophetically

The first one to address the remnant of the future was Moses (Deut. 4:27-31; 28:58-68; 31:29). He spoke concerning the tribulation period of "the latter days" (Deut. 4:30; 31:29). It is in this same eschatological sense that eleven of the prophets spoke concerning the remnant of Israel. It was their concern to give the believing remnant an eschatological hope that would carry them through the judgments to come. The following prophets ministered encouragement and hope to the remnant of "the day of the Lord," i.e., the tribulation. Again, they are presented in chronological order:

1. Joel prophesied concerning the tribulation remnant (2:32).
2. Hosea spoke concerning the tribulation remnant (5:15–6:3).
3. Amos prophesied both concerning the tribulation remnant (9:8-10) and the millennial remnant[37] (9:11-15).
4. Micah spoke both of the tribulation remnant (2:12-13; 5:3, 7-9) and the millennial remnant (4:6-8; 7:18).
5. Isaiah spoke concerning both the tribulation remnant (10:20-23; 11:11-16; 24:13-15; 25:4; 59:20; 63:7–64:12;[38] 66:8-9) and the millennial remnant (4:2-6; 66:19-20).
6. Zephaniah mentioned the tribulation remnant (3:11-12) and the millennial remnant (3:13-20).
7. Jeremiah spoke of both the tribulation remnant (30:7-11; 31:7) and the millennial remnant (23:3-8).

---

[37] The millennial remnant will merge with the nation as a whole, for in the millennial kingdom, *all Israel will be saved* (Rom. 11:26). The term "millennial remnant" is used here simply to distinguish it from the tribulation remnant when God will be sifting out the unregenerate of the nation (cf. Zech. 13:8-9). This will leave behind the purified remnant that will inherit the millennial kingdom.

[38] Isaiah 63:7–64:12 is a confession of the future tribulation remnant.

8. Ezekiel spoke of the tribulation remnant (20:33-44; 34:17-22) and the millennial remnant (11:17-21; 36:16-32; 39:22, 25-29).
9. Daniel mentioned both the tribulation remnant (12:1, 10) and the millennial remnant (12:2-3).
10. Zechariah spoke of both of the tribulation remnant (11:4, 7; 12:7-14; 13:1, 8-9) and the millennial remnant (8:6-13).
11. Malachi spoke of the tribulation remnant (3:2-3; 4:1-3).

The Old Testament prophets were not the only ones in the Scriptures to speak about the remnant of prophecy. Jesus the Messiah addressed the tribulation remnant and forewarned it of the horrors it would endure (Mt. 24:15-31). He also spoke of the coming blessing for the millennial remnant. He called His disciples the "little flock" and promised them (with the exclusion of Judas Iscariot) that their Father had chosen them to receive the kingdom (Lk. 12:32). He promised His apostles that when He came to sit on His glorious throne, they, too, would *sit upon twelve thrones, judging the twelve tribes of Israel* (Mt. 19:28). He likewise told them that, because they had stood by Him in His trials, they would share fellowship with Him in His kingdom and *sit on thrones judging the twelve tribes of Israel* (Lk. 22:28-30).

Paul and John also mentioned the prophetic remnant. Paul spoke of a day when *all Israel* would be saved (Rom. 11:25-29). This must be the national Israel that he had been speaking of throughout chapters 9–11 (Rom. 9:4, 6, 27, 31; 10:19, 21; 11:1-2, 7, 25-26). However, it is the purged-out remnant of the tribulation period (cf. Jer. 30:7, 11, 23-24; 31:1-9; Ezek. 20:33-44; Zech. 13:7-9). This remnant will finally merge with and become the millennial remnant. John also spoke of the prophetic remnant during the tribulation and mentioned four distinct groups:
1. The 144,000 witnesses, 12,000 from each tribe of Israel (Rev. 7:1-8; 14:1-5)

2. The two Jewish witnesses (Rev. 11:1-13)
3. Persecuted Jewish believers (Rev. 12:17)
4. Martyred Jewish believers (Rev. 6:9-11)

The Remnant Considered Contemporarily

When thinking of the contemporary or present remnant, it is appropriate to begin with the concept of the Messiah fulfilling some of the functions of this remnant. In treating the concept of the Suffering Servant, the book of Isaiah develops the thought that the true Messiah is also the perfect Israel.[39] In other words, there is a certain overlap between Israel as the servant and the Messiah as the greater Servant (cf. Isa. 42:1-9, 18-22; 43:1-7, 10, 21-24; 44:1-5, 18-23; 48:9-11; 49:1-13, especially v. 3). Where national Israel fails, the Messiah succeeds. He fulfills the functions that the remnant is truly called to accomplish.

It is no wonder, then, that the New Testament writers often identify Jesus as the perfect Israel, the One who will fulfill the God-ordained functions of the remnant. They describe Him with images and symbols that were used in the Hebrew Bible to designate the nation Israel. For example, He is called "My son," the One who God called out of Egypt (Mt. 2:15; cf. Hos. 11:1; Exod. 4:22). He also called Himself "the true vine" (Jn. 15:1; cf. Isa. 5:1-12; Jer. 12:10; Ps. 80:8-19; Mt. 21:33-45). Therefore, Jesus, as the Messiah, fulfills the role of the contemporary remnant without negating the function of this role in God's purpose for Israel.

There are many others in the New Testament who, having trusted in Jesus as Messiah and Savior, became a part of the present remnant. They were Jews who accepted the Jewish Messiah and, therefore, became a part of contemporary believing remnant

---

[39] For a thorough, verse-by-verse study of Isaiah and the rabbinic interpretation of the Suffering Servant passages, see: Arnold G. Fruchtenbaum, *Ariel Bible Commentary: The Book of Isaiah* (San Antonio, TX: Ariel Ministries, 2022).

of Israel: Zacharias and Elizabeth (Lk. 1:5-25, 57-80); Joseph and Mary (Mt. 1:18-25; Lk. 1:26-56); the shepherds (Lk. 2:8-20); Anna and Simeon (Lk. 2:21-38); John the Baptist (Mt. 3:1-17; 11:2-19; Lk. 3:1-22); the apostles (Mt. 16:13-17; Mk. 8:27-30; Lk. 9:18-21; Jn. 6:69; 17:12); Peter (Gal. 2:14); Timothy's mother, a Jewish woman who was a believer (Acts 16:1); Aquila and his wife Priscilla, Jews who had to leave Rome (Acts 18:2); Apollos (Acts 18:24-28); many thousands of Jews who were among those *who have believed* (Acts 21:20); Jewish believers called "the circumcision" in contrast to the Gentile believers (Rom. 15:8-12; cf. 11:13-14, 17-21); and the twelve tribes in the church (Jas. 1:1; cf. 1 Pet. 1:1; 2:4-10; Acts 8:1, 4; Gal. 2:7-9). These individuals came from the nation of Israel. The Messiah was sent to them as their Savior (Acts 13:16-17, 23-24; cf. Lk. 2:32), and for them He is presently exalted in order to grant repentance (Acts 5:31). These believing Jews mentioned in the New Testament form a small part of the present-day remnant. For nearly two thousand years, individuals have been called from the Jewish fold by the Good Shepherd, and along with those from the Gentile fold, they form one flock with one Shepherd (Jn. 10:14-16). They have entered the kingdom by the narrow gate (Mt. 7:13-14) and now function as the true remnant of Israel because they follow the Messiah (Mt. 5:1-16). They are a part of *the Israel of God* (Gal. 6:16), who have had their hearts circumcised and now receive their praise from God, not men (Rom. 2:28-29; cf. Deut. 10:16; 30:6; Jer. 4:4; 9:25-26).

The supreme example of the present-day remnant, however, is the apostle Paul. In fact, according to his own words, he is the prototype of the contemporary remnant (Rom. 11:1). He describes his relationship to the nation of Israel in eleven different ways, calling himself:

1. *an Israelite* (Rom. 11:1; 2 Cor. 11:22)
2. *of the nation of Israel* (Phil. 3:5)
3. Israel, *my nation* (Acts 24:17)
4. *a Hebrew of the Hebrews* (Phil. 3:5)
5. a Hebrew (2 Cor. 11:22)
6. *a descendant of Abraham* (Rom. 11:1; 2 Cor. 11:22)
7. *of the tribe of Benjamin* (Rom. 11:1; Phil. 3:5)
8. *a Jew* (Acts 21:39; 22:3)
9. a Jew *by nature* (Gal. 2:14-15)
10. *my brethren, my kinsmen according to the flesh, who are Israelites* (Rom. 9:3-4)
11. *my fellow countrymen*, literally, "my flesh" (Rom. 11:13-14)

At this point, four observations concerning the present-day remnant are appropriate, especially as it relates to the larger body of Messiah, the church. First, from what has been seen above in the Scriptures, it is obvious that the Jew remains a Jew when he comes to faith in Jesus as His Messiah and Savior. He cannot stop being what he was born to be. His Jewishness, which springs from his relationship to Abraham, Isaac, and Jacob, remains the same.[40] Second, when the Jew does come to faith, he becomes a part of the present-day remnant. What that means will be seen below. Third, now that the Jew has become a part of the believing remnant, he must maintain a three-fold citizenship (in the following order): (1) a citizen of heaven (Phil. 3:20-21); (2) a citizen of dispersed and exiled Israel (Acts 24:17; Rom. 11:1; 2 Cor. 11:22; Phil. 3:5); and (3) a citizen of a local country where he currently resides, unless he lives in Israel (Rom. 13:1-7; 1 Tim. 2:1-4; Titus 3:1-2; 1 Pet. 2:13-17; cf. Acts 16:35-39; 22:22-29; 23:25-30; 25:13-22). The fourth and final observation is that it must be obvious that there are certain valid distinctions within the body of

---

[40] For more information on this concept, see: Fruchtenbaum, *The Remnant of Israel*, pp. 1-16.

Messiah. The apostle Paul certainly saw himself as a part of that body (cf. 1 Cor. 12:13), but at the same time, he maintained a full personal, cultural, and national identity with the Jewish people—despite the fact that he was the *apostle to the Gentiles* (Rom. 11:13).

This reality, however, raises a question concerning six New Testament passages that speak about the unity in the body of Messiah, where there is no distinction between the Jew and the Gentile. These passages are Romans 3:9; 10:12; 1 Corinthians 1:24; 12:13; Galatians 3:28; and Colossians 3:11. The solution to the question regarding distinction versus unity is to be found in the fact that the above-listed passages are in a different context. They speak about how one becomes a believer (Rom. 3:9; 10:12; 1 Cor. 1:24; Gal. 3:28) as well as how one is to be accepted in the body of Messiah (1 Cor. 12:13; Col. 3:11). They do not disagree with the notion that there is a definite diversity in the body as well. Even the above passages that speak about male and female or master and slave being one in Messiah must be harmonized with other passages that speak about a diversity in the same realms, even in the same books (e.g., 1 Cor. 7:20-24; Col. 3:22–4:1 on slaves and masters; 1 Cor. 11:3-16; 14:34 on females and males). In other words, there is a definite oneness and unity in the body of Messiah, which exists because of the nature of the gospel and the work of the Spirit. At the same time, there is a definite plurality and diversity in the body of Messiah. This diversity is personal, sexual, cultural, economic, social, and national. Does this make the Jewish believer "better" than the non-Jewish believer? Of course not. It in no way makes the Jew in the body superior to the non-Jew, any more than it makes the non-Jew in the body inferior to the Jew. In the body of Messiah, there is a diversity within a unity, which means, among other things, that there is a nationality within a universality and a racial within an interracial. Galatians 2:11-15 provides a negative example of this concept, while 1 Corinthians

9:19-22 and Philippians 3:4-7 provide a positive example. It simply means that the Jew in the body must be free to function as a part of the present-day remnant in the manner that God has called him.

The Remnant Systematically Developed

Having surveyed the biblical concept of the remnant of Israel in a chronological fashion, it remains only to develop it in a systematic fashion—that is, what are the universal functions of the remnant that cross time and space? When this question is answered, the function of the present-day remnant in relation to the Holocaust can be better defined.

Basically, the believing remnant of Israel has eight universal functions. First, the remnant is to possess the promises of God (cf.

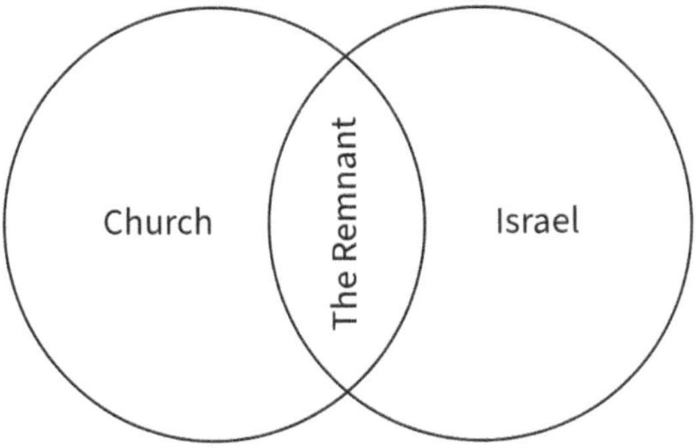

[Diagram: Two overlapping circles labeled "Church" and "Israel" with the intersection labeled "The Remnant"]

Above: Both Testaments have always seen two Israels: Israel the whole, meaning all Jews who are descendants of Abraham, Isaac, and Jacob; and the remnant of Israel, which are those Jews who believe what God has revealed to Moses, the prophets, and finally Jesus the Messiah. Jews who believe in Jesus the Messiah continue to be Jews. Therefore, since the birth of the church in Acts 2, the believing remnant of Israel belongs both to the church and Israel. It is this remnant through whom God will fulfill His program, not the entire nation. God keeps the nation of Israel alive because of the believing remnant, and the believing remnant is therefore responsible for keeping the entire nation alive. The reason that all attempts to annihilate the Jews have failed is because there has always been a believing remnant among the Jewish people.

Dan. 9:1-27; Rom. 11:25-27). The covenant promises, sovereignly and graciously given by God, are only possessed and experienced by the believing remnant. Without the remnant, the promises of God in relation to the nation of Israel would go unclaimed.

Second, the remnant is to prove the faithfulness of God (cf. Dan. 1:1-21; Rom. 11:25-27). This is logically related to the first function, for if the promises of God go unclaimed, they testify to God's unfaithfulness in His original election of Israel. But because the promises are claimed by the remnant, the faithfulness of God is demonstrated. Even in the most difficult times of punishment, there is a part of the nation that displays God's faithfulness and reliability. The believing remnant, sometimes even unto death, trusts and obeys God, which once again demonstrates that God is trustworthy. The majority of the nation may believe that God is unfaithful to His Word and may curse Him to His face, but there will always be a small portion, a vocal minority, that will continually praise Him for His faithfulness.

Third, the remnant is to preserve the nation of Israel (cf. Amos 7:1-6; Isa. 1:9; 65:8; Rom. 9:29). There are times when God leaves the nation "few in number," only to bring some to their knees in surrender and submission to His perfect plan, even to "the latter days" (Deut. 4:27-31). It is this believing remnant, this "few in number," that sustains the nation as a whole. Many times, it was the prophets themselves that stood alone between God and the nation, which was only a hair's breadth away from extinction (cf. Isa. 65:8; Amos 3:7; 7:1-6). In other words, the remnant functions as a preservative within the nation, protecting Israel from decay and destruction from within because of her infectious corruption. A repetition of a quote by Keil is entirely appropriate at this point. In commenting on Deuteronomy 30:1-10, he notes that a remnant would always exist, "since even in times of the greatest apostasy on the part of the nation there would always be a holy seed which could not die out."[41] Otherwise, the nation would have been utterly and permanently rejected, rendering the promises of God null and void, which is an impossible outcome.

Fourth, the remnant is to persevere with the nation of Israel (e.g., Jer. 43:4-7; Ezek. 3:10-15; Dan. 1:1-21; 2:49; 3:1-30; 6:1-28; Neh. 1:1–2:10; Num. 14:5-10, 30). The believing remnant is not to flee from the nation when it is under the judgment of God but rather is to suffer along with the nation. There may be times when God Himself removes the remnant before the judgment falls (e.g., in A.D. 70; cf. Lk. 21:20-24), but unless He does the removing, the remnant must stay with their brethren. It will become obvious below why this must be an imperative for the remnant.

Fifth, the believing remnant is to pray for the nation of Israel (cf. Num. 14:11-21; Amos 7:1-6; Dan. 9:3-19; Neh. 1:1-11; Rom. 9:1-3; 10:1). This is one of the reasons that the remnant is not to desert the nation of Israel when she is under judgment. It must pray with and for the nation, which is proof of its love. Prayer is always more effective when it comes from within the crucible itself. This gives prayer reality and power. When the remnant prays for the sinning nation, God intervenes for His own glory (Jas. 5:17-18; Isa. 48:9).

Sixth, the believing remnant is to press God to fulfill the covenant promises (cf. Dan. 9:3-19; Neh. 1:1-11; Rev. 6:9-11). This is a major part of the content of the remnant's prayer on behalf of the nation. The remnant is to pray God's Word back to Him, especially the covenant promises, and then to press God to fulfill them. Prayer that is based on God's contractual arrangements is

---

[41] Keil and Delitzsch, "Deuteronomy," p. 451.

prayer that goes straight to the heart of God. He said it, the remnant prays it, and He fulfills it in His own time.

Seventh, the believing remnant is to proclaim the truth of God to the nation (cf. Jer. 1:1-19; 2:1–45:5; Ezek. 2:1-10; 3:1-27; 11:14-21; 14:1–24:27; 33:1–48:35; Dan. 1:1–2:3; 8:1–12:13; Acts 2:14-41; 3:12–4:31; 5:12-42; 6:8–7:60; 13:13-41). This is the preeminent reason that the remnant is not to forsake the suffering nation in her hour of pain. The Jewish people must hear God's truth, especially when He has their attention through severe discipline. There are always some from within the nation who will respond and become a part of the believing remnant. In fact, that is one way that God brings the remnant to the surface.

Eighth, the believing remnant is to provoke the nation of Israel to jealousy (Rom. 11:13-14). The Gentile believers are to do the same during this age of grace (Rom. 11:11-12). The remnant is to remain in touch with the nation, displaying the blessings of the New Covenant, in order that the nation might be driven back to God. This is part of God's faithfulness to the nation as a whole. In fact, that has been Paul's teaching in the entire section of Romans 9–11, and yet the church is surprised that God demonstrates such grace to the nation of Israel. Zimmerli comes to this conclusion when he says:

> The Christian church has largely forgotten this preaching of the Apostle. And, therefore, in our day it falls to the lot of the Christian church to be startled by that faithfulness of God which has opposed his merciful history to the human program of a final solution (to the Jewish question).[42]

All eight of these functions of the believing remnant were manifested during the Holocaust to a greater or lesser degree. One is

---

[42] Walther Zimmerli, *Israel und die Christen: Hören und Fragen* (Neukirchen, Germany: Neukirchener Verlag, 1964), p. 80.

not able to measure the depth of the eight functions, but it is possible to see them at work, especially in the lives of thousands of Jewish believers who not only suffered in the Holocaust but also perished with their kinsmen according to the flesh. This is borne out by the numerous written and oral records of Jewish and Gentile testimony.[43] The founder of the International Board of Jewish Missions, Jacob Gartenhaus (1896–1984), states:

> During the Nazi genocidal onslaught against the Jews of Europe, Jewish converts numbering nearly *one and a quarter million* suffered the same fate as did non-Christian Jews. Most of these were slaughtered by the Nazis or met death through the horrors of the concentration camps.[44]

Believers and unbelievers alike testify to the fact that the remnant of Israel was used in a great way by God in ministering to the nation as a whole during the Holocaust.

---

[43] In previous footnotes, several titles were listed that contain testimonies of Jewish believers during the Holocaust. The following are a few additional titles. For testimonies concerning the remnant functioning during the Holocaust from Jewish sources, see: Eliezer Berkovits, *With God in Hell: Judaism in the Ghettos and Deathcamps* (New York, NY: Sanhedrin Press, 1979), pp. 12-14; Donat, *The Holocaust Kingdom*, pp. 28-31; Heller, *On the Edge of Destruction*, pp. 183-209; and Poliakov, *Harvest of Hate*, p. 296. From Messianic Jewish sources, see: James C. Hefley, *The New Jews* (Carol Stream, IL: Tyndale House Publishers, 1974), pp. 57-67, 103-114; Arthur W. Kac, ed., *The Messiahship of Jesus: What Jews and Jewish Christians Say* (Chicago, IL: Moody Press, 1980), p. 141; Zola Levitt, *Meshumed!* (Chicago, IL: Moody Press, 1979). For Messianic Jews who led a large revival among Jews around the turn of the century, see Jacob Gartenhaus, *Famous Hebrew Christians* (Grand Rapids, MI: Baker Book House, 1976). These authors, for the most part, died before the Holocaust, but their ministries lived on in the hearts of the Messianic Jewish disciples who had to face Hitler and the Nazis. They were prepared to function as the believing remnant because of the godly testimony and biblical training that they received from their teachers.

[44] Gartenhaus, *Famous Hebrew Christians*, p. 25.

Israel's Adversary

Having studied Israel's election and defined her remnant, it is now appropriate to expose her adversary. God sovereignly and graciously chose the nation Israel to be His uniquely elected people in the world. Apart from a small but faithful remnant, the nation consistently defected from its divinely ordained purpose, thereby bringing unending suffering upon itself. The ultimate cause behind Israel's defection from God has always been Satan, the nation's adversary and preeminent anti-Semite. His goal has always been to disrupt God's plans and purposes. It is therefore not surprising that he is attacking the elected nation—in particular, the faithful remnant—for much of the plan of God is inseparably bound to the people of Israel. Walvoord makes this point perfectly clear:

> The trials of Israel stem from the basic conflict between divine purpose and satanic opposition. The very fact that God selected Israel as a special means of divine revelation makes the nation the object of special satanic attack. Satanic hatred of the seed of Abraham is manifested from the beginning of God's dealings with Abraham and continues through the entire course of human history culminating in the rebellion at the end of the millennium…
>
> Undoubtedly one of the principal causes for Israel's suffering has been the unending opposition of Satan to the fulfillment of God's purpose in the nation.[45]

As Feinberg asserts, it is only because of the sustaining hand of God that the nation still exists: "Throughout the centuries Satan has longed to blot out Israel, but she knows God's protecting hand."[46]

---

[45] John F. Walvoord, *Israel in Prophecy* (Grand Rapids, MI: Zondervan Publishing House, 1962), pp. 101-02; see also p. 103.

[46] Feinberg, *Israel at the Center of History & Revelation*, p. 53.

The purpose of this segment of the book is to briefly survey the satanic strategy in the Old Testament, then in the New Testament, and then to once again relate it to the Holocaust.

The Old Testament Perspective

Satan's strategy in the Hebrew Bible can be seen in two particular phases: first, in his attack on the godly line in general; and second, in his attack on the nation Israel in particular.

The attack on the godly line in general began in Genesis 3. Following Satan's attack on the first couple, God put a division between the seed of the woman and the seed of Satan (Gen. 3:15). As the nation would later look back on this record, it would be continually reminded that two lines of division existed in the world by God's design: the pro-Semite line and the anti-Semite line. This "enmity" is the satanic cause of anti-Semitism, as Pastor Terryl Delaney states:

> What causes this deep-seated hatred toward the Jewish people? In one word—Satan... In this great prototype of the Gospel [Gen. 3:15], God spells out the conflict of the ages. The serpent is Satan, and his seed is the children of darkness; the woman is Israel, and her seed is Christ. The English word *enmity* comes from the same root as the word *enemy*. Thus, we see in this great prophecy that Satan will be the enemy of Israel and his hatred for her will exist until her seed, the Messiah, crushes the old serpent's head. Anti-Semitism finds its source in the mind of Satan.[47]

What began in the Garden of Eden continues to this very day until the Messiah returns. This is affirmed by Daniel Fuchs, Missions Director and President of Chosen People Ministries:

---

[47] Terryl Delaney, "Why Do People Hate the Jews?" *The Chosen People* 88 (November 1981): 10.

The struggle which started in Genesis continues through the ages. Later God chose a people, Israel, so that there might be a line for the Lord Jesus Christ. We must never forget that enmity of Satan against the Jews is because God chose them as His channel of blessing for the world.[48]

Satan's attack on the godly in general is further illustrated in the life of Job (e.g., 1:6-12; 2:1-6). As the Israelites would again look back on this historical narrative, they would be reminded that behind many of their struggles and sufferings was the invisible war between God and Satan (cf. Ezek. 14:14, 20; Jas. 5:11). This would be a particularly relevant message for those who, like Job, belonged to the believing remnant.

The attack on the nation Israel in particular can be seen on three major fronts. First, Satan stood up against Israel, provoking David to number the people (1 Chron. 21:1; cf. Ps. 109:6). In reality, God was using Satan as a tool to discipline Israel (2 Sam. 24:1), but David was nevertheless led away from trusting God by taking the census. He was moved to trust numbers and soldiers instead. Second, Satan stood up against Joshua the high priest in Zechariah's day (Zech. 3:1-2). As Joshua was ministering before the Lord, Satan stood at the high priest's right hand to accuse him, but the Lord rebuked him. This situation adequately prepared the way for the return of the priestly ministry in the post-captivity community. Third, Satan attempted to argue over the body of Moses, but Israel's guardian angel, Michael (Dan. 12:1), rebuked him again in the name of the Lord (Jude 9). This dispute demonstrates the tenacity of the devil against Israel and her theocratic legislator. It also exhibits God's sovereign, but unseen, angelic agents ministering on behalf of the nation.

---

[48] Daniel Fuchs, "Satan's Rebellion Against God," *The Chosen People* 88 (November 1981): 6.

The New Testament Perspective

In the New Testament, Satan's strategy can be seen in two particular phases: in his attack on the Man-child (i.e., Jesus the Messiah) at His first advent; and in his attack on the woman (i.e., the nation Israel) at Jesus' second advent. The key passage for the record of this two-fold attack is Revelation 12. In capsule form, the apostle John, himself a part of the present-day believing remnant, recorded the satanic strategy during the period that encompasses the two advents of the Messiah. John is not concerned with the interadvent period at this point but rather the two comings alone, for Satan launches his two most significant attacks on these two fronts.

Before reviewing these assaults, it should be noted that three significant features of Satan are recorded in Revelation 12:

1. His titles, such as "the great dragon" (12:9; cf. vv. 3-4, 7, 13, 16-17, referring to his power), "the serpent of old" (12:9; cf. v. 15; referring to his deception), "the devil" (12:9; cf. v. 12; referring to his slander or accusations), and "Satan" (12: 9; referring to his resistance)
2. His functions, such as deceiving the whole world (12:9) and accusing the brethren (12:10)
3. His opposition, such as the merits of Messiah's death (12: 11), the word of the believers' testimony (12:11,17), their spirit of martyrdom (12:11), and their obedience to the commandments of God (12:17)

The Attack on the Man-child at the First Advent

Satan launched his first attack on Messiah at His birth (Rev.12:1-5). This began with slaughter of the babes by Herod, the precursor to Satan's final Antichrist (Mt. 2:13-21). Is it any wonder that the Lord called Satan "a murderer from the beginning" (Jn. 8:44)? The attack, however, did not stop with the birth of the Messiah but continued through Jesus' temptation (Mt. 4:1-11; Mk. 1:12-13; Lk. 4:1-13, esp. v. 13), His controversies with the Pharisees (e.g., Mt. 22:15-22; Mk. 12:13-17; Lk. 20:20-26; Jn. 8:44), His interception with Peter (Mt. 16:16-23; Lk. 22:31-32), His confrontation with Judas Iscariot (Lk. 22:3-6; Jn. 6:70-71; 13:21-30), and finally with His crucifixion (Col. 2:13-15).

The Attack on the Woman at the Second Advent

Satan will launch his second attack on Israel in the middle of the tribulation (Rev. 12:13-17). As God protected Jesus at His birth as well as during the other satanic attacks, so He will miraculously protect the believing remnant during this period. It is at this time, as Barnhouse says, that "Satan flings himself against the Jews in one final paroxysm of fury."[49] This is the time that Satan's superman, the Antichrist, will be on the loose, attempting to utterly destroy Israel (cf. Rev. 13; 2 Thess. 2:3-12; Mt. 24:15; Dan. 9:24-27). It will be the time of *Jacob's trouble* (Jer. 30:7ff.; Ezek. 20:33-38; Mt. 24:15-22) when two-thirds of the Jews in the land will be slaughtered, going through the worst holocaust that they will ever have to face (cf. Zech. 13:7-9).[50]

One question still remains concerning this final attack by Satan on the woman. When the devil is thrown down to the earth and when he knows that he only has *a short time* (Rev. 12:9, 12), why does he set out to persecute Israel (Rev. 12:13)? Two possible answers may be given. First, Satan cannot attack the Man-child, who is now waiting in heaven for His eventual rule over the nations

---

[49] Donald G. Barnhouse, *The Invisible War: The Panorama of the Continuing Conflict Between Good &Evil* (Grand Rapids, MI: Zondervan, 1977), p. 281.

[50] For details regarding the tribulation, see: Arnold G. Fruchtenbaum, *The Footsteps of the Messiah: A Study of the Sequence of Prophetic Events* (San Antonio, TX: Ariel Ministries, 2022, Fifth Edition).

(Rev. 12:5). Jesus is not only out of reach but also no longer a defenseless child. He is the Messianic King, having all the authority of God (Rev. 12:10). So, second, Satan must turn his fury on the woman, the nation Israel, who gave birth to the child. If he can wipe her off the face of the earth, Messiah cannot come back at His second advent. Without a covenant people to receive His covenant promises, the program of God comes to a grinding halt. Jesus told the religious leaders of His day, those who led the nation in their rejection of His Messiahship, that until they said, "Blessed is He who comes in the name of the Lord," they would not see Him again (Mt. 23:37-39). This confession must come from the religious leaders themselves. That is why Satan's repeated attacks against the nation have been against the leaders (e.g., Moses, David, Joshua the high priest). In other words, the second advent of Messiah is conditioned upon the Jewish people coming to faith being led by their religious leaders, and their salvation is the major purpose for the time of Jacob's trouble (cf. Ezek. 20:33-38; Zech. 13:8-9; Lk. 21:20-24; Rom. 11:25-27).

This concept puts the Holocaust in a completely different light. Through the centuries, including the Holocaust years, Satan has been attempting to annihilate the Jewish people. Before the first coming of Messiah, his attacks were aimed at cutting off the Messianic line, thus preventing the birth of the Savior. After the first coming, his attacks aimed at preventing Messiah's return. For millennia, he has tried to eradicate the Jewish people so that there would be no covenant people left for whom the Savior could return. All of the covenant promises would then go unfulfilled (an impossibility because of God's character), and the program of God would collapse. The Holocaust was one of Satan's best shots (perhaps his best shot up to this point) to accomplish this demonic goal. Greenberg realizes this when he says, "Since there can be no covenant without the covenant people, the fundamental existence of Jews and Judaism is thrown into question by this genocide."[51]

Not only was Hitler demon possessed and governed by Satan,[52] but he paved the way for the final Hitlerian ruler, the Antichrist. In speaking of Hitler, Price makes the following insightful remark:

> Are we to see more in this man [Hitler] than just a defeated tyrant who articulated, and then implemented, a particularly virulent type of anti-Semitism? Were his aspirations for Nordic superiority at the cost of the annihilation of an entire nationality of people and his designs for personal aggrandizement merely the apparitions of a madman consumed with a pathological hatred for the Jews? Or was he the precursor of an even more sinister figure who will soon follow upon the stage of world history to reap an even greater horror upon the Jews?[53]

The Holocaust was a satanic onslaught that fell short of its intended goal: the extermination of the entire Jewish race (i.e., genocide). Nevertheless, it carried with it all the demonic fury that Satan could muster through Hitler and his Nazis. This reality is affirmed in a dramatic way by author and professor of philosophy Israel Knox:

> The animosity of the Nazis for the Jews was irrational and pathological, and the resolve to bring about their total liquidation by means of a carefully planned process of genocide was at once so shrewd and so diabolical that only such as were equally demonic could envisage it and anticipate it, least of all the Jews, who,

---

[51] Greenberg, "Cloud of Smoke, Pillar of Fire," p. 8. For additional details regarding Satan and his attempts to prevent the first and second coming of the Messiah, see: Fruchtenbaum, *The Footsteps of the Messiah*, pp. 525-543.

[52] See: Jean-Michel Angebert, *The Occult and the Third Reich: The Mystical Origins of Nazism and the Search for the Holy Grail* (New York, NY: McGraw-Hill Book Comp., 1974); Abram Poljak, *Hitler – Warlord and Spiritualist* (Marshfield, MO: First Fruits of Zion, 2019, Seventh Edition).

[53] Price, *Next Year in Jerusalem*, pp. 111-12.

though the victims of persecution throughout two millennia, were not practitioners of it...

In Milton's *Paradise Lost*, Lucifer avers: "Evil, be thou my good." When evil is no longer just a deviation from the good, a heresy *within* the sphere of good, but is itself enthroned as the good, then the moral universe has been turned upside down and the sovereignty of Satan has been established. The Holocaust Kingdom was the kingdom of Satan and those who served him. Isaiah's exhortation: "Woe unto those who call evil good, and good evil," was exchanged for Lucifer's challenge: "Evil, be thou my good"—and the logic of the Holocaust was now crystal-clear: it was the logic of a party, a country, a people that proclaimed Lucifer, in the guise of Hitler, to be king, and decided to call evil good and to conduct themselves accordingly.[54]

There awaits in the wings of history another holocaust, more demonic and more satanic than that of Nazi Germany. It will be the final holocaust for the Jewish people. Merrill Unger describes the satanic madness that will govern the final tribulation period just prior to Jesus' return to set up His Messianic kingdom:

The mad cry will arise: "On to Jerusalem! Annihilate the Jew! Banish the names of God and Christ from the earth!" It will be the most desperate and devastating outburst of anti-Semitism the world has ever seen, the heinous culmination of demonic malignity and hatred against God and His plans for the earth. It will end in colossal defeat and wholesale destruction of the impious armies by the glorious revelation of the all-conquering Christ from heaven, defending His earthly people Israel, slaying His enemies, consigning the beast and false prophet to Gehenna and

---

[54] Jacob Glatstein, Israel Knox, and Samuel Margoshes, *et al.*, eds., *Anthology of Holocaust Literature* (New York, NY: Atheneum, 1978), pp. xviii-xix, xxii-xxiii.

Satan to the abyss, and setting up His own righteous and peaceful Kingdom upon the earth (Rev. 19:11–20:3).[55]

Conclusion

In summary, it has been determined that the Jewish people stand in a very unique relationship to God, to man, and to Satan. This position has been established, first of all, through her election. Israel's election by God stands secure, no matter what the spiritual condition of the nation, because it is sovereign, gracious, and eternal. There are seven basic purposes for this election: (1) to be a blessing to the entire earth; (2) to be a special nation to God; (3) to be a kingdom of priests on God's behalf; (4) to be a witness to the one, true God; (5) to demonstrate God's gracious and faithful dealings available to all men; (6) to be entrusted with the oracles of God; and (7) to bring God's Messiah into the world. As a result of this high and holy election, Israel was to respond in loving obedience. If she refused to fulfill her calling, severe discipline would inevitably follow. Sadly, this is the pathetic history of God's chosen nation and people, down to and including the Holocaust.

Although most of Israel's history is strewn with the wreckage of disobedience and judgment, nevertheless, a true and faithful remnant has always existed. The nation's past, present, and future are dramatically marked by the ministry of Israel's remnant, including the period of the Holocaust. The remnant's ministry or functions include: (1) to possess the promises of God; (2) to prove the faithfulness of God; (3) to preserve the nation as a whole; (4) to persevere with the nation in her hour of discipline; (5) to pray for the nation during these periods of judgment; (6) to press God to fulfill His covenant promises to the nation; (7) to proclaim the truth of

---

[55] Merrill F. Unger, *Biblical Demonology: A Study of the Spiritual Forces Behind the Present World Unrest* (Wheaton, IL: Van Kampen Press, 1952), pp. 208-209.

God to the nation, especially during periods of discipline; and (8) to provoke the nation to jealousy over the Messiahship of Jesus.

To fully understand Israel's dismal history, with all of its suffering and pain, one must see the biblical testimony concerning her perennial adversary, Satan. The true author and instigator of all anti-Semitism is this opposer and enemy of God. Behind every Hitler in history stands the imposing figure of Satan and his demons, always seeking to annihilate the Jewish people. If he can accomplish such a feat, the entire program of God will immediately collapse. However, the God of Israel will never allow this, for His eternal Word stands behind the nation's election, which will eventually be fulfilled in her faithful remnant. Then, and only then, will all of God's covenant purposes be fulfilled in His covenant people. No Hitler can deter such a plan and program.

Above: This collection of stone memorial plaques depicts the names of Jewish communities that were wiped out in pogroms or during the Holocaust (photo: © AdobeStock).

On this page: Roughly ten walking minutes from the gates of Auschwitz-Birkenau, there is a museum that houses art by the Canadian-born sculptor Rick Wienecke. One of Wienecke's sculptures is a memorial titled "The Unknown Child." A little boy presses against the inside of a crematorium door. His arm reaches through the closed door, desperately grasping for a place where he will be safe. This art piece does not answer the question "Where was God during the Holocaust?" (Photos: Christiane Jurik)

The Perspective of a Biblical Theodicy

Having focused on the perspectives of contemporary Judaism, the biblical covenants, and the nation Israel, it is now imperative that the difficult problem of a biblical theodicy be addressed.

The *Encyclopedia of Philosophy* offers the following definition of theodicy:

> Christianity (like Judaism and Islam) is committed to a monotheistic doctrine of God as absolute in goodness and power and as the creator of the universe *ex nihilo*. The challenge of the fact of evil to this faith has accordingly been formulated as a dilemma: If God is all-powerful, he must be able to prevent evil. If he is all-good, he must want to prevent evil. But evil exists. Therefore, God is either not all-powerful or not all-good. A theodicy (from [the Greek terms] *theos*, god, and *dike*, justice) is accordingly an attempt to reconcile the unlimited goodness of an all-powerful God with the reality of evil.[1]

In a world deeply troubled with evil and suffering, theodicy is worthy of any man's thinking and pondering. Only the unthinking

---

[1] John Hick, "Evil, The Problem of," in P. Edwards, ed., *Encyclopedia of Philosophy* (New York, NY: Macmillan, 1972), Vol. 3, p. 136.

and unfeeling would dare ignore the deep problems of the twentieth century. Professor of Systematic Theology at the Free University of Amsterdam Gerrit C. Berkouwer, has captured the extreme importance of such a theodicy in the modern world:

> Theodicy is a justification of God's providential rule. It attempts to prove that in spite of all enigmas and all criticisms God's governing of the world is holy, good, and just. Theodicy is an attempt to defend God against all complaints or accusations by demonstrating the meaningfulness and purposefulness of God's activity in the world and in human life. It presupposes the seriousness of all sorts of doubts and criticisms and assumes that there are empirical facts which cause tensions and pose problems in connection with the Divine rule.[2]

As seen in the previous chapters of this work, the Holocaust poses an immense problem for those attempting to devise a biblical theodicy, especially among Jewish philosophers, theologians, and rabbis. The existential reality of Nazi evil and suffering has caused many Jewish thinkers to reject any possibility of developing an adequate theodicy. In their minds, God's action, or lack of action, during the rise and fall of the Third Reich can never be justified. Primo Levi, an Italian Jew and survivor of Auschwitz, recounts the persistent memories of the personal evil and suffering that he saw and experienced during his enslavement:

> They crowd my memory with their faceless presences, and if I could enclose all the evil of our time in one image, I would choose this image which is familiar to me: an emaciated man, with head dropped and shoulders curved, on whose face and in whose eyes not a trace of a thought is to be seen.[3]

---

[2] Gerrit Cornelis Berkouwer, *Studies in Dogmatics: The Providence of God* (Grand Rapids, MI: Eerdmans Publishing Company, 1952).

[3] Primo Levi, *Survival in Auschwitz: The Nazi Assault on Humanity*, translated by Stuart Woolf (New York, NY: Collier Books, 1958), p. 82.

Left and below: Suppression of the uprising in the Warsaw ghetto, 1943. Jewish resistance members are captured and escorted by the Waffen-SS to an assembly point for deportation (photos: www.wikipedia.org).

Alexander Donat, a survivor who escaped both the Warsaw ghetto and Hitler's death camps, later wrote to his grandson about the evil of the Holocaust and its implications for religious Judaism:

> The Holocaust was for every survivor a crucial religious experience. Day-in and day-out we cried out for a sign of God's presence. In the ghettoes and in the death camps, before gallows and the doors of gas chambers, when confronted with *ultimate incredible evil*, we cried: "Lord, where art thou?" We sought Him, and we didn't find Him. The acute awareness of *God's puzzling and humiliating absence* was always with us. Memory of this experience is always with us…
>
> The far-reaching religious implications of the Holocaust have by no means been explored, nor has the process of coming to grips

with its meaning been completed. It implies a profound revolution in the basic tenets of Judaism, and the rise of a new set of Judaic values (italics added).[4]

Is it any wonder that a theologian like Heschel, who also experienced the devastating evil of the Holocaust, could say, "The world is in flames, consumed by evil. Is it possible that there is no one who cares?"[5]

The evil that annihilated six million Jews continues to fester under the religious skin of Judaism. How could a God of love and power allow six million Jews to be slaughtered in such a manner, with over one million of them being children? The vast number of six million is too much to handle. However, for a biblical theodicy, the number is not the deciding factor. One innocent child poses as much of a problem as one million innocent children. Even radical Jewish theologian Richard L. Rubenstein recognizes this truth: "A God who tolerates the suffering of even one innocent child is either infinitely cruel or hopelessly indifferent."[6] Judaism has for centuries recognized this principle. The Talmud, for example, declares that destroying a single life in Israel is equivalent to destroying the entire world, and saving a single life in Israel is equivalent to saving the entire world.[7] Therefore, an adequate theodicy will answer the issue of evil and suffering, be it in the lives of six or six million.

In dealing with evil and theodicy, it must be remembered that three different kinds of evil have to be confronted. First, there is the problem of *metaphysical evil*, or the nature and source of evil. In other words, what is evil, and who is its author? Second, there

---

[4] Donat, "A Letter to My Grandson," pp. 43-44.

[5] Abraham J. Heschel, *God In Search of Man: A Philosophy of Judaism* (New York, NY: Farrar, Straus and Giroux, 1955), p. 367.

[6] Rubenstein, *After Auschwitz: Radical Theology and Contemporary Judaism*, p. 87.

[7] See: *b. Sanhedrin* 37a:13.

is the problem of *moral evil*, or the reality and responsibility of evil. Again, to rephrase this problem, who is responsible for evil? How is it that man chooses to commit evil? And third, there is the problem of *physical evil*, or the suffering of innocent people by events not determined by their own moral choices. In other words, why do people suffer from natural catastrophes? If God is in sovereign control of the natural world, why are there so many natural disasters? This chapter will not deal with the problem of physical evil since it does not relate specifically to the Holocaust itself.[8]

A further word must be added at this point before embarking on the task that lies ahead. In approaching the problem of evil and theodicy, it must be remembered that man faces certain inherent limitations in penetrating these issues. Berkouwer suggests that three factors limit one's knowledge in these matters.[9]

First, there is the common failure to reckon with the real and concrete wrath of God as it is revealed in Scripture. This failure, in turn, greatly impoverishes one's experience with the holiness of God. When considering evil in all of its forms, one must keep in mind that God is not only presently revealing His wrath from

---

[8] For an excellent summary of the problem of physical evil and the reasons for its existence, see Norman Geisler, *The Roots of Evil: Revised, Third Edition – With a Response to Rabbi Kushner's "When Bad Things Happen to Good People"* (Matthews, NC: Bastion Books, 2013), n.p. In this work, Geisler provides the following eleven reasons for the existence of physical evil: (1) Some physical evil comes to us directly from our own free choices. (2) Some physical evils come to us indirectly from the exercise of our freedom. (3) Some physical evils come to us directly from the free choices of others. (4) Some physical evil comes to us indirectly from the free choices of others. (5) The Bible declares that much suffering and all human death are the result of Adam's sin. (6) Some physical evil may be a necessary by-product of other good activities. (7) Some evils may come upon us as the result of the choices of evil spirits. (8) Some physical evils are God-given warnings of greater physical evils. (9) Some physical suffering may be used by God as a warning about moral evils. (10) Some physical evil may be permitted as a condition of greater moral perfection. (11) Finally, some physical evil occurs because higher forms live on lower ones.

[9] Berkouwer, *Studies in Dogmatics: The Providence of God*, pp. 256-275.

heaven (Rom. 1:18ff.) but will also do so in the future for all eternity (2 Thess. 1:6-10). In other words, God has not yet made His final statement concerning evil.

Second, there is human guilt as a real limitation to one's thought and understanding. Real moral guilt not only accounts for much human evil and suffering but also prevents the human mind from clearly penetrating the midst of divine providence in matters of suffering and evil.

Third, the neglect of the church's doxology also places a severe limitation on one's perception and experience of evil and suffering. The church is assured that God has all things under His sovereign control and that He is working all things together for her good (Rom. 8:28-39). The church may not always understand God's superintendence over His creation, but she can rest in faith that He is about His business and will eventually bring all things to the light of His holiness (cf. Rom. 11:33-36; 1 Cor. 4:5; 13:12).

Berkouwer summarizes this point in regard to an adequate theodicy: "With this we deal with the profoundest point in all reflection on the problem of theodicy: is it possible to stand in this evil world and sing a doxology in the face of the incomprehensibility of God's world rule?"[10]

Robert Duncan Culver, pastor, preacher, and professor of theology at Wheaton College, reaffirms that this incomprehensibility of God's world rule is at the heart of a true biblical theodicy when he says: "Now it is a matter of considerable importance that the Bible nowhere attempts to justify God (theodicy) in allowing evil in the world... Furthermore, the Bible makes no bones about assigning the existence of evil to the permission of God's government: providence."[11]

---

[10] Ibid., p. 266.

[11] Robert D. Culver, "The Nature and Origin of Evil," *Bibliotheca Sacra* 129 (April–June 1972): 107.

Philosopher of religion John Hick also affirms that "mystery" is the only positive answer to innocent suffering:

> Our 'solution,' then, to this baffling problem of excessive and undeserved suffering is a frank appeal to the positive value of mystery. Such suffering remains unjust and inexplicable, haphazard and cruelly excessive. The mystery of dysteleological[12] suffering is a real mystery, impenetrable to the rationalizing human mind.[13]

This chapter will first look at theodicy from a philosophical perspective and then from a theological perspective. Philosophically, there are several positions that are unacceptable to a biblical theist, while there are other positions that are commensurate with a biblical stance. Both of these alternatives will be surveyed. Finally, theologically, there are several major biblical doctrines that make it quite reasonable to expect evil and suffering to flourish for a time within the sovereign plan of God. These doctrines will likewise be surveyed, along with the divine purposes for allowing evil and suffering as they relate to the church, the Gentiles, and the Jews (cf. 1 Cor. 10:32).

---

[12] In this context, the term "dysteleology" refers to the philosophical perspective that rejects the idea of purposeful design or an ultimate cause in existence. In other words, the term encapsulates the concept that nature lacks teleology, or inherent purpose.

[13] John Hick, *Evil and the God of Love* (New York, NY: Palgrave Macmillan, 2010; second edition reissued with a new preface), p. 335.

A Philosophical Perspective of Theodicy

In examining the problem of evil and suffering from a philosophical viewpoint, it becomes obvious that certain positions and responses are totally unacceptable to a biblical theist. However, there are other positions that conform to the biblical revelation and are therefore acceptable to a biblical theist. The unacceptable positions will be dealt with first, followed by the acceptable ones.

Unacceptable Philosophical Positions

The systematic theologian and philosopher Norman Geisler suggests six philosophical positions that ultimately must prove unacceptable to the biblical theist.[14] The first two concern evil itself, while the last four concern God. All six positions fall short of the biblical revelation concerning God and evil. Additionally, they contain certain philosophical weaknesses. Therefore, it is not surprising that all of these positions seek to modify, and thus ultimately distort, the biblical stance concerning God and evil.

Illusionism

The first unacceptable philosophical position concerns evil and can be called "illusionism." The existence of evil itself is denied. Evil is viewed as an illusion rather than a reality. This position denies biblical revelation. According to the Scriptures, evil is real enough to cause God's real judgment to fall upon humanity and to cause Jesus, God's only Son and Savior, to come and die for sin (cf. Ps. 9:7-8; Isa. 45:21-22; 53:1-2; 66:15-16; Jer. 1:16; Hos. 6:7; Mal. 3:5; Jn. 3:16-19, 36; 1 Jn. 1:5–2:2).

---

[14] Norman Geisler, *The Roots of Evil* (Grand Rapids, MI: Zondervan Publishing House, 1978), pp. 15-40.

Even philosophically, illusionism proves less than satisfactory. If evil were an illusion, then where did this illusion originate? Plus, if evil is merely an illusion, then why does it seem so real? Finally, what practical difference does it make if one views evil as an illusion or as reality, especially if the evil of the Holocaust has devoured him?

Dualism

The second unacceptable philosophical position also concerns the nature of evil and can be designated as "dualism." In this position, evil is not denied as in illusionism, but rather it is said to have eternally co-existed with good while still dwelling independently in its own realm. In other words, good and evil are co-existing and eternal entities. This view is closely related to the modern thought called "process theology," where God is seen as bipolar, encompassing all things (i.e., panentheism) and in the process of growth.[15] Once again, this position is far from the biblical revelation, which declares that God is the only uncreated, eternal Being (cf. Gen. 21:33; Ps. 90:2). God is affirmed by the biblical testimony as infinitely holy and totally apart from any form of evil, either in His being or His actions (1 Jn. 1:5; Jas. 1:13). God is not in process. He is totally constant (Mal. 3:6; Heb. 13:8; Jas. 1:17).

Philosophically, dualism proves unsatisfactory as well. How can one relate both good and evil to God's non-contradictory nature? How can an evolving, semi-omnipotent God bring about any kind

---

[15] For details, see: David Ray Griffin, *God, Power, and Evil: A Process Theodicy* (Philadelphia, PA: The Westminster Press, 1976). For views of process theology within Judaism, especially as related to the Holocaust, see: Jerome Eckstein, "The Holocaust and Jewish Theology," *Midstream* 23 (April 1977): 36-45; Jakob J. Petuchowski et al., "Symposium: The God We Worship," *Dimensions in American Judaism* 2 (Fall 1967): 26-27. For a critique of this position from within Judaism, see: Jacob B. Agus, "God and the Catastrophe," *Conservative Judaism* 18 (Summer 1964): 18-19. For an evangelical evaluation and critique of process theology, see: Geisler, "Process Theology," pp. 237-284.

of moral victory in the world, especially if He needs man's assistance? How can one turn to an impotent God in times of suffering, let alone in times of loving worship?

Finitism

The third unacceptable philosophical position concerns the nature of God Himself and can be called "finitism." In this position, evil is seen as real, but the traditional view of God as omnipotent is rejected. God is all-loving but not all-powerful. In other words, God is incapable of destroying evil.[16] Of course, this is in direct contradiction to the biblical revelation of God as the omnipotent Creator (cf. Gen. 17:1; Job 42:2; Rev. 19:6).

Finitism also raises some philosophical questions. Why did God create the world if He could not control evil? How can a finite God assure one of His final triumph over evil? Is not every finite being created? Who then created this finite God?

Sadism

The fourth unacceptable philosophical position also concerns the nature of God and can be called "sadism." Once again, the reality of evil is affirmed, while the nature of God is radically challenged. In contrast to finitism, which sees God as impotent, sadism maintains His omnipotence but denies His all-loving nature. Either He is unconcerned about evil or He actually delights in it. While some Jewish Holocaust theologians might opt for the finitism position,

---

[16] For Jewish religious leaders who apply finitism to the Holocaust, see: Harold S. Kushner, *When Bad Things Happen to Good People* (New York, NY: Schocken Books, 1981), pp. 113-148; Lelyveld, *Atheism Is Dead*, pp. 158, 176-77; Eckstein, "The Holocaust and Jewish Theology," pp. 36-45; Simon Friedeman, "God in Buchenwald," *The Jewish Spectator* 34 (October 1969): 20-22. For one modern expression of finitism outside of Judaism but still related to theodicy, see: Griffin, *God, Power, and Evil: A Process Theodicy*, pp. 251-274.

few (if any) would claim the sadism position, for it would deny the entire loving covenantal framework within which Judaism itself stands (cf. Deut. 7:6-11). Of course, this concept of sadism is denied by the biblical revelation (cf. Ps. 145:9, 15-16; 2 Cor. 13:11; Heb. 12:5-6; 1 Jn. 4:7-8, 16).

Sadism raises some pertinent philosophical questions. If God is limited in His love, then He must be limited in His moral nature, which means that there is no ultimate moral standard by which to measure Him. Is this concept not incompatible with His nature? Why would He destroy that which He created?

Impossibilism

The fifth unacceptable philosophical position likewise concerns the nature of God and can be called "impossibilism." This position affirms the reality of evil and suffering but seeks to transform the nature of God to accommodate such evil and suffering. Impossibilism maintains that God is all-powerful and all-loving but that it is impossible for Him to either foresee or destroy evil without going contrary to His own will. This view denies the clear revelation of Scripture, for God is both all-knowing (cf. Prov. 15:3; Jer. 23:23-25; Heb. 4:13) and capable of creating a world where evil is possible but does not occur (cf. Job 42:2; Lk. 1:37).

Impossibilism raises some philosophical questions. Is not God outside of time and therefore unbound by the concept of foreseeing? Does foreseeing necessitate foreordaining?

Atheism

The sixth and final unacceptable philosophical position does not seek to modify the nature of God to accommodate the reality of evil and suffering but rather seeks to deny His very existence. This view is called "atheism." Instead of making evil an illusion, it claims that God is an illusion. The very presence and reality of evil prove that God does not exist at all. Of course, the biblical revelation assumes the existence of God (Gen. 1:1) and maintains that only a fool would deny such a divine existence (Ps. 14:1; 53:1), especially in light of the fact that God has revealed Himself to all humanity in a general way (cf. Ps. 19:1-6; Acts 14:15-17; 17:22-31; Rom. 1:18-32). A few Jewish Holocaust theologians have come very close to this position.[17] The unrestrained evil of Nazism has driven them to Jewish atheism. The God of the forefathers must be dead.

Atheism raises certain philosophical questions. How can one deny that God exists without actually implying at the same time that He does exist? In other words, does not the denial of God's existence necessitate a prior postulate equal to God? In maintaining that the very existence of evil proves that God does not exist, is not the atheist ignoring the time element involved in eliminating evil? How can the present existence of evil prove that God does not exist when the future might bring with it the divine defeat of such evil? Is it not possible that so-called unjust suffering might have some divine purpose in this world or the world to come?

In summary, illusionism, dualism, finitism, sadism, impossibilism, and atheism have proven unsatisfactory both from the perspective of the biblical revelation and because they leave certain philosophical questions unanswered. These six philosophical positions must, therefore, be rejected as having no sound justification for a theodicy involving the Holocaust.

---

[17] For example, see: Jennifer Lassley, "A Defective Covenant: Abandonment of Faith among Jewish Survivors of the Holocaust," *International Social Science Review* 90, no. 2 (2015): 1-17. https://www.jstor.org/stable/intesociscierevi.90.2.03.

Acceptable Philosophical Positions

Having examined and rejected six major philosophical positions regarding evil and suffering, it is now appropriate to survey any other positions that may be acceptable to the theist and, therefore, applicable to the Holocaust. Two fundamental philosophical positions will be examined and deemed acceptable when applied to the evil of the Holocaust. Both will be contrasted with other possible positions on the specific issues addressed, and their implications will be developed.

The two acceptable positions are closely related. The first deals with the possibility of a divine Creator and, more specifically, with the kind of divine Creator who is both infinite and personal. This position is called "theism." The second view deals with the possibility of a divine creation and, more specifically, with the kind of divine creation that is moral and fallen. This position is called "depravity." Theism deals with God's person, while depravity deals with His action, specifically in the kind of world that He has created. Only an understanding of both of these positions can bring a satisfactory explanation of evil and suffering (i.e., theodicy), especially the evil and suffering of the Holocaust.

Theism

Two basic options are open to a theism that adequately seeks to explain the evil in our world. These options were originally presented by Geisler, who classified them as "the greatest world" and "the greatest way" theodicies.[18]

"The greatest world" theodicy was advocated by Augustine of Hippo (354–430) and Gottfried Wilhelm Leibniz (1646–1716). It maintains that of all the worlds that God could have created,

---

[18] This discussion on theism is based on Geisler, *The Roots of Evil* (1978), pp. 43-52.

this present one is the best. The present evil in the world is absolutely necessary in order to highlight the good in the world. It is also maintained that the very nature of God demands this view of the world. If God is the best of all beings (which He is), then the world that He creates must also be the best of all worlds (i.e., the world must reflect His character).

There are at least two basic reasons that "the greatest world" theodicy is not the best theistic explanation of evil: First, it tends to pronounce evil as good, or at least have a distorted view of evil; and second, it tends to justify evil in view of some alleged overall good that it is supposed to portray.

A better option open to a theism that adequately seeks to explain the evil in the world is "the greatest way" theodicy. This view has been advocated by various individuals, including Thomas Aquinas (1225–1274). It does not maintain that this world is the best of all possible worlds. Quite the contrary, it insists that this world is thoroughly run over by evil and suffering. However, it also maintains that this present evil world is the best possible way to the best possible world.

In order to provide a full understanding of "the greatest way" theodicy, Geisler applies it first to the metaphysical problem of evil and then to the moral problem of evil.

The metaphysical problem of evil can be stated in the following manner: God is the Author of everything; therefore, He must be the Author of evil as well. The solution to this problem is to be found in what Augustine called "privation."[19] Evil is not a thing or a substance, but rather a privation or lack of something that should rightly be there. Augustine substantiated this concept with two postulates. First, God is totally good, and therefore, all created things are good as well. They were created good but then became

---

[19] See: Thomas Aquinas, "Question 75, Article 1," *The Summa Theologiæ of St. Thomas Aquinas*; accessible at https://www.newadvent.org/summa/2075.htm#article1.

evil through privation or corruption. Second, evil does not exist in itself but only in another as a corruption of it; therefore, evil is an ontological parasite.[20] Augustine went on to clarify that privation is distinct from mere absence or negation. Rather, it is the lack of something that ought to be there (e.g., the lack of sight in a rock is merely an absence, but in a blind man it is a true privation).

The obvious question that naturally arises from this view is this: What is the source of such a privation? Augustine answered this question in two ways. First, God is the supreme and incorruptible good. He, therefore, created His creation good—in fact, *very good* (Gen. 1:31). Then His creation underwent corruption and experienced privation (cf. Gen. 3). God, in His perfection, cannot be destroyed, but His creation can. If something is created or composed, then it can, by its very nature, be destroyed or decomposed. Second, it was free choice that led to privation. Man, in his finitude, has been given free moral choices, and these choices are what leads to privation. Therefore, the metaphysical problem of evil is not really metaphysical at all; it is moral. Moral pride leads to free choice contrary to the revealed will of God, thus producing the evil of privation. Therefore, free choice arising out of moral pride is the first cause of evil. There is no other cause, especially metaphysical. It must therefore be concluded that the ultimate solution to the metaphysical problem of evil is moral.

Having applied "the greatest way" theodicy to the metaphysical problem of evil, Geisler then applies it to *the moral problem of evil.* This is both logical and necessary since the ultimate solution to the metaphysical problem of evil is moral.

---

[20] The phrase "ontological parasite" makes reference to a branch of philosophy that deals with the nature of being and existence. By describing evil as an ontological parasite, the statement suggests that evil depends on something else for its existence, much like a parasite depends on a host. According to Augustine, evil is a negative force that feeds on or distorts the inherent goodness of another thing.

There are two sources for the moral problem of evil. First, man, in his finitude, makes evil possible. Second, free choice by man is what has led to the reality of evil. Many Holocaust theologians appeal to this free moral choice in man as the ultimate cause of the Holocaust.[21] It was not God who caused it, but man in his morally depraved condition. However, the question must be asked: Why did an absolute good God make creatures with free moral choice when He knew that they would choose evil? Geisler answers that only one of two responses can apply. First is the response of "necessitarianism." This view can be traced back to pantheism, Plotinus (the founder of Neoplatonism, ca. 205–270), and Spinoza (1632–1677). For the pantheist, creation flows necessarily from the very nature of God. It basically affirms that God, by His very nature, had to create. This answer must be rejected as unnecessary and incorrect, for God does not have to do anything other than that which He wills to do. A second response is, therefore, better. It is the response of "self-determinism." God created His world with free choice because He simply chose to do so. It was His own free choice, not made under any compulsion or restraint. This reflects his sovereign rule over everything.

What purpose could there be for such a creation? Perhaps three answers could be given. First, God simply wanted or willed to do so. Second, God is love; perhaps He simply had a desire to share this love with others outside the members of the Trinity. And third, perhaps He desired to be worshipped and enjoyed by His creation forever for who He is and for what He does. Whatever the purpose of creating man with free moral choice, even when He knew that man would sin, God will ultimately be glorified forever for His decision.

---

[21] For example, see: Robert Gordis, *A Faith for Moderns* (New York, NY: Bloch Publishing Co., 1971), pp. 159-252; Abraham Joshua Heschel, *The Insecurity of Freedom* (New York, NY: Schocken Books, 1966); Dennis Prager and Joseph Telushkin, *The Nine Questions People Ask About Judaism* (New York, NY: Simon & Schuster, 1986), p. 35.

Depravity

The second acceptable philosophical position deals with God's action, specifically in the kind of world that He might have created. Is this present evil world the only acceptable creation that would accurately reflect the true nature of the God of biblical theism or were there other possible worlds that He could have created that would have reflected His perfections and purposes just as well?

Again, Geisler suggests that only four possible options come into view when considering the various worlds that God could have made. The first moral option was *no world*. The theistic God could have chosen not to create any world at all. In reality, this is really not an option, for it is meaningless to try to make a moral judgment where no moral comparison is possible. To have a comparison, there must be commonality. There is no commonality between nothing and something. Therefore, it must be recognized that a non-world has no moral or metaphysical status. Actually, the comparison is not really between no world and a morally evil one; it should have been between no world and the best of all possible worlds that will result from this present world. That is the kind of theodicy that has been developed. If that is the case, then this present world is definitely better than no world, for this present world is the way to the best of all worlds.

The second moral option was an *amoral world*. God could have chosen to make a world without free creatures in it. Then man would have been more like a robot, free from all moral decisions and therefore all moral responsibility. Like the first moral option, there really is no moral comparison that can be made between a moral world and an amoral world. Robots or animals and human beings are not comparable in any moral fashion. Since man is finite and corruptible, he will always have moral choices to make. Robots and animals do not have such free moral choices.

The third moral option was a *morally innocent world*. God could have brought about a world where creatures were free but would never sin. This would have been a world where free humans would simply never choose to exercise their free choice to do evil.

Geisler suggests three responses to this potential option. First, it is possible that no such world would ever have materialized. Not everything that is logically possible actually happens. Second, producing a free world where humans never choose to sin may not be possible without tampering with human freedom. This would end any idea of a free moral world. Plus, it would certainly end the love shared between God and His morally free creatures. And third, a world where evil never occurred is morally inferior because it never called man to higher and nobler causes and achievements. The higher virtues of life, those that really reflect on the Creator, are hammered out on the anvil of evil and suffering. This present world calls for all the best in man.

The fourth and last moral option was a *morally fallen world*. God could have created a world where human beings were free and also did evil. This is the world that He *did* create. It is not the best of all worlds, but it is the way to the best of all worlds.

Some theists argue that God's love will eventually win over all human beings (i.e., "soul-making"). This form of universalism neglects two major factors. First, the Bible does not affirm such a matter. Quite the contrary, the Old and New Testaments alike, if taken at face value, continually affirm that God will eventually separate the righteous from the unrighteous, the former to eternal blessing and the latter to eternal judgment (e.g., Dan. 12:1-2; Mt. 25:46; 2 Thess. 1:5-10). And second, this view is a distortion of God's love. Love does not coerce or pressure. It waits patiently for a reciprocal response of love (1 Cor. 13:4-7). It allows the loved one to decide for himself (i.e., "soul-deciding"). God, in His love for His creatures, granted them the free choice of responding or not responding to His matchless love and grace.

Conclusion

One final question must be answered in regard to the philosophical perspective of theodicy. Granted that this present world is the best way to the best possible world and that this world is a morally fallen world, was it still necessary for God to allow so much evil and suffering in it? In other words, why has God allowed so much evil and suffering in this world that He created, especially the suffering of six million Jewish people? Could He not have accomplished His divine purposes for this world, as well as the world to come, with a lesser degree of evil and suffering in this present world?

Of course, God could have prevented the terrible degree of evil and suffering in the Holocaust because He is omnipotent—and if He could have, He would have, all other things being equal, for He is all-loving. However, apparently all other things were not equal, for God is also omniscient, which means that the degree of evil and suffering He permits is the exact amount required to accomplish the greatest good for mankind and the greatest glory for Himself (if not in this present world, certainly in the one to come). A major part of the problem is that man is not all-knowing, and therefore, in his finitude, he must trust that God knows best and does best. This is not always easy, especially when one is caught in the fury of the evil and suffering of the Holocaust. That is why the Mishnah says, "It is not in our hands [to explain the reason] either of the security of the wicked, or even of the afflictions of the righteous."[22]

---

[22] *Pirkei Avot* 4:15, retrieved from www.sefaria.org.

In conclusion, it has been demonstrated that the only acceptable philosophical positions are those that affirm a theistic explanation of evil. The best theodicy holds that this world is the surest way to the best world. This theodicy acknowledges that evil is a privation and that God has created man with free, moral choices. These free, moral choices lead, on one hand, to good, while on the other hand, they lead to evil. This world, which is the best possible way to obtain the best possible world, is where the greatest number of people are given maximal eternal joy, while at the same time, the freedom of all creatures is respected. Only a philosophical perspective like this can make any sense out of the insanity of the Holocaust.

A Theological Perspective of Theodicy

Having examined the problem of evil and suffering from a philosophical viewpoint, it is now imperative that the theological viewpoint be considered. It must be affirmed that the investigation of certain specific doctrinal positions as well as certain specific biblical purposes will point to the fact that it is both reasonable and logical to expect God to forestall His eventual and ultimate solution to the problem of evil and suffering. First, then, specific doctrinal positions will be related to a biblical theodicy for the Holocaust, followed by specific biblical purposes (i.e., for the church, the Gentile, and the Jew).

Specific Doctrinal Positions

Some theologians have tried to relate certain specific doctrinal positions to a biblical theodicy.[23] Using selected categories of systematic theology, they have addressed themselves to the issue of evil

---

[23] For example, see: Norman L. Geisler, "God, Evil, and Dispensations," in Donald K. Campbell, *Walvoord: A Tribute* (Chicago, IL: Moody Press, 1982), pp. 95-112

and suffering. It is needful that several more categories of systematic theology be applied to this same problem.

The first category to be investigated is *bibliology*, the doctrine of the Bible. Two specific factors come into focus. First, related to the time periods of the Bible, is the unique portrayal of the dispensations. Each one of these specific time periods or economies is set up by God to test man in some specific ways in regard to His clearly revealed will,[24] and each one of these historical dispensations ends in utter failure and judgment. Geisler suggests that at least two purposes surface in God's dispensational plan for the ages:

> First, He wants to prove to the universe (of rational creatures) that creatures always fail and bring evil (not good) on themselves when they disobey God's commands. Second, and conversely, God wants to prove that it is always right to obey His commands, for when individuals do, they bring good and blessing on themselves. In that way, heaven can be full of free creatures and yet justly rule out any rebellion again.[25]

A second factor also comes into focus in the doctrine of the Bible. Related to the supernatural origin of the Scriptures is the role of biblical prophecy and its fulfillment. The Bible does not predict that the world will end on a positive, victorious note but rather that it will end in utter rebellion and judgment at Messiah's return (cf. 2 Thess. 1:3–2:12; Rev. 19:11-21). As the world has bathed itself in evil and suffering for all of its existence, it will end in the same bitter fashion. The Bible truly gives an accurate picture of the world in its rebellion against its Creator, with all of the expected consequences for both man and God and man with man. This is especially true of the prophetic picture of the nation Israel,

---

[24] Fruchtenbaum, *The Word of God: Its Nature and Content*, pp. 123-147.

[25] Geisler, "God, Evil, and Dispensations," p. 104.

including the suffering of the Holocaust. Goldberg notes: "Did not Moses, our teacher, indicate what would happen to the Jewish people when they set aside God's truth (Leviticus 26, Deuteronomy 28)? Did not the prophets warn Israel that if they turned away from God's revealed truth, they would suffer the consequences?"[26]

The second category is *theology proper*, the doctrine of God. God must always act in total accordance with His nature, and His attributes reveal His character. Whatever the Holocaust meant, it certainly cannot be viewed apart from God's attributes. His holiness, justice, love, goodness, truth, freedom, omnipotence, immutability, omnipresence, omniscience, and sovereignty must all be brought to bear on the evil and suffering of the Holocaust. Whatever happened during that brief period, it in no way compromised any of these attributes of God.

One example will suffice to illustrate this point. In 2 Peter 3:9 and 15a, Peter makes a statement that reflects upon one aspect of the character of God: patience. The apostle states:

> [9]*The Lord is not slow about His promise* [of the second coming of Jesus], *as some count slowness, but **is patient** toward you, not willing for any to perish, but for all to come to repentance...* [15a]*and regard **the patience** of our Lord as salvation...* (emphasis added).

The second coming of the Lord will mark the end of all evil and suffering (2 Pet. 3:10-13), but as yet this anticipated coming has not arrived. Why has God so long delayed the return of the Messiah, which would alleviate such suffering and misery? The answer to this question is based on His character: God is patient. It is His great desire that all come to repentance, which leads to salvation. He does not want anyone to perish in judgment. Therefore, He

---

[26] Louis Goldberg, "For More Objectivity in Jewish–Christian Relations," in Arthur W. Kac, *The Messiahship of Jesus: What Jews and Jewish Christians Say* (Chicago, IL: Moody Press, 1980), p. 83.

delays His return so that those who will come to repentance, perhaps even through much suffering as in the Holocaust, might experience the greater good of salvation. His patience is prompted by His love, which is another one of His attributes.

The third category is *angelology*, the doctrine of angels, including Satan and demons. Two important factors relate to this doctrine. First, God's angels were certainly at work on behalf of the elect of the church, especially the remnant of Israel, the Jewish believers, who suffered in the Holocaust (cf. Heb. 1:13-14). Second, it is also true that Satan and his demons were heavily at work trying to stamp out the nation of Israel, for Satan is the author of all anti-Semitism. It must be remembered that evil first found itself expressed in the fall of Satan (cf. Isa. 14:12-15; Ezek. 28:11-19; 1 Tim. 3:6; Rev. 12:3-4).

The fourth category is *anthropology*, the doctrine of man. Suffering will not only produce God's greater glory but also man's (e.g., 2 Cor. 4:17). Suffering will also produce man's greater good (e.g., Gen. 50:20; Job 23:10; Rom. 5:20; 8:28). This truth is sufficient as a theodicy in and of itself, but added to it is the biblical teaching on man's free, moral nature. Humans are free, moral creatures, responsible for all of their actions and reactions. Each Nazi and each Jew must account for their moral choices in this life. It is a part of creaturely existence.

The fifth category is *hamartiology*, the doctrine of sin. Certainly, the Holocaust bears witness to the biblical testimony concerning man's sinfulness, both his sinful nature (e.g., Ps. 51:5; 58:3; Eph. 2:3; 4:18) and his sinful acts (e.g., 1 Jn. 1:8-10). The Bible well describes humans as potentially capable of any crime on the face of the earth. Apart from the grace of God, every person could be transformed into a Hitler.

The sixth category is *soteriology*, the doctrine of salvation. At least two factors can be related to this doctrine. First, it was evil itself that brought the Messiah to His eternally appointed death (e.g., Col. 2:13-15; Heb. 2:14-15; 1 Pet. 3:18). He who was without sin came to remove sin and all of the suffering that results from it (2 Cor. 5:21). Second, it is certainly true that people only come to God for salvation in their moments of personal need, sometimes in frantic moments of suffering and desperation. Is it as C. S. Lewis said: "But pain insists upon being attended to. God whispers to us in our pleasures, speaks in our conscience, but shouts in our pain: it is His megaphone to rouse a deaf world."[27] It is impossible to determine how many Jews came to a saving faith in the Messiahship of Jesus during the Holocaust, but it was probably well into the thousands. Certainly, this outcome must be considered a greater good as well as leading to a greater world.

The seventh category is *ecclesiology*, the doctrine of the church. Again, two factors can be related to this doctrine. First, the Holocaust brought out the unique commitment of the body of Messiah, the true church, as Gentile believers sought to hide many Jews from the invading Nazis. These believers truly laid down their lives as Jesus had (1 Jn. 3:16-18). But second, the Holocaust also brought out the true nature of the false church, the apostate church, which not only denied the Savior but also thousands of Jews and non-Jews fleeing from the Nazis. In fact, in many cases, the apostate church actually helped in the slaughter of the helpless victims.[28]

The eighth category is *eschatology*, the doctrine of last things. Once again, at least two factors can be related to this doctrine. First, if the Holocaust demonstrates anything, it is that worse is to

---

[27] C. S. Lewis, *The Problem of Pain* (New York, NY: HarperCollins, 2001), p. 92.

[28] For example, see: John S. Conway, *The Nazi Persecution of the Churches, 1933-1945* (New York, NY: Macmillan Publishing, 1969); Ernst Christian Helmreich, *The German Churches under Hitler: Background, Struggle, and Epilogue* (Detroit, MI: Wayne State University Press, 1979); Robert P. Ericksen, Susannah Heschel, eds., *Betrayal: German Churches and the Holocaust* (Minneapolis, MN: Augsburg Fortress Press, 1999).

come (e.g., Zech. 13). In fact, the Holocaust is almost a precursor of what the Jewish people must face in the future, just prior to the Lord's return (Mt. 24). God is going to allow Israel to suffer her worst persecution yet, and then all Israel will be saved (Rom. 11). The time of Jacob's trouble is in the future, hovering over the Jewish people like a knife ready to fall (Jer. 30). Second, the future holds a positive outlook, for God's eternal judgment will come and a new world will follow, one without any evil or suffering (Dan. 12:1-3; 2 Thess. 1:3–2:12; 2 Pet. 3:1-13; Rev. 19:11–22:21). Israel will once again find herself in her rightful place as the head of the nations (e.g., Deut. 28:1-14; Zech. 14:16-21). Israel awaits her future worst holocaust, but it will certainly be her last.[29]

The ninth category is *Christology*, the doctrine of the Messiah in His person and work. As mentioned above in soteriology, Jesus certainly came to die for all the evil and suffering in the world, but He also came with a unique relationship to the Jewish people. In His incarnation, the Lord was born, lived, died, and rose again as a Jew on Jewish soil (e.g., Rom. 1:1-4). He knew and loved His brethren according to the flesh, and He will one day return and reign as their Davidic King and Messiah (e.g., Lk. 1:26-38; Rev. 5:1-14; 12:5; 19:11-16). As He wept over Jerusalem because of her rejection of His Messiahship (Mt. 23:37-39), so He must certainly have wept over her bitter calamity of the twentieth century. In fact, His lament over the city of Jerusalem undoubtedly saw her destruction down through the ages (Lk. 21:20-24).

The tenth and final category is *pneumatology*, the doctrine of the Holy Spirit. The Spirit's work must be obvious to anyone observing the Holocaust from a biblical and theological perspective. His restraining ministry prevented two-thirds of the Jewish people

---

[29] See: Fruchtenbaum, *The Footsteps of the Messiah*, pp. 275-300; Rubenstein, *After Auschwitz: Radical Theology and Contemporary Judaism*, pp. 135, 198; Daniel Fuchs, "Satan and the Final Holocaust," *The Chosen People*, July 1982, pp. 12-13; Harold A. Sevener, "The Holocaust: Will It Ever Happen Again?" *The Chosen People*, July 1982, pp. 3-6.

from being slaughtered (Gen. 6:3; 2 Thess. 2:6-9). His convicting and regenerating ministries brought many Jews and non-Jews into a saving knowledge of the Messiah (Jn. 3:3-8; 16:7-11; Tit. 3:4-7). He was at work before, during, and after the Holocaust in bringing glory to the Savior (Jn. 15:26; 16:14).

The brief survey of the major doctrines of the Bible has revealed that rather than being lost and behind the scenes, God was at work in a mighty way during the Holocaust. However, His activity was undoubtedly only known and appreciated by those who knew and believed His Word. The greatest theodicy is always perceived by the hearts of the faithful. This survey has also made it reasonable and logical to see evil and suffering as major factors in God's total plan for the ages. He is truly using this evil world to bring about greater glory for Himself as well as greater good for man.

Specific Biblical Purposes

Having related certain specific doctrinal positions to a biblical theodicy, it is now fitting to relate certain specific biblical purposes to this same theodicy. The Bible divides humanity into three major groups: the church, the Gentiles, and the Jews (e.g., 1 Cor. 10:32). It will now be demonstrated that although all three groups experience evil and suffering for some similar purposes, each group individually also experiences them for unique purposes.

The first group is *the church*. Why does the church experience evil and suffering in this present world? The New Testament lists eleven reasons and purposes:

1. To share in the Messiah's sufferings (Rom. 8:16-17; 2 Cor. 1:5; Phil. 3:10; Col. 1:24; 1 Pet. 4:13-14)
2. To draw believers near to the Messiah, their faithful High Priest (Heb. 2:17-18; 4:14-16; 10:19-25)
3. To conform believers to the image of the Messiah (Rom. 8:26-30)

4. To cause believers to grow in the faith (Rom. 5:3-4; Jas. 1:2-4; 2 Pet. 1:2-11)
5. To purify the believers' faith and give them a greater love for the Messiah (1 Pet. 1:3-9; 4:1-3)
6. To discipline or train believers so they can share in His holiness (Heb. 12:5-11; 1 Cor. 5:1-13; 11:17-34; cf. Heb. 2:10; 5:8)
7. To give believers a life message of comfort (2 Cor. 1:3-7)
8. To prepare believers for glory and honor (Rom. 5:2; 8:17-18; 2 Cor. 4:16-18; 1 Pet. 1:6-7)
9. To give believers a greater experience of His grace (2 Cor. 12:7-10)
10. To glorify God (1 Pet. 4:12-19)
11. To remind believers of "old" truth (2 Pet. 1:12-15)

The second group is *the Gentiles*. Why do unbelieving Gentiles experience evil and suffering in this present world? The New Testament lists three specific purposes:

1. To be exposed to God's present wrath for suppressing the truth (Jn. 3:16-19, 36; Rom. 1:18-32)
2. To act as a forewarning against God's future wrath (Eph. 2:3; 2 Thess. 1:3-10; cf. 1 Pet. 4:17-18)
3. To be drawn to the Spirit's convicting and regenerating ministry (1 Tim. 2:4; 2 Pet. 3:9; 1 Jn. 2:2; cf. Jn. 3:1-8; 16:7-11; Tit. 3:5)

The third group is *the Jewish people*. Why do unbelieving Jews experience evil and suffering in this present world? The Bible records four major purposes:

1. To receive punishment for specific covenant violations (e.g., Lev. 26; Deut. 28–30)
2. To vindicate God's own name before the Gentiles (e.g., Ezek. 20:1-32, 44; 36:22, 32)

3. To receive discipline for the rejection of the Messiahship of Jesus[30] and for preventing the spread of His gospel, two things that resulted in the worldwide dispersion of the Jewish people in A.D. 70 (e.g., Lk. 21:20-24; Eph. 2:3; 1 Thess. 2:13-16)
4. To surface the godly, believing remnant (Rom. 11:13-14, 25-29; cf. Jer. 30:1–31:37)

Summary and Conclusion

This present evil and suffering world is the best way to the best world to come. In fact, much of the present suffering leads to positive benefits even in this age, in the midst of the darkness itself. Whether it be the church, the unbelieving Gentiles, or the unbelieving Jews, God is permitting evil and suffering—and indeed even using it—for man's better good as well as His ultimate glory.

Theodicy is the justification of the moral actions of God. There are several different and often opposing views offering themselves for such a justification. It has been seen that, philosophically, biblical theism is the best offering for all of the problems involved in a true theodicy. The infinite, personal Creator has created a world that allows for personal, moral choices by His creatures, thus preserving true moral freedom. At the same time, He is using this present evil world as the best possible way to the eventual best possible world.[31]

---

[30] While acknowledging that the rejection of the Messiahship of Jesus brought judgment upon the Jewish people as a whole (i.e., the worldwide scattering in A.D. 70), this is not to imply that every generation of Jews is personally responsible for the death of the Messiah (deicide charge), nor that only the Jews of the first century were solely responsible for that same death (e.g., Acts 4:27-28). Every human being is responsible for the death of Messiah (e.g., 2 Cor. 5:18-21; 1 Jn. 2:2) as well as God Himself (e.g., Isa. 53:6, 10; Acts 4:28).

[31] It must be observed that the premillennial scheme of biblical interpretation best suits this kind of theodicy, that is, the best possible way to "the best possible world." See: Alva J.

It has also been seen that, theologically, biblical theism best reflects all of the major categories of systematic theology. In fact, after reviewing the categories, it is possible to see why God's permissive toleration of evil and suffering in this present world is both reasonable and logical. It is in accord with His own nature and truth. This assertion, however, does not imply that we can presently know *all* of the answers in a truly biblical theodicy, for God has not yet revealed His final word on this most difficult problem. There is still room for mystery (Deut. 29:29; Rom. 11:33).

Finally, the Word of God makes it quite clear that God has several different purposes or reasons for allowing evil and suffering in His world. Whether it be the church, the Gentiles, or the Jews, God is working all things according to His sovereign and gracious will in order that He will be ultimately glorified and that man will ultimately experience the greater good. The Holocaust is one of many violent eruptions that the Jewish people have faced and will face again in the future. Those responsible for such atrocities will ultimately pay for their evil choices and actions (Gen. 12:3), but in the meantime, it is hoped that Israel will learn the painful lessons that God is trying to teach her.

It is only fitting to close this chapter with the very words of Holy Scripture, words that have comforted God's people down through the centuries, especially as they faced the onslaught of evil and suffering:

Shall not the Judge of all the earth deal justly? (Gen. 18:25b)

The Rock! His work is perfect, For all His ways are just; A God of faithfulness and without injustice, Righteous and upright is He. (Deut. 32:4)

McClain, *The Greatness of the Kingdom* (Chicago, IL: Moody Press, 1968), pp. 527-531, where he elaborates on a premillennial philosophy of history.

Concluding Thoughts

The Holocaust is a major fact of history, perhaps the most significant fact of history for most Jews, and yet it certainly cannot be considered any less significant to the God who created those very same Jews. It is probably still too short a time since the destruction of the six million to formulate any mutually agreed-upon religious beliefs from within Judaism itself. Perhaps the passing of six million more years will still not be enough time for the Jewish community to come to grips with the theological meaning of the Holocaust. It is likely that, because of the basic approach to the Scriptures within Judaism, some mutually agreed-upon solution is virtually impossible. When one dismisses the presupposition of divine revelation, as much of Judaism does for *all* of the Scriptures, then it becomes impossible to arrive at any meaningful and agreed-upon solutions to life and death, to time and eternity.

Committed evangelicals who submit themselves to the full authority of an inerrant Bible can arrive at some firmly established answers to life and death, time and eternity. This work *begins* with this assumption and commitment. God has sovereignly, graciously, and eternally established four major covenants with the nation of Israel. They blueprint Israel's total relationship with God in the past, present, and future. They lay out God's plan and purpose for the nation in time and eternity. God's commitments to the nation and the nation's commitments to God are firmly and permanently fixed. The fifth covenant, the Mosaic, adds many details to the nation's walk with God without abolishing any of the promises of the previous four (i.e., the Abrahamic, the Palestinian, the Davidic, and the New). The Mosaic Covenant adds fine print to the other covenants. Since all five of these covenants are still in force in some way or another, it can be concluded that Israel's suffering (including the Holocaust) must be a consequence of violating one or all of these covenants.

Through the above covenants, God has created Israel as a unique, elect nation. No other nation in the world has been chosen as Israel has. She occupies a special relationship with God and always will. It is true, however, that for the most part, the nation as a whole has not enjoyed the privileges of her election nor fulfilled the obligations of this election. Still, God will not reject His election of the nation, even though He may have to take it through severe and harsh discipline. When the nation as a whole refuses to fulfill its calling, there is always a faithful portion within the nation that will. This is the believing remnant of God. God has always had and always will have a remnant according to grace (Rom. 11:5). It is the remnant that not only enjoys the privileges of its election (as well as fulfills its obligations) but also sustains the nation as a whole. It ministers to and on behalf of the nation.

Along with the nation's election and the faithful remnant within the nation, there is an underlying reason for Israel's perennial sufferings: She has an adversary. Without negating any individual or corporate responsibility within the nation, it still must be admitted that Satan is out to destroy not only the nation as a whole but also the remnant in particular. Satan is locked in battle with God Himself. However, the only way that he can get to God is through the people of God, namely, either Israel or the church. His demonic strategy has permeated Israel's history from its very inception and will continue into her future, possibly through other Hitlers as well. It is certain that each major wave of worldwide Jewish persecution is building upon the previous waves until they all finally crash into the worst Holocaust of all, with the worst Hitler of all: the tribulation period with Satan's masterpiece, the Antichrist.

This satanic adversary is one of the major reasons for the present evil and suffering in the world. Any theodicy that is a biblical theodicy must include the evil and suffering caused by Satan and his demons. This evil fury is most dramatically seen throughout Jewish history.

Along with the satanic source of evil are man's own free moral choices. Although greatly influenced by Satan, the various Hitlers of the world cannot escape their moral culpability. It is therefore both reasonable and logical to see a biblical theism as the proper response to the evil of the Holocaust. This world is not the best of all possible worlds. Quite the contrary, it is a totally evil and corrupt world, but this does not mean that God is finished with this world. He is sovereignly and providentially moving history toward a new world. Therefore, although this is not the best world, it certainly is the best way to the best world. The present suffering (including the Holocaust) is working toward the eventual glorification of God and the benediction of man. Even in the midst of this present evil and suffering, God is accomplishing His own purposes for all men, be they Jews or Gentiles, believers or unbelievers. Admittedly, it is not always possible to see these purposes in this life, but the life to come will reveal them most clearly. In the meantime, some mystery must remain.

Israel must await her future Messianic glory. In the meantime, she moves ever so precariously toward her future holocaust. However, it must be remembered that until that time, and including that time, Israel remains *the apple of God's eye* (Deut. 32:8-10;

Zech. 2:8). To tamper with Israel is to invite the judgment of God, either in a national or individual way (Gen. 12:3). As the rabbis rightly stated, "He who plans evil against Israel is as if he had planned evil against God."[1] When Israel suffers, God suffers. One day, He will truly prove to be the Savior of the nation, for *in all their affliction He was afflicted, and the angel of His presence saved them; in His love and in His mercy He redeemed them; and He lifted them and carried them all the days of old* (Isa. 63:9). God's eternal covenant program cannot be broken, for the very character of God depends upon it. It is as the prophet Samuel declared so long ago: *For the* LORD *will not abandon His people on account of His great name, because the* LORD *has been pleased to make you* [Israel] *a people for Himself* (1 Sam. 12:22; cf. Rom.11:25-36).

---

[1] *Tanna Debei Eliyahu Rabbah 7*; available in Hebrew on www.sefaria.org.

Indices

Index of Names

The following index lists the names of authors cited in this work along with the corresponding page numbers. Whenever possible, the lifespans of the authors have been included within brackets.

Agus, Jacob B. (1911–1986), 94, 277
Akiba ben Joseph, Rabbi (ca. 50–135), 42, 280
Aquinas, Thomas (1225–1274), 238, 294
Augustine of Hippo (354–430), 237, 238, 239

Bamberger, Bernard J. (1904–1980), 89, 281
Barnhouse, Donald Grey (1895–1960), 123, 218, 281
Baron, David (1855–1926), 135
Bemporad, Jack (b. 1933), 84, 277
Berdyaev, Nicholas A. (1874–1948), 77, 281
Berenbaum, Michael (b. 1945), 64, 87, 277, 281
Berkouwer, Gerrit C. (1903–1996), 226, 229, 230, 281
Berkovits, Eliezer (1908–1992), 12, 33, 34, 36, 38, 40, 46, 47, 76, 78, 96, 277, 281
Besdin, Abraham R. (1922–1993), 91, 277, 282, 292

Borowitz, Eugene B. (1924–2016), 82, 83, 86, 282
Brown, Michael (1938–2023), 17, 49, 277
Buber, Martin (1878–1965), 69
Bulka, Reuven Pinchas (1944–2021), 19, 277
Bush, George (1796–1859), 110, 282

Cain, Seymour (b. 1914), 1
Carmy, Shalom (b. 1949), 35, 277
Cassuto, Umberto (1883–1951), 111, 282
Chafer, Lewis Sperry (1871–1952), 106, 117, 118, 132, 133, 180, 277, 282
Charny, Israel W. (b. 1931), 90, 90, 277
Clemens, Samuel Langhorne (Pseudonym: Mark Twain, 1835–1910), 126, 126, 127, 282
Cooper, David L. (1886–1965), 127, 283
Cranfield, Charles (1915–2015), 192, 196, 283

Culver, Robert Duncan (1916–2015), 230, 277

Delaney, Terryl (b. 1943), 215, 278
Dimont, Max Isaac (1912–1992), 77, 144, 283
Donat, Alexander (1905–1983), 14, 15, 30, 227, 278, 283
Dorff, Elliot (b. 1943), 48, 278

Eban, Abba (1915–2002), 90, 283
Eckstein, Jerome (1925–2009), 55, 278
Edersheim, Alfred (1825–1889), 184
Eichrodt, Walther (1890–1978), 187, 195, 283
Ellison, H. L. (1903–1983), 147, 278
Esh, Shaul (1921–1968), 31, 278
Ettinger, Shmuel (1919–1988), 16, 284
Evans, Robert L. (1866–1960), 123, 183, 184, 189, 284

Fackenheim, Emil L. (1916–2003), 13, 76, 92, 93, 94, 278, 284
Feinberg, Charles L. (1909–1995), 134, 135, 214, 284
Frank, Anne (1929–1945), 11
Frankl, Victor E. (1905–1997), 12, 284
Friedeman, S. Simon (1910–2001), 54
Fruchtenbaum, Arnold G. (b. 1943), xiii, xv, xvii, 10, 160, 162, 199, 284
Fuchs, Daniel, 215, 278

Geisler, Norman (1932–2019), 232, 237, 238, 239, 240, 241, 242, 245, 285
Gertel, Elliot B. (b. 1954), 45, 278
Glatstein, Jacob (1896–1971), 58, 285, 288
Godet, Frédéric Louis (1812–1900), 165, 285
Goldberg, Louis (1923–2002), 157, 246, 285
Goldman, Solomon (1893–1953), 140, 285
Gordis, Robert (1908–1992), 84, 278, 285
Granatstein, Melvin (b. 1941), 26, 31, 278
Greenberg, Irving (b. 1933), 34, 35, 39, 43, 50, 56, 81, 82, 95, 173, 219, 279, 286

Hammer, Reuven (Robert Alan) (1933–2019), 73, 279
Hertz, Joseph (1872–1946), 132
Heschel, Abraham Joshua (1907–1972), 28, 32, 37, 70, 71, 72, 228, 279, 283, 286
Hick, John (1922–2012), 231, 286
Hilberg, Raul (1926–2007), 5, 136, 287
Hitler, Adolf (1889–1945), 5, 14, 25, 46, 66, 80, 92, 93, 118, 119, 123, 124, 146, 147, 153, 172, 180, 220, 221, 223, 227, 247, 257, 286, 287, 290
Howe, Leroy T., 18

Jacob, Edmond (1909–1998), 174
Jewett, Paul (1920–1991), 5
Jocz, Jakob (1906–1983), 20, 25, 287

Karff, Samuel (1931–2020), 48, 279
Katz, Steven T. (b. 1944), 22, 287
Kazin, Alfred (1915–1998), 17, 287
Keil, Carl Friedrich (1807–1888), 110
Kidner, Frank Derek (1913–2008), 113, 288
Knox, Israel (1904–1986), 153, 220, 285, 288, 291, 294

Leibniz, Gottfried Wilhelm (1646–1716), 237
Lelyveld, Arthur J. (1913–1996), 71, 288
Levi, Primo (1919–1987), 226
Levin, Nora (1916–1989), 48, 279, 288
Lewis, C. S. (1898–1963), 248
Lincoln, Charles Fred (1887–1976), 103, 279
Luther, Martin (1483–1546), 4, 164, 289

Machen, John Gresham (1881–1937), 186, 289
Magurshak, Dan, 18, 289
Matt, Hershel Jonah (1922–1987), 27
Maybaum, Ignaz (1897–1976), 79, 289
Mayer, Carl (1902–1974), 77, 289
McClain, Alva J. (1888–1968), 169
Muntz, J. Palmer (1897–1992), 135, 290

Neusner, Jacob (1932–2016), 13, 16, 19, 24, 96, 284, 290

Newell, William R. (1868–1956), 162, 290
Nygren, Anders (1890–1978), 161, 290

Oehler, Gustav F. (1812–1872), 186, 290
Olan, Levi A. (1903–1984), 54, 55, 279

Peli, Pinchas H. (1930–1989), 44, 279
Pentecost, J. Dwight (1915–2014), 104, 108, 128, 129, 130, 131, 151, 279, 290
Plotinus, founder of Neoplatonism, ca. 205–270, 240
Polish, Daniel (b. 1942), 86
Prager, Dennis (b. 1948), 84, 87, 290
Price, Walter K. (ca. 1924–2017), 39, 51, 120, 220, 290

Rabinovitch, Nachum Eliezer (1928–2020), 26, 39, 91, 279
Rad, Gerhard von (1901–1971), 111, 196, 292
Robertson, Archibald T. (1863–1934), 165, 290
Robinson, H. Wheeler (1872–1945), 174, 290
Robinson, Jacob (1889–1977), 2
Rowley, Harold H. (1890–1969), 187, 189, 195, 197, 291
Rubenstein, Richard L. (1924–2021), 16, 59, 60, 61, 146, 228, 279, 291

Samuels, Mark E. (1927–2017), 92, 280
Sanders, E. P. (1937–2022), 42, 280

Sauer, Erich (1898–1959), 192, 198, 291
Schachter-Shalomi, Meshullam Zalman (1924–2014), 45, 291
Schlesinger, George (1925–2013), 32, 280
Schulweis, Harold M. (1925–2014), 20, 32, 66, 291
Shapiro, Morris (1920–2010), 73, 87, 280
Sherwin, Byron L. (1946–2015), 70, 280
Silverman, David Wolf (1926–2021), 53, 280
Simon, Ernst (1899–1988), 49
Smith, Norman, 52
Soloveitchik, Joseph (1903–1993), 27, 36, 37, 137, 282, 292, 294
Sontag, Frederick (1924–2009), 68, 86, 280
Spinoza, Baruch de (1632–1677), 240
Stitskin, Leon D. (1911–1978), 101, 280
Stuhlmueller, Carroll (1923–1994), 189, 292

Talmon, Jacob (1916–1980), 41, 172, 280, 292
Telushkin, Joseph (b. 1948), 84, 87, 290

Toussaint, Stanley D. (1928–2017), 166, 292

Unger, Merrill F. (1909–1980), 221

Walvoord, John F. (1910–2002), 106, 107, 140, 167, 214, 282, 285, 292
Waskow, Arthur I. (b. 1933), 66, 292
Weinberg, Werner (1915–1997), 15, 280
Wenham, Gordon J. (b. 1943), 158, 181, 293
Westermann, Claus (1909–2000), 168, 293
Wiesel, Elie (1928–2016), 11, 13, 22, 30, 42, 44, 57, 62, 64, 65, 69, 74, 75, 88, 90, 95, 278, 280, 281, 282, 293
Williamson, Clark (1935–2021), 3
Wolff, Hans Walter (1911–1993), 175, 293
Wouk, Herman (1915–2019), 175, 293
Wyschogrod, Michael (1928–2015), 24, 29, 46, 122, 280, 293

Zimmerli, Walther (1907–1983), 194, 212, 294

Bibliography

Articles

Agus, Jacob B. "God and the Catastrophe." *Conservative Judaism* 1964; 18(4, Summer):13-21.

Bemporad, Jack. "Toward a New Jewish Theology." *American Judaism* 1964-65; 14(2, Winter):9-51.

Berenbaum, Michael. "Teach It to Your Children." *Sh'ma: A Journal of Jewish Ideas* 1981; 11(213, May 1):100-101.

Berkovits, Eliezer. "Crisis and Faith." *Tradition: A Journal of Orthodox Thought* 1974; 14(4, Fall):5-19.

Besdin, Abraham R. "Reflections on the Agony and the Ecstasy." *Tradition: A Journal of Orthodox Thought* 1971; 11(4, Spring):64-70.

Bronznick, Norman M. "A Theological View of the Holocaust." *Journal of Jewish Education* 1973; 42(4, Summer):13-28.

Brown, Michael. "On Crucifying the Jews." *Judaism: A Quarterly Journal of Jewish Life and Thought* 1978; 27(4, Fall):476-488.

Bulka, Reuven P. "Logotherapy As a Response to the Holocaust." *Tradition: A Journal of Orthodox Jewish Thought* 1975; 15(1-2, Spring-Summer):89-96.

Cain, Seymour. "The Question and the Answers After Auschwitz." *Judaism: A Quarterly Journal of Jewish Life and Thought* 1971; 20(3, Summer): 263-278.

Carmy, Shalom. "The Courage to Suffer: Isaiah 53 and Its Context." *Gesher* 1979; 7:102-124.

Chafer, Lewis Sperry. "Editorials: The Jew – A World Issue." *Bibliotheca Sacra: A Theological Quarterly* 1945; 102(406, April-June):129-30.

Charny, Israel W. "Teaching the Violence of the Holocaust." *Journal of Jewish Education* 1968; 38(2, March):15-24.

Culver, Robert Duncan. "The Nature and Origin of Evil." *Bibliotheca Sacra: A Theological Quarterly* 1972; 129(514, April-June):106-115.

Delaney, Terryl. "Why Do People Hate the Jews?" *The Chosen People* 1981; 88(November):10.

Donat, Alexander. "A Letter to My Grandson." *Midstream* 1970; 16(6, June/July):41-45.

Dorff, Elliot N. "God and the Holocaust." *Judaism: A Quarterly Journal of Jewish Life and Thought* 1977; 26(1, Winter):27-34.

Eckardt, Alice L. "Rebel Against God." *Face to Face: An Interreligious Bulletin* [Special Issue: "Building a Moral Society: Aspects of Elie Wiesel's Work"] 1979; 6(Spring):18-20.

Eckstein, Jerome. "The Holocaust and Jewish Theology." *Midstream* 1977; 23(April):36-45.

Ellison, H. L. "The Impact of Auschwitz on Theology Today." *The Hebrew Christian* 1981; 54(Autumn):89.

Esh, Shaul. "The Dignity of the Destroyed: Towards a Definition of the Period of the Holocaust." *Judaism: A Quarterly Journal of Jewish Life and Thought* 1962; 11(2 Spring):99-111.

Fackenheim, Emil L. "Jewish Faith and the Holocaust: A Fragment." *Commentary* 1968; 46(August):32-33.

_____. "The People Israel Lives." *The Christian Century* 1970; 87(May):563-568.

_____; Wiesel, Elie; Schwarzschild, Steven G. "Jewish Values in the Post-Holocaust Future: A Symposium." *Judaism: A Quarterly Journal of Jewish Life and Thought* 1967; 16(3, Summer):266-299.

Friedeman, Simon. "God in Buchenwald." *The Jewish Spectator* 1969; 34(October):20-22.

Friedrich, Otto. "The Kingdom of Auschwitz." *The Atlantic Monthly* 1981; 248(September):30-60.

Fuchs, Daniel. "Satan and the Final Holocaust." *The Chosen People* 1982; (July):12-13.

Fuchs, Daniel. "Satan's Rebellion Against God." *The Chosen People* 1981; 88(November):6.

Gertel, Elliott B. "Because of Our Sins." *Tradition: A Journal of Orthodox Thought* 1976; 15(4, Spring):68-82.

Goldberg, Louis. "Another Holocaust?" *Issues* 1982; 3:1-4.

Gordis, Robert. "The Nature of Man in the Judeo-Christian Tradition." *Judaism: A Quarterly Journal of Jewish Life and Thought* 1953; 2(2, April 1):101-109.

Granatstein, Melvin. "Theodicy and Belief." *Tradition: A Journal of Orthodox Thought* 1973; 13(3, Winter):36-47.

Greenberg, Irving Y. "Orthodox Judaism and the Holocaust." *Gesher* 1979; 7:55-82.

Hammer, Robert (Reuven) A. "The God of Suffering." *Conservative Judaism* 1976; 31(1-2, Fall-Winter):34-41.

Heschel, Abraham Joshua. "The Divine Pathos: The Basic Category of Prophetic Theology." *Judaism: A Quarterly Journal of Jewish Life and Thought* 1953; 2(1, January):61-67.

Howe, Leroy T. "Theology and the Death Camps." *The Christian Century* 1969; 86(February):251-252.

Karff, Samuel E. "Aggadah-The Language of Jewish 'God Talk,'" *Judaism: A Quarterly Journal of Jewish Life and Thought* 1970; 19(2 Spring):158-173.

Laney, J. Carl. "A Fresh Look at the Imprecatory Psalms." *Bibliotheca Sacra: A Theological Quarterly* 1981; 138(January-March):35-45.

Lassley, Jennifer. "A Defective Covenant: Abandonment of Faith among Jewish Survivors of the Holocaust." *International Social Science Review* 2015; 90(2):1-17.

Levin, Nora, "The Human in the Holocaust: A Homily." *Sh'ma: A Journal of Jewish Ideas* 1981; 11(213, May):97-100

Lincoln, Charles Fred. "The Biblical Covenants." *Bibliotheca Sacra: A Theological Quarterly* 1943; 100(398):309-323.

Matt, Herschel J. "Man's Choice and God's Design." *Judaism: A Quarterly Journal of Jewish Life and Thought* 1972; 21(2, Spring):211-221.

Olan, Levi A. "An Organicist View." *Dimensions in American Judaism* 1967; 2(Fall):27.

Peli, Pinchas H. "In Search of Religious Language for the Holocaust." *Conservative Judaism* 1979; 32(Winter):9-16.

Pentecost, J. Dwight. "The Purpose of the Law." *Bibliotheca Sacra: A Theological Quarterly* 1971; 128(July - September):227-233.

Petuchowski, Jakob J.; Martin, Bernard; Gittelsohn, Roland B.; Olan, Levi A. "Symposium: The God We Worship." *Dimensions in American Judaism* 2 1967; 2(Fall):20-27

Rabinovitch, Nachum L. "The Religious Significance of Israel." *Tradition: A Journal of Orthodox Thought* 1974; 14(4, Fall):20-28.

Rubenstein, Richard L. "Auschwitz and Covenant Theology." *The Christian Century* 1969; 86(May 21):716-718.

Ryrie, Charles Caldwell. "The End of the Law." *Bibliotheca Sacra: A Theological* 1967; 124(July - September):239-247.

Samuels, Marc E. "In Praise of Doubt." *Judaism: A Quarterly Journal of Jewish Life and Thought* 1971; 20(4, Fall):456-460.

Sanders, E. P. "R. Akiba's View of Suffering," *The Jewish Quarterly Review* 1973; 63(4, April):332-51.

Schlesinger, George N. "Arguments from Despair." *Tradition: A Journal of Orthodox Thought* 1979; 17(4, Spring):15-26.

Sevener, Harold A. "The Holocaust: Will It Ever Happen Again?" *The Chosen People*, 1982; (July):3-6.

Shapiro, Morris. "For Yom Hashoah." *Conservative Judaism* 1974; 28(3, Spring):57-59.

Sherwin, Byron L. "The Impotence of Explanation and the European Holocaust." *Tradition: A Journal of Orthodox Thought* 1972; 12(3-4, Winter-Spring):99-106.

Silverman, David Wolf, "The Holocaust: A Living Force." *Conservative Judaism* 1976; 31(1-2, Fall – Winter):21-25

Simon, Ernst. "The Jews as God's Witness to the World." *Judaism: A Quarterly Journal of Jewish Life and Thought* 1966; 15(3, Summer):306-318.

Smith, Norman. "Holocaust." *The Jewish Spectator* 1973; 38(5, May).

Sontag, Frederick. "The Holocaust God." *Encounter* 1981; 42(2 Spring):163-167.

Spiegelman, Marvin J. "On the Holocaust and Jewish Education." *Journal of Jewish Education* 1973; 43(1, Fall):36-37.

Stitskin, Leon D. "A Rejoinder." *Tradition: A Journal of Orthodox Thought* 1978; 17(2 Spring):91-95.

Talmon, Jacob L. "European History as the Seedbed of the Holocaust." *Jewish Quarterly* 1973; 21(1-2):3-22. Published online May 2013.

Weinberg, Werner. "On Being a Survivor." *The Christian Century* 1981; 98(12):378-381.

Wiesel, Elie. "Eichmann's Victims and the Unheard Testimony." *Commentary* 1961; 32(6, December 1):510-516.

_____. "Freedom of Conscience—A Jewish Commentary." *Journal of Ecumenical Studies* 1977; 14(Fall):638-649.

_____. "Telling the Tale." *Dimensions in American Judaism* 1968; 2(3, Spring):9-12.

Wyschogrod, Michael. "Auschwitz: Beginning of a New Era? Reflections on the Holocaust." *Tradition: A Journal of Orthodox Thought* 1977; 17(1, Fall):63-78.

———. "Faith and the Holocaust." *Judaism: A Quarterly Journal of Jewish Life and Thought* 1971; 20(3, Summer):286-294.

Books

Abelson, Cyril M. "Bias and the Bible," in: Aryeh Carmell, Cyril Domb, eds., *Challenge: Torah Views on Science and Its Problems*, 2nd rev. ed. New York, NY: Association of Orthodox Jewish Scientists, Feldheim Publishers, 1978.

Angebert, Jean-Michel. *The Occult and the Third Reich: The Mystical Origins of Nazism and the Search for the Holy Grail*. New York, NY: McGraw-Hill Book Company, 1974.

Anonymous. "I Believe," in: Eliezer L. Ehrmann, ed., *Readings in Modern Jewish History: From the American Revolution to the Present*. New York, NY: KTAV Publishing House, 1977, for BJE of Metropolitan Chicago.

Bamberger, Bernard J. *The Search for Jewish Theology*. New York, NY: Behrman House, 1978.

Barnhouse, Donald Grey. *Genesis: A Devotional Exposition*. Grand Rapids, MI: Zondervan Publishing House, 1973.

———. *The Invisible War: the Panorama of the Continuing Conflict between Good & Evil*. Grand Rapids, MI: Zondervan Publishing House, 1977.

Baron, David. *Israel in the Plan of God*. Grand Rapids, MI: Kregel Publications, 1983.

Baron, David. *The History of Israel: Its Spiritual Significance*. London, UK: Morgan & Scott, Ltd., 1925.

Bartini, Kalman. "Shir V'heydo," in: Murray J. Kohn, *The Voice of My Blood Cries Out: The Holocaust as Reflected in Hebrew Poetry*. New York, NY: Shengold Publishers, 1979.

Ben-Sasson, H. H., ed. *A History of the Jewish People*. George Weidenfeld and Nicolson Ltd, trans. Cambridge, MA: Harvard University Press, 1976.

Berdyaev, Nicolas A. *The Meaning of History*. George Reavey, trans. London, UK: Centenary Press, 1936.

Berenbaum, Michael. *The Vision of the Void: Theological Reflections on the Works of Elie Wiesel*. Middleton, CT: Wesleyan University Press, 1979.

Berkouwer, Gerrit Cornelius. *Studies in Dogmatics: The Providence of God*. Lewis Smedes, trans. Grand Rapids, MI: Eerdmans, 1952.

Berkovits, Eliezer. "The Hiding God of History," in: Yisrael Gutman and Livia Rothkirchen, eds., *The Catastrophe of European Jewry: Antecedents, History, Reflections*. Jerusalem, Israel: Yad Vashem, 1976.

_____. *Faith After the Holocaust*. Brooklyn, NY: KTAV Publishing House, 1973.

_____. *God, Man and History: A Jewish Interpretation*. Middle Village, NY: Jonathan David Publishers, 1965.

_____. *With God in Hell: Judaism in the Ghettos and Deathcamps*. New York, NY: Sanhedrin Press, 1979.

Besdin, Abraham R. *Reflections of the Rav: Lessons in Jewish Thought – Volume One Adapted from Lectures of Rabbi Joseph B. Soloveitchik*. Rev. ed. Hoboken, NJ: KTAV Publishing House, 1993.

Bonhoeffer, Dietrich. *Letters and Papers from Prison*. Reginald H. Fuller, trans. Eberhard Bethge, ed. New York: NY: Macmillan Company, 1971. Published originally as *Prisoner for God*.

Borowitz, Eugene B. *How Can a Jew Speak of Faith Today?*. Philadelphia, PA: Westminster Press, 1969.

Bradbury, John W., ed. *The Sure Word of Prophecy*. 2nd ed. New York, NY: Fleming H. Revell Co., 1944.

Buber, Martin. *Eclipse of God: Studies in the Relation between Religion and Philosophy*. 1st ed. New York, NY: Harper & Row, 1957.

Bush, George. *Notes on Genesis*. 2 vols. Minneapolis, MN: Klock & Klock Christian Publishers (Limited Classical Reprint Library), 1981.

Campbell, Donald K., ed. *Walvoord: A Tribute*. Chicago, IL: Moody Press, 1982.

Cargas, Harry James. *In Conversation with Elie Wiesel*. New York, NY: Paulist Press, 1976.

Carmell, Aryeh; Domb, Cyril; eds. *Challenge: Torah Views on Science and Its Problems*. 2nd rev. ed. New York, NY: Association of Orthodox Jewish Scientists, Feldheim Publishers, 1978.

Cassuto, Umberto. *A Commentary on the Book of Genesis, Part II from Noah to Abraham*. 2 vols. Israel Abrahams, trans. Jerusalem, Israel: Magnes Press, 1961.

Chafer, Lewis Sperry. *Systematic Theology, Vol. 4, Ecclesiology, Eschatology*. Dallas, TX: Dallas Seminary Press, 1975.

_____. *Systematic Theology, Vol. 5: Christology*. 8 Vols. Dallas, TX: Dallas Seminary Press, 1975.

Clemens, Samuel Langhorne (Pseudonym: Mark Twain). "Concerning the Jews," in: Janet Smith, ed., *Mark Twain on the Damned Human Race, American Century Series*. New York, NY: Hill and Wang, 1962.

Cohen, Abraham. *Everyman's Talmud: The Major Teachings of the Rabbinic Sages*. New York, NY: Schocken Books, 1975.

Conway, John S. *The Nazi Persecution of the Churches, 1933-1945*. New York, NY: Basic Books, 1968.

Cooper, David L. *What Men Must Believe or God's Gracious Provision for Man*. Los Angeles, CA: Biblical Research Society, 1963.

Cranfield, Charles E. B. "Love," in: Alan Richardson, ed., *A Theological Word Book of the Bible*. New York, NY: Macmillan Company, 1951.

_____. *A Critical and Exegetical Commentary on the Epistle to the Romans, Vol. 1, Romans 1–8*. 2 vols. New York, NY: T&T Clark, 1975.

Croner, Helga; Klenicki, Leon; eds. *Issues in the Jewish-Christian Dialogue: Jewish Perspectives on Covenant, Mission and Witness*. New York, NY: Paulist Press, 1979.

Cutler, Donald, ed. *The Religious Situation: 1968*. Boston, MA: Beacon Press, 1968.

Dawidowicz, Lucy S., ed. *A Holocaust Reader*. West Orange, NJ: Behrman House, 1976 (Library of Jewish Studies).

_____. *The War Against the Jews: 1933–1945*. New York, NY: Bantam Books, 1975.

Diller, Jerry V., ed. *Ancient Roots and Modern Meanings: A Contemporary Reader in Jewish Identity*. New York, NY: Bloch Publishing Co, 1978.

Dimont, Max I. *Jews, God and History*. New York, NY: The New American Library, 1962.

Dobschiner, Joanna-Ruth. *Selected to Live*. Old Tappan, NJ: Fleming H Revell Co, 1973.

Donat, Alexander. *The Holocaust Kingdom: A Memoir*. New York, NY: Holocaust Library, 1965.

Eban, Abba. *My People: The Story of the Jews*. New York, NY: Behrman House, 1968.

Edersheim, Alfred. *The History of the Jewish Nation: After the Destruction of Jerusalem Under Titus*, rev. by Henry A. White. Grand Rapids, MI: Baker Book House, 1979 (reprint of the 1895 edition).

Edwards, Paul, ed. *Encyclopedia of Philosophy*. 8 Vols. New York. NY: Macmillan Company, 1972.

Ehrmann, Eliezer L., ed. *Readings in Modern Jewish History: From the American Revolution to the Present*. New York, NY: KTAV Publishing House, 1977.

Eichrodt, Walther. *Theology of the Old Testament*, 2 vols. John A. Baker, trans. Philadelphia, PA: Westminster Press, 1961–1967.

Eisenberg, Azriel L., ed. *Witness to the Holocaust*. New York, NY: Pilgrim Press, 1981.

Ericksen, Robert P.; Heschel, Susannah; eds. *Betrayal: German Churches and the Holocaust*. Minneapolis, MN: Augsburg Fortress Press, 1999.

Ettinger, Shmuel. "The Modern Period," in: H. H. Ben-Sasson, ed., *A History of the Jewish People*. Cambridge, MA: Harvard University Press, 1976.

Evans, Robert L. *The Jew in the Plan of God*. Neptune, NY: Loizeaux Brothers, 1950.

Fackenheim, Emil L. "The Human Condition After Auschwitz," in: Jacob Neusner, ed., *Understanding Jewish Theology: Classical Issues and Modern Perspectives*. New York, NY: KTAV Publishing House, 1973.

_____. *Quest for Past and Future: Essays in Jewish Theology*. Boston, MA: Beacon Press, 1970.

_____. *The Jewish Return into History: Reflections in the Age of Auschwitz and a New Jerusalem*. New York, NY: Schocken Books, 1978.

Federbush, Shimon, ed. *Torah u-Melukhah*. Jerusalem, Israel: Mossad Harav Kook, 1961.

Feinberg, Charles L. *Israel at the Center of History & Revelation*. Portland, OR: Multnomah Press, 1980.

Fleischner, Eva, ed. *Auschwitz: Beginning of a New Era? Reflections on the Holocaust: Papers Given at the International Symposium on the Holocaust held at the Cathedral of Saint John the Divine New York City June 3 to 6 1974*. New York, NY: KTAV Publishing House, 1977.

Frank, Anne. *The Diary of a Young Girl: The Revised Critical Edition*. Arnold J. Pomerans and B. M. Mooyaart-Doubleday, trans.; David Barnouw and Gerrold van der Stroom, eds. New York, NY: Doubleday, 2003.

Frankl, Victor E. *Man's Search for Meaning: An Introduction to Logotherapy*. Ilse Lasch, trans. New York, NY: Pocket Books, 1984.

_____. *Man's Search for Ultimate Meaning*. New York, NY: Basic Books, 2000.

Fruchtenbaum, Arnold G. *Ariel Bible Commentary: The Book of Isaiah*. San Antonio, TX: Ariel Ministries, 2022.

_____. *Ariel Bible Commentary: The Book of Romans*. San Antonio, TX: Ariel Ministries, 2022.

_____. *Jesus was a Jew*, rev. ed. San Antonio, TX: Ariel Ministries, 2021.

_____. *The Footsteps of the Messiah: A Study of the Sequence of Prophetic Events*, 4th ed. San Antonio, TX: Ariel Ministries, 2021.

_____. *The Remnant of Israel: The Theology, History, and Philosophy of the Messianic Jewish Community*, 4th ed. San Antonio, TX: Ariel Ministries, 2021.

_____. *The Word of God: Its Nature and Content*, 3rd ed. San Antonio, TX: Ariel Ministries, 2019.

Frydland, Rachmiel. *When Being Jewish Was a Crime*. Nashville, TN: Thomas Nelson, 1978.

Gartenhaus, Jacob. *Famous Hebrew Christians*. Grand Rapids, MI: Baker Book House, 1976.

Geehan, E. R., ed. *Jerusalem and Athens: Critical Discussions on the Philosophy and Apologetics of Cornelius Van Til*. Phillipsburg, NJ: Presbyterian and Reformed Publishing Company, 1971.

Geisler, Norman L. "God, Evil, and Dispensations," in: Donald K. Campbell, ed., *Walvoord: A Tribute*. Chicago, IL: Moody Press, 1982.

_____. "Process Theology," in: Stanley N. Gundry and Alan F. Johnson, eds., *Tensions in Contemporary Theology*. Chicago, IL: Moody Press, 1980.

_____. *The Roots of Evil*. Grand Rapids, MI: Zondervan Publishing House, 1978.

Glatstein, Jacob; Israel Knox; Samuel Margoshes; eds. *Anthology of Holocaust Literature*. New York, NY: Atheneum, 1978.

Glatzer, Nahum N., ed. *Modern Jewish Thoughts: A Source Reader*. New York, NY: Schocken Books, 1977.

Godet, Frédéric Louis. *Commentary on St. Paul's Epistle to the Romans*. Alexander Cusin, trans. Grand Rapids, MI: Kregel Publications, 1977.

Goldberg, Louis. "For More Objectivity in Jewish–Christian Relations," in: Arthur W. Kac, ed., *The Messiahship of Jesus: What Jews and Jewish Christians Say*. Chicago, IL: Moody Press, 1980.

_____. *Leviticus: A Study Guide Commentary*. Grand Rapids, MI: Zondervan Publishing House, 1980.

_____. *Our Jewish Friends*. Neptune, NJ: Loizeaux Brothers, 1983.

Goldman, Solomon. *Soncino Books of the Bible: Samuel*. 1st ed. London, UK: Soncino Press, 1949.

Gordis, Robert. *A Faith for Moderns*. New York, NY: Bloch Publishing Co., 1971.

Graeber, Isacque; Britt, Steuart Henderson; eds. *Jews in a Gentile World: The Problem of Anti-Semitism*. New York, NY: Macmillan Company, 1942.

Grant, Myrna. *The Journey: The Story of Rose Warmer's Triumphant Discovery*. Wheaton, IL: Tyndale House Publishers, 1978.

Greenberg, Irving Y. "Cloud of Smoke, Pillar of Fire: Judaism, Christianity, and Modernity after the Holocaust," in: Eva Fleischner, ed., *Auschwitz: Beginning of a New Era? Reflections on the Holocaust*. New York, NY: KTAV Publishing House, 1977.

Griffin, David Ray. *God, Power, and Evil: A Process Theodicy*. Philadelphia, PA. Westminster Press, 1976.

Gundry, Stanley N.; Johnson, Alan F.; eds. *Tensions in Contemporary Theology*. Chicago, IL. Moody Press, 1980.

Gutman, Yisrael; Rothkirchen, Livia; eds. *The Catastrophe of European Jewry: Antecedents, History, Reflections*. Jerusalem, Israel: Yad Vashem, 1976.

Hausner, Gideon. *Justice in Jerusalem*. New York, NY: Holocaust Library, 1966.

Hefley, James C. *The New Jews*. Wheaton, IL: Tyndale House Publishers, 1974.

Heller, Celia S. *On the Edge of Destruction: Jews of Poland Between the Two World Wars*. New York, NY: Schocken Books, 1977.

Helmreich, Ernst Christian. *The German Churches under Hitler: Background, Struggle, and Epilogue*. Detroit, MI: Wayne State University Press, 1979.

Hertz, Joseph H., ed. *The Pentateuch and Haftorahs: Hebrew Text, English Translation and Commentary*, 2nd ed. London, UK: Soncino Press, 1981.

Heschel, Abraham Joshua. "Reflections on Being a Jew," in: Nahum N. Glatzer, ed., *Modern Jewish Thoughts: A Source Reader*. New York, NY: Schocken Books, 1977.

_____. *God In Search of Man: A Philosophy of Religion*. New York, NY: Farrar, Strauss, & Giroux, 1955.

_____. *Man Is Not Alone: A Philosophy of Religion*. New York, NY: Farrar, Strauss, & Giroux, 1979.

_____. *The Earth Is the Lord's: The Inner World of the Jew in Eastern Europe*. Ilya Schor, illus. Woodstock, VT: Jewish Lights Publishing, 1995.

_____. *The Insecurity of Freedom*. New York, NY: Schocken Books, 1966.

———. *The Prophets*, 2 vols. New York, NY: Harper & Row, 1975.

Hick, John. "Evil, The Problem of," in: P. Edwards, ed., *Encyclopedia of Philosophy, Volume 3, Epictetus – Hilbert, David*. New York, NY: Macmillan Company, 1972.

———. *Evil and the God of Love*. New York, NY: Palgrave Macmillan, 2010, 2nd ed.

Hilberg, Raul. *The Destruction of the European Jews, Vol. 1*. 3 vols. New York, NY: Harper & Row, 1979.

Hirschmann, Maria Anne. *Hansi: The Girl Who Left the Swastika*. Wheaton, IL: Tyndale House Publishers, 1973.

Hitler, Adolf. *Mein Kampf*. Ralph Manheim, trans. London, UK: Hutchinson, 1969.

Jacob, Edmond. *Theology of the Old Testament*. Arthur W. Heathcote; Philip J. Allcock; trans. New York, NY: Harper & Row Publishers, 1958.

Jenni, E. "The Remnant of Israel," in: Cecil Roth and Geoffrey Wigoder, eds., *Encyclopedia Judaica (16 Vols.), Volume 14*. 1st ed. Jerusalem: Israel, Keter Publishing House, 1971.

———. Jenni, E. "The Remnant of Israel," in: Fred Skolnik and Michael Berenbaum, eds. *Encyclopedia Judaica (22 Vols.), Vol. 17, Ra–Sam*. 2nd ed. Farmington Hills, MI: Thomson Gale & Jerusalem, Israel: Keter Publishing House, 2006.

Jewett, Paul K. "X. Concerning Christ, Christians, and Jews," in: E. R. Geehan, ed., *Jerusalem and Athens: Critical Discussions on the Philosophy and Apologetics of Cornelius Van Til*. Phillipsburg, NJ: Presbyterian and Reformed Publishing Company, 1971.

Jocz, Jakob. *The Jewish People and Jesus Christ After Auschwitz: A Study in the Controversy Between Church and Synagogue*. Grand Rapids, MI: Baker Book House, 1981.

Josephus, Flavius. *The Works of Flavius Josephus, Vol I, The Wars of the Jews*. 4 Vols. William Whiston, trans. Grand Rapids, MI: Baker Book House, 1982.

Kac, Arthur W., ed. *The Messiahship of Jesus: What Jews and Jewish Christians Say*. Chicago, IL: Moody Press, 1980.

———. *The Rebirth of the State of Israel: Is It of God or of Men?*. Chicago, IL: Moody Press, 1958.

———. *The Spiritual Dilemma of the Jewish People: Its Cause and Cure*. Chicago, IL: Moody Press, 1963.

Kaiser, Walter C. Jr. "The Blessing of David: The Charter for Humanity," in: John H. Skilton, ed., *The Law and the Prophets: Old Testament Studies*

Prepared in Honor of Oswald Thompson Allis. Nutley, NJ: Presbyterian and Reformed Publishing Company, 1974.

Katz, Steven T. "Jewish Faith After the Holocaust: Four Approaches," in: Geoffrey Wigoder, Louis I. Rabinowitz, and Jonathan Omer-Man, eds., *Encyclopedia Judaica Yearbook 1975–76: Events of 1974–75*. Jerusalem, Israel: Keter Publishing House, Encyclopaedia Judaica, 1976.

Kazin, Alfred. "The Heart of the World," in: Eva Fleischner, ed., *Auschwitz: Beginning of a New Era? Reflections on the Holocaust*. New York, NY: KTAV Publishing House, 1977.

Kidner, Frank Derek. *Genesis: An Introduction and Commentary, The Tyndale Old Testament Commentaries*. Downers Grove, IL: InterVarsity Press, 1967.

Kiel, Carl Friedrich; Delitzsch, Franz. *Biblical Commentary on the Books of Samuel*. James Martin, trans. Clark's Foreign Theological Library, 4th ser., Vol. IX. Edinburgh, Scotland: T&T Clark, 1886.

_____. *Commentary on the Old Testament in Ten Volumes, Volume I: The Pentateuch, Three Volumes in One*. James Martin, trans. Grand Rapids, MI: Eerdmans, 1981.

_____. "The Fifth Book of Moses (Deuteronomy)," in: Carl Friedrich Keil and Franz Delitzsch, *Commentary on the Old Testament in Ten Volumes Volume I: The Pentateuch, Three Volumes in One*. James Martin, trans. Grand Rapids, MI: Eerdmans, 1973.

_____. "The First Book of Moses (Genesis)," in: Carl Friedrich Keil and Franz Delitzsch, *Commentary on the Old Testament in Ten Volumes Volume I: The Pentateuch, Three Volumes in One*. James Martin, trans. Grand Rapids, MI: Eerdmans, 1981>

_____. "The Fourth Book of Moses (Numbers)," in: Carl Friedrich Keil and Franz Delitzsch, *Commentary on the Old Testament in Ten Volumes Volume I: The Pentateuch, Three Volumes in One*. James Martin, trans. Grand Rapids, MI: Eerdmans, 1981.

_____. "The Second Book of Moses (Exodus)," in: *Commentary on the Old Testament in Ten Volumes Volume I: The Pentateuch, Three Volumes in One*. James Martin, trans. Grand Rapids, MI: Eerdmans, 1981.

Knox, Israel. "Introduction" in: Jacob Glatstein, Israel Knox, Samuel Margoshes, eds. *Anthology of Holocaust Literature*. New York, NY: Atheneum, 1978.

Kohn, Murray J. *The Voice of My Blood Cries Out: The Holocaust as Reflected in Hebrew Poetry*. New York, NY: Shengold Publishers, 1979.

Kushner, Harold S. *When Bad Things Happen to Good People*. New York, NY: Schocken Books, 1981.

Lelyveld, Arthur. *Atheism Is Dead: A Jewish Response to Radical Theology*. Cleveland, OH: World Publishing Co, 1958.

Levi, Primo. *Survival in Auschwitz: The Nazi Assault on Humanity*. Stuart Woolf, trans. New York, NY: Collier Books, 1961. Originally appeared in English under the title *If This Is a Man*.

Levitt, Zola. *Meshumed!*. Chicago, IL: Moody Press, 1979.

Lewis, C.S. *The Problem of Pain*. New York, NY: HarperCollins, 2001.

Littell, Franklin H.; Locke, Hubert G.; eds. *The German Church Struggle and the Holocaust*. Detroit, MI: Wayne State University Press, 1974.

_____, ed. *Religious Liberty in the Crossfire of Creeds*. Philadelphia, PA: Ecumenical Press, 1978.

Luther, Martin. *A Commentary on Saint Paul's Epistle to the Galatians*. Philadelphia, PA: John Highlands, 1891.

_____. *Luther's Works, Vol. 54, Table Talk*. Theodore G. Tappert, trans. & ed.; Helmut T Lehmann, general ed. Philadelphia, PA: Fortress Press, 1967.

Machen, John Gresham. *The Christian View of Man*. London, England: Banner of Truth Trust, 1937.

Magurshak, Dan. "The 'Incomprehensibility' of the Holocaust: Tightening Up Some Loose Usage," in: Michael R. Marrus, ed., *The Nazi Holocaust – Part 1: Perspectives on the Holocaust*. Westport, CT: Meckler, 1989.

Markell, Jan. *Angels in the Camp: A Remarkable Story of Peace in the Midst of the Holocaust*. Wheaton, IL: Tyndale House Publishers, 1979.

Marrus, Michael R., ed. *The Nazi Holocaust – Part 1: Perspectives on the Holocaust*. Westport, CT: Meckler, 1989.

Martin, Linette. *Hans Rookmaaker: A Biography*. Downers Grove, IL: InterVarsity Press, 1979.

Matczak, Sebastian A., ed. *God In Contemporary Thought: A Philosophical Perspective*. New York, NY: Learned Publications, 1977.

Maybaum, Ignaz. *The Face of God after Auschwitz*. Amsterdam, Netherlands: Polak & Van Gennep Ltd , 1965.

Mayer, Carl. "Religious and Political Aspects of Anti-Semitism," in: Isacque Graeber and Steuart Henderson Britt, eds., *Jews in a Gentile World: The Problem of Anti-Semitism*. New York, NY: Macmillan Company, 1942.

McClain, Alva J. *Law and Grace*. Chicago, IL: Moody Press, 1954.

_____. *The Greatness of the Kingdom*. Chicago, IL: Moody Press, 1968.

McQuaid, Elwood. *Zvi*. West Collingswood, IL: The Spearhead Press, 1978.

Miller, Basil. *Martin Niemoeller: Hero of the Concentration Camp.* Grand Rapids, MI: Zondervan Publishing House, 1942.

Millgram, Abraham Ezra, ed. *Great Jewish Ideas.* B'nai B'rith Great Books Series, Vol. 5. Washington, D.C.: B'nai B'rith Department of Adult Jewish Education, 1964.

Mitchell, Joseph R.; Mitchell, Helen Buss. *The Holocaust: Readings & Interpretations.* Guilfoord, CT: McGraw-Hill/Dushkin, 2001.

Montefiore, C. G.; Loewe, H. M. J.; eds. *A Rabbinic Anthology.* Cambridge, UK: Cambridge University Press, 1974, 2012.

Muntz, J. Palmer. "The Jew in History and Destiny," in: John W. Bradbury, ed. *The Sure Word of Prophecy.* 2nd ed. New York, NY: Fleming H. Revell Co., 1944.

Neusner, Jacob. *The Way of Torah: An Introduction to Judaism,* 2nd ed. Encino, CA: Dickenson Publishing, 1974.

_____. *Understanding Jewish Theology: Classical Issues and Modern Perspectives.* New York, NY: KTAV Publishing House, 1973.

Newell, William R. *Romans: Verse by Verse.* Chicago, IL: Moody Press, 1938.

Nygren, Anders. *Commentary of Romans.* Carl C. Rasmussen, trans. Philadelphia, PA: Fortress Press, 1949.

Oehler, Gustav Friedrich. *Theology of the Old Testament,* rev. by George E. Day, 2nd ed. New York, NY: Funk & Wagnalls, 1884.

Overduin, Jack (Jacobus). *Faith and Victory in Dachau.* Harry der Nederlanden, trans. Ontario, Canada: Paideia Press, 1978. First published in Dutch as *Hel en Hemel van Dachau.*

Pentecost, J. Dwight, *Things to Come: A Study in Biblical Eschatology.* Grand Rapids, MI: Dunham Publishing Co, 1958.

Poliakov, Léon. *Harvest of Hate: The Nazi Program for the Destruction of the Jews of Europe.* Rev. ed. New York, NY: Holocaust Library, 1979.

Polish, Daniel F. "Witnessing God after Auschwitz," in: Helga Croner and Leon Klenicki, eds. *Issues in the Jewish-Christian Dialogue: Jewish Perspectives on Covenant, Mission and Witness.* New York, NY: Paulist Press, 1979.

Poljak, Abram. *Hitler: Warlord and Spiritualist,* 7th ed. Marshfield, MO: First Fruits of Zion, 2019.

Prager, Dennis; Telushkin, Joseph. *Nine Questions People Ask About Judaism.* New York, NY: Simon & Schuster, 1986.

Price, Walter K. *Next Year in Jerusalem [Le-shanah ha-baah bi-Yerushalayim].* Chicago, IL: Moody Press, 1975.

Richardson, Alan, ed. *A Theological Word Book of the Bible*. New York, NY: Macmillan Company, 1951.

Robertson, Archibald Thomas. *Word Pictures in the New Testament: Volume 4 – The Epistles of Paul*. Nashville, TN: Broadman Press, 1931.

Robinson, H. Wheeler. *Corporate Personality in Ancient Israel*, rev. ed. Philadelphia, PA: Fortress Press, 1980.

Robinson, Jacob. "Holocaust," in: Cecil Roth and Geoffrey Wigoder, eds., *Encyclopedia Judaica. Vol 8: He-Ir*, 1st ed. Jerusalem, Israel: Keter Publishing House, 1971.

Robinson, Jacob; Feldman, Nira; Yahill, Lenii; *Israel Pocket Library: Holocaust*. Jerusalem, Israel: Keter Publishing House, 1974.

Rosenbaum, Irving J. *The Holocaust and Halakhah*. Jerusalem, Israel: KTAV Publishing House, 1976.

Rosenfeld, Alvin H. *A Double Dying: Reflections on Holocaust Literature*. Bloomington, IN: Indiana University Press, 1980.

Roth, Cecil; Wigoder, Geoffrey; eds. *Encyclopedia Judaica*. 16 Vols. 1st ed. Jerusalem, Israel: Keter Publishing House, 1971.

Rowley, Harold Henry. *The Biblical Doctrine of Election*. London, England: Lutterworth Press, 1950.

_____. *The Faith of Israel: Aspects of Old Testament Thought*. London, England: SCM Press, 1956.

Rubenstein, Richard L. "Symposium of Jewish Belief," in: Jerry V. Diller, ed., *Ancient Roots and Modern Meanings: A Contemporary Reader in Jewish Identity*. New York, NY: Bloch Publishing Co, 1978.

Rubenstein, Richard L. *After Auschwitz: Radical Theology and Contemporary Judaism*. Indianapolis, IN: Bobbs-Merrill, 1966.

Ryrie, Charles Caldwell. *The Basis of the Premillennial Faith*. 1st ed. Neptune, NJ: Loizeaux Brothers, 1953.

Sauer, Erich. *From Eternity to Eternity: An Outline of the Divine Purposes*. G.H. Lang, trans. Grand Rapids, MI: Eerdmans, 1957.

Sauer, Erich. *The Dawn of World Redemption: A Survey of Historical Revelation in the Old Testament*. G. H. Lang, trans., Grand Rapids, MI: Eerdmans, 1951.

Schachter-Shalomi, Meshullam [Zalman M Schachter]. "Homeland and Holocaust: Issues in the Jewish Religious Situation-Commentary," in: Donald R. Cutler, ed., *The Religious Situation: 1968*. Boston, MA: Beacon Press, 1968.

Schulweis, Harold M. "Suffering and Evil," in: Abraham E. Millgram, ed., *Great Jewish Ideas*. B'nai B'rith Great Books Series, Vol. 5. Washington, D.C.: B'nai B'rith Department of Adult Jewish Education, 1964.

Simon, Ulrich. *A Theology of Auschwitz: The Christian Faith and the Problem of Evil*. London, UK: Victor Gollancz, Ltd., 1967.

Skilton, John H, ed. *The Law and the Prophets: Old Testament Studies Prepared in Honor of Oswald Thompson Allis*. Nutley, NJ: Presbyterian and Reformed Publishing Company, 1974.

Skolnik, Fred; Berenbaum, Michael, eds. *Encyclopedia Judaica*. 22 Vols. 2nd ed. Farmington Hills, MI: Thomson Gale & Jerusalem, Israel: Keter Publishing House, 2006.

Smith, Janet, ed. *Mark Twain on the Damned Human Race, American Century Series*. New York, NY: Hill and Wang, 1962.

Soloveitchik, Joseph B. "Chapter III: The World Is Not Forsaken," in; Abraham R. Besdin, ed., *Reflections of the Rav: Lessons in Jewish Thought – Volume One Adapted from Lectures of Rabbi Joseph B. Soloveitchik*. Hoboken, NJ: KTAV Publishing House, 1993.

_____. "Kol Dodi Dofek," in: Shimon Federbush, ed., *Torah u-Melukhah*. Jerusalem, Israel: Mossad Harav Kook, 1961.

Stuhlmueller, Carroll. "God in the Witness of Israel's Election," in: Sebastian A. Matczak, ed., *God In Contemporary Thought: A Philosophical Perspective*. New York, NY: Learned Publications, 1977.

Talmon, Jacob L. "European History as the Seedbed of the Holocaust," in: *Holocaust and Rebirth – Sho'ah veha-tekumah: A Symposium*. Efraim Zuroff, trans. Jerusalem, Israel: Yad Vashem, 1974.

Tana, Shlomo. "Reyach Ha'esh," in: Murray J. Kohn, *The Voice of My Blood Cries Out: The Holocaust as Reflected in Hebrew Poetry*. New York, NY: Shengold Publishers, 1979.

ten Boom, Corrie. *A Prisoner and Yet…*. Fort Washington, PA: Christian Literature Crusade, 1954.

ten Boom, Corrie. *The Hiding Place: The Triumphant True Story of Corrie ten Boom*. New York, NY: Bantam Books, 1974.

Toussaint, Stanley D. *Behold the King: A Study of Matthew*. 1st ed. Portland, OR: Multnomah Press, 1980.

Unger, Merrill F. *Biblical Demonology: A Study of the Spiritual Forces Behind the Present World Unrest*. Wheaton, IL: Van Kampen Press, 1952.

von Rad, Gerhard. *Genesis: A Commentary*, rev ed.; John H. Marks, trans. Philadelphia, PA: Westminster Press, 1972.

_____. *Old Testament Theology: The Theology of Israel's Historical Traditions*. 2 vols., D. M. G. Stalker, trans. New York, NY: Harper & Row, 1962, 1965.

Walvoord, John F. *Israel in Prophecy*. Grand Rapids, MI: Zondervan Publishing House, 1962.

_____. *Matthew: Thy Kingdom Come*. Chicago, IL: Moody Press, 1974.

_____. *The Millennial Kingdom*. Grand Rapids, MI: Dunham Publishing Co, 1959.

Waskow, Arthur I. *Godwrestling*. New York, NY: Schocken Books, 1978.

Weinberger, Alexander Moishe; Leeson, Muriel. *I Escaped the Holocaust*. Beaverlodge, Alberta, Canada: Horizon House, 1978.

Wenham, Gordon J. *The Book of Leviticus*. The New International Commentary on the Old Testament. Vol. 3. Grand Rapids, MI: Wm. B. Eerdmans Publishing Co., 1979.

Wenham, John William. *The Enigma of Evil: Can We Believe in the Goodness of God?*. Grand Rapids, MI: Zondervan Publishing House, 1985. First published in 1974 by Inter-Varsity Press, Downers Grove, IL, under the title *The Goodness of God*.

Westermann, Claus. *Blessing: In the Bible and the Life of the Church*. Keith Crim, trans. Philadelphia, PA: Fortress Press, 1978. Original title *Der Segen in der Bibel und im Handeln der Kirche*.

Wiesel, Elie. "Eichmann's Victims and the Unheard Testimony," in: Joseph R. Mitchell and Helen Buss Mitchell, *The Holocaust: Readings & Interpretations*. Guilforod, CT: McGraw-Hill/Dushkin, 2001.

_____. "Freedom of Conscience—A Jewish Commentary," in: Franklin H. Littell, ed., *Religious Liberty in the Crossfire of Creeds*. Philadelphia, PA: Ecumenical Press, 1978.

_____. "Talking and Writing and Keeping Silent," in: Franklin H. Littell and Hubert G. Locke, eds., *The German Church Struggle and the Holocaust*. Detroit, MI: Wayne State University Press, 1974.

_____. *A Beggar in Jerusalem*. Lily Edelman and the author, trans. New York, NY: Schocken Books, 1970

_____. *Legends of Our Time*. New York, NY: Schocken Books, 1982.

_____. *Night*. Stella Rodway, trans. New York, NY: Avon Books, 1960

_____. *One Generation After*. Lily Edelman and Elie Wiesel, trans. New York: NY, Random House, 1965.

_____. *Report to the President – President's Commission on the Holocaust*. Washington, D.C., US Govt. Print. Office, 1979.

_____. *The Town Beyond the Wall*. Stephen Becker, trans. New York, NY: Schocken Books, 1982.

Wigoder, Geoffrey; Rabinowitz, Louis I.; Omer-Man, Jonathan, eds. *Encyclopedia Judaica Yearbook 1975–76: Events of 1974–75*. Jerusalem, Israel: Keter Publishing House, Encyclopaedia Judaica, 1976.

Williamson, Clark M. *Has God Rejected His People? Anti-Judaism in the Christian Church*. Eugene, OR: Wipf & Stock, 2017.

Wolff, Hans Walter. *Anthropology of the Old Testament*. Margaret Kohl, trans. Philadelphia, PA: Fortress Press, 1974.

Wouk, Herman. *This is My God: The Jewish Way of Life*, rev. ed. New York, NY: Pocket Books, 1974.

Wyschogrod, Michael; Soulen, R. Kendall (ed.). *Abraham's Promise – Judaism and Jewish Christian Relations*. Grand Rapids, MI: Willliam B. Eerdmans, 2004.

Yad Vashem, Holocaust and Rebirth - Sho'ah veha-tekumah: A Symposium. Efraim Zuroff, trans. Jerusalem, Israel: Yad Vashem, 1974.

Zimmels, Hirsch Jakob. *The Echo of the Nazi Holocaust in Rabbinic Literature*. New York, NY: KTAV Publishing House, 1977.

Zimmerli, Walther. *Israel und die Christen: Hören und Fragen*. Neukirchen, Germany: Neukirchener Verlag des Erziehungsvereins, 1964.

_____. *Old Testament Theology in Outline*. David E. Green, trans. Atlanta, GA: John Knox Press, 1978.

Other items

Aquinas, Thomas. "Question 75, Article 1." *The Summa Theologiæ*. Vol. II–I. 2nd rev. ed. Literally translated by Fathers of the English Dominican Province, 1920. Available online: https://www.newadvent.org/summa/2075.htm#article1. Accessed 18 Dec 2023.

Ki-moon, Ban. "'One and a Half Million Jewish Children Perished in the Holocaust,' Message for the International Day of Commemoration in Memory of the Victims of the Holocaust, 27 January 2012." United Nations: Information Service, Press release UNIS/SGSM/316, 25 Jan 2012. Available online: https://unis.unvienna.org/unis/en/pressrels/2012/unissgsm316.html. Accessed 18 Dec 2023.

Soloveitchik, Joseph B. "Kol Dodi Dofek," in: Shimon Federbush, ed., *Torah u-Melukhah*. Jerusalem, Israel: Mossad Harav Kook, 1961. Translated by David Z. Gordon and available at https://www.sefaria.org/Kol_Dodi_Dofek?tab=contents. Accessed 18 Dec 2023.

Scripture Index

Genesis

Genesis 1:1 236
Genesis 1:26-28 171
Genesis 1:31 239
Genesis 2:18-25 171
Genesis 3:15 215
Genesis 4:7 85
Genesis 4:23 85
Genesis 6:3 250
Genesis 9:8-17 188
Genesis 12:1 186
Genesis 12:1-3 . 106, 108, 109, 125,
.... 148, 185, 189
Genesis 12:3 109, 111, 112, 114, 115,
    116, 118, 120, 122, 123, 124,
    125, 127, 147, 151, 177, 253,
.... 258
Genesis 12:7 128
Genesis 12:10-20 121
Genesis 13:14-17 ...... 106, 109, 125
Genesis 13:15 128
Genesis 13:15-16 109
Genesis 15:1-6 109
Genesis 15:1-21 125
Genesis 15:4-7 106
Genesis 15:7-17 109
Genesis 15:7-21 107
Genesis 15:8-21 108
Genesis 15:13-14 132
Genesis 15:13-16 ...... 133, 137, 143
Genesis 15:14 132
Genesis 15:16 132
Genesis 15:18-21 109

Genesis 17:1 234
Genesis 17:1-8 106
Genesis 17:1-21 125
Genesis 17:5-7 185
Genesis 17:7 .... 107, 157
Genesis 17:7-8 128
Genesis 17:7-19 126
Genesis 17:9-14 107
Genesis 17:19 107
Genesis 18 .... 73, 173
Genesis 18:19 194
Genesis 18:25 253
Genesis 20:1-18 121
Genesis 21:33 233
Genesis 22:15-18 125
Genesis 22:17-18 156
Genesis 22:18 .... 185, 189
Genesis 26:2-5 .... 107, 125
Genesis 26:4 189
Genesis 26:5 186
Genesis 27:1-46 113
Genesis 27:18-33 125
Genesis 27:27-29 125
Genesis 27:29 .... 114, 115
Genesis 28:3-15 125
Genesis 28:12-15 107
Genesis 28:14 .... 185, 189
Genesis 30:25-30 115
Genesis 34 165
Genesis 39:1-5 115
Genesis 43:32 133
Genesis 46:31-34 133
Genesis 49:5-7 165
Genesis 50:20 247

Exodus

Exodus 1:8-14 121
Exodus 1:15-21 121
Exodus 2:16-22 121
Exodus 3:12 190
Exodus 3:13-15 191
Exodus 3:18 190
Exodus 4:22 .... 190, 205
Exodus 4:22-23 .... 121, 190
Exodus 5 73
Exodus 5:1-2 191
Exodus 5:1-3 190
Exodus 5:1-14:31 121
Exodus 6:6-7 190
Exodus 7:16 190
Exodus 8:1 190
Exodus 8:20 190
Exodus 8:25-26 133
Exodus 9:1 190
Exodus 9:13 190
Exodus 9:16 192
Exodus 10:3-26 190
Exodus 17:8-16 121
Exodus 18:1-27 121
Exodus 19:3-4 188
Exodus 19:4-6 .... 191, 194
Exodus 19:5 .... 154, 191
Exodus 19:5-6 191
Exodus 20:2-3 191
Exodus 20:3-6 .... 166, 190
Exodus 20:5-6 173
Exodus 21:2 154
Exodus 23:22 185
Exodus 23:25 190
Exodus 25:1 155
Exodus 28:41 190
Exodus 29:45-46 190
Exodus 32 73
Exodus 32:6-35 196
Exodus 34:6-7 173
Exodus 34:28 154

Leviticus

Leviticus 7:35 190
Leviticus 11:44-45 191
Leviticus 16 175
Leviticus 18:5 168
Leviticus 18:24-28 177
Leviticus 19:2 191
Leviticus 20:7 191
Leviticus 20:23 177
Leviticus 20:26 191
Leviticus 26 ... 44, 45, 157, 158, 168,
 .... 170, 246, 251
Leviticus 26:1-46 165
Leviticus 26:11-13 190
Leviticus 26:22 176
Leviticus 26:29 .... 170, 171
Leviticus 26:33 146
Leviticus 26:33-45 170
Leviticus 26:36-45 .... 146, 202
Leviticus 26:39 176
Leviticus 26:40-42 129
Leviticus 26:40-45 157
Leviticus 26:44-45 .... 188, 190
Leviticus 27:28-29 177

Numbers

Numbers 3:3 190
Numbers 10:29-32 121
Numbers 13:1-20:13 114
Numbers 14:5-10 211
Numbers 14:11-21 211
Numbers 14:31-33 176
Numbers 16 74
Numbers 20:14-21 116
Numbers 22-24 178
Numbers 22:1-24:25 114
Numbers 24:2-9 125
Numbers 24:3-9 114
Numbers 24:9 .... 115, 185
Numbers 24:20 121
Numbers 24:21 121
Numbers 31:16 178

Deuteronomy

Deuteronomy 4:5-8 ... 189, 192, 195

Scripture Index | 285

Deuteronomy 4:5-36 192
Deuteronomy 4:20 191
Deuteronomy 4:23-27 166
Deuteronomy 4:23-31 ...... 131, 176
Deuteronomy 4:27 134
Deuteronomy 4:27-31168, 170, 203,
.... 210
Deuteronomy 4:29-31 132
Deuteronomy 4:30.... 170, 172, 203
Deuteronomy 4:30-31 157
Deuteronomy 4:32-37 186
Deuteronomy 4:37 187
Deuteronomy 4:40 175
Deuteronomy 5:7-10 166
Deuteronomy 5:9-10 173
Deuteronomy 5:29 175
Deuteronomy 6:4 191
Deuteronomy 6:4-9 .... 171, 194
Deuteronomy 6:5 195
Deuteronomy 6:6-7 192
Deuteronomy 7:1-6 177
Deuteronomy 7:1-11 166
Deuteronomy 7:6 ...... 186, 191, 195
Deuteronomy 7:6-11 .... 113, 235
Deuteronomy 7:7-8 .... 53, 187
Deuteronomy 7:9-10 173
Deuteronomy 7:11-14 189
Deuteronomy 8:11-20 196
Deuteronomy 9:4-6 187
Deuteronomy 10:8 190
Deuteronomy 10:12 195
Deuteronomy 10:14 195
Deuteronomy 10:14-15 186
Deuteronomy 10:16 206
Deuteronomy 11:13 195
Deuteronomy 11:13-28 166
Deuteronomy 11:22 195
Deuteronomy 11:26-28 194
Deuteronomy 11:26-32 165
Deuteronomy 11:29 168
Deuteronomy 12:2-3 177
Deuteronomy 12:23-25 175
Deuteronomy 12:28 175
Deuteronomy 14:2 .... 186, 191
Deuteronomy 17:2-7 166
Deuteronomy 17:12 190

Deuteronomy 17:14-20 197
Deuteronomy 18:5-7 190
Deuteronomy 19:9 195
Deuteronomy 20:16-18 177
Deuteronomy 21:5 190
Deuteronomy 21:23 168
Deuteronomy 23:3-6 114
Deuteronomy 24:16 173
Deuteronomy 25:17-19 121
Deuteronomy 26:18 191
Deuteronomy 26:18-19 191
Deuteronomy 27:1-26 166
Deuteronomy 27:9-10 190
Deuteronomy 27:12-13 137
Deuteronomy 27:26 168
Deuteronomy 28 246
Deuteronomy 28-3044, 45, 168, 170,
.... 251
Deuteronomy 28:1-14 249
Deuteronomy 28:1-30:30 165
Deuteronomy 28:9 191
Deuteronomy 28:10 191
Deuteronomy 28:15-68 116
Deuteronomy 28:32-59 176
Deuteronomy 28:36-68 170
Deuteronomy 28:53-57 ..... 170, 171
Deuteronomy 28:58-68 203
Deuteronomy 28:63-68 ..... 129, 132
Deuteronomy 28:64 134
Deuteronomy 28:64-68 ..... 146, 168
Deuteronomy 29:10-13 190
Deuteronomy 29:14-29 194
Deuteronomy 29:29 .. 193, 194, 253
Deuteronomy 30:1-3 . 129, 131, 132
Deuteronomy 30:1-4 170
Deuteronomy 30:1-8 109
Deuteronomy 30:1-10116, 128, 129,
.... 132, 137, 146, 210
Deuteronomy 30:1-20 196
Deuteronomy 30:3 132
Deuteronomy 30:3-6 129
Deuteronomy 30:4-8 129
Deuteronomy 30:5 129
Deuteronomy 30:6 .... 130, 206
Deuteronomy 30:7 .... 116, 129

Deuteronomy 30:9 129
Deuteronomy 30:15-20 194
Deuteronomy 30:16 195
Deuteronomy 30:19-20 181
Deuteronomy 31:14-29 166
Deuteronomy 31:16-17 37
Deuteronomy 31:29 .... 172, 203
Deuteronomy 32:4 253
Deuteronomy 32:8-9 .... 187, 189
Deuteronomy 32:8-10 257
Deuteronomy 32:9 190
Deuteronomy 32:26 134
Deuteronomy 32:39 48

Joshua

Joshua 1:2-7 132
Joshua 2:1-21 121
Joshua 2:9-11 192
Joshua 6:22-25 121
Joshua 7:1-26 177
Joshua 8:30-35 166
Joshua 9:22-23 116
Joshua 24:2-3 113
Joshua 24:9-10 114
Joshua 24:14-15 190
Joshua 24:14-28 194

Judges

Judges 1:16 121
Judges 4:11 121
Judges 5:23 115
Judges 11:17 116

1 Samuel

1 Samuel 2:12-36 166
1 Samuel 8:1-22 197
1 Samuel 12:22 258
1 Samuel 15:1-8 121
1 Samuel 15:6 121
1 Samuel 17:4-47 115

2 Samuel

2 Samuel 3:10-18 166
2 Samuel 7 141
2 Samuel 7:1-17 139
2 Samuel 7:12-16 .... 109, 140
2 Samuel 7:13 .... 107, 142
2 Samuel 7:14 .... 143, 148
2 Samuel 7:14-15 142
2 Samuel 7:16 142
2 Samuel 7:23-24 190
2 Samuel 23:5 142
2 Samuel 24:1 216

1 Kings

1 Kings 11:9-13 143
1 Kings 11:9-39 139

2 Kings

2 Kings 6:24-29 171
2 Kings 8:12 176
2 Kings 15:16 176
2 Kings 17:1-41 .... 143, 176
2 Kings 17:7-23 133
2 Kings 22:8-20 166

1 Chronicles

1 Chronicles 16:13 190
1 Chronicles 16:16-17 107
1 Chronicles 16:16-18 126
1 Chronicles 16:24-31 191
1 Chronicles 17:1-15 139
1 Chronicles 17:12 .... 107, 142
1 Chronicles 17:14 142
1 Chronicles 21:1 216
1 Chronicles 22:9-10 142
1 Chronicles 22:10 107

2 Chronicles

2 Chronicles 13:5 142
2 Chronicles 21:7 142
2 Chronicles 28:17 116
2 Chronicles 34:14-28 166
2 Chronicles 36:11-21 133
2 Chronicles 36:15-17 176
2 Chronicles 36:17-21 143
2 Chronicles 36:22-23 137

Ezra

Ezra 1:1-7 137
Ezra 5:1-2 137
Ezra 6:14 137

Nehemiah

Nehemiah 1:1-11 211
Nehemiah 1:1-2:10 211
Nehemiah 1:17-20 137
Nehemiah 7:5-6 137
Nehemiah 10:28-29 194
Nehemiah 10:28-39 166
Nehemiah 13:1-3 114

Esther

Esther 3:1-15 122
Esther 4:7-8 122
Esther 5:9-14 122
Esther 6:12-13 122
Esther 7:3-6 122

Job

Job 1-3 173
Job 1:6-12 216
Job 2:1-6 216
Job 5:17 42
Job 13 74
Job 23:10 247

Job 42:2 .... 234, 235

Psalms

Psalm 9:7-8 232
Psalm 10 74
Psalm 13 74
Psalm 14:1 236
Psalm 19:1-6 236
Psalm 19:8 156
Psalm 33:12 .... 190, 192
Psalm 37:20-22 116
Psalm 42 74
Psalm 44 74
Psalm 51:5 247
Psalm 53:1 236
Psalm 58:3 247
Psalm 67:1-7 189
Psalm 72:1-20 189
Psalm 78:10 169
Psalm 80:8-19 205
Psalm 83:1-6 116
Psalm 89 .... 74, 139
Psalm 89:1-4 142
Psalm 89:1-49 139
Psalm 89:28-29 142
Psalm 89:30-33 142
Psalm 89:36-37 142
Psalm 90:2 233
Psalm 100:3 190
Psalm 102:18-22 192
Psalm 105:8-10 107
Psalm 105:8-11 126
Psalm 109:6 216
Psalm 109:9-10 177
Psalm 109:12-13 177
Psalm 109:26-31 116
Psalm 119:21 166
Psalm 127-128 171
Psalm 132:11 142
Psalm 135:4 191
Psalm 137:8-9 177
Psalm 137:17 116
Psalm 144:15 192
Psalm 145:9-16 235
Psalm 147:19-20 .... 186, 192

Proverbs

Proverbs 3:11-12 .... 42, 196
Proverbs 15:3 235

Isaiah

Isaiah 1:9 .... 199, 210
Isaiah 2:4 149
Isaiah 5:1-12 205
Isaiah 9:7 .... 107, 142
Isaiah 10:5-14 121
Isaiah 10:5-19 143
Isaiah 10:24-27 143
Isaiah 11:11-16 137
Isaiah 13:1-14:23 .... 122, 143
Isaiah 13:16-18 177
Isaiah 14:12-15 247
Isaiah 14:21 177
Isaiah 14:24-27 .... 121, 143
Isaiah 15-16 114
Isaiah 19:1-20:4 121
Isaiah 19:23-25 190
Isaiah 28:14-22 137
Isaiah 30:30-32 143
Isaiah 33:22 191
Isaiah 37:21-29 143
Isaiah 41:8-16 190
Isaiah 42:1-22 205
Isaiah 42:6 191
Isaiah 42:12 191
Isaiah 42:23-25 143
Isaiah 43:1 .... 187, 190
Isaiah 43:1-10 190
Isaiah 43:1-24 205
Isaiah 43:7 191
Isaiah 43:10-12 191
Isaiah 43:21 191
Isaiah 44:1-8 190
Isaiah 44:1-23 205
Isaiah 44:21 190
Isaiah 44:23 191
Isaiah 44:28 137
Isaiah 45:4 190
Isaiah 45:5 191
Isaiah 45:7 48
Isaiah 45:15 .... 38, 198
Isaiah 45:21-22 232
Isaiah 45:23 191
Isaiah 46:13 191
Isaiah 48:9 211
Isaiah 48:9-11 205
Isaiah 48:20 190
Isaiah 49:1-13 205
Isaiah 49:6 191
Isaiah 51:2 186
Isaiah 51:4 191
Isaiah 52:3-6 121
Isaiah 52:7 154
Isaiah 52:13-53:12 176
Isaiah 53:1-2 232
Isaiah 54:7-9 188
Isaiah 54:10 188
Isaiah 55:3 .... 107, 142, 150
Isaiah 55:8-11 192
Isaiah 57:15 72
Isaiah 59:21 149
Isaiah 60:1-2 191
Isaiah 60:1-3 191
Isaiah 60:1-22 137
Isaiah 61:4-9 137
Isaiah 61:8 .... 107, 149, 150
Isaiah 61:9 149
Isaiah 63:9 258
Isaiah 63:16 190
Isaiah 64:8 190
Isaiah 65:8 .... 199, 210
Isaiah 65:15-16 167
Isaiah 66:15-16 232

Jeremiah

Jeremiah 1:1-19 212
Jeremiah 1:16 232
Jeremiah 2:1-45:5 212
Jeremiah 2:2-3 191
Jeremiah 4:1-2 189
Jeremiah 4:4 206
Jeremiah 6:11-12 176
Jeremiah 9:25-26 .... 114, 206
Jeremiah 11:2-5 166
Jeremiah 12 74

Jeremiah 12:10 205
Jeremiah 16:14-15 137
Jeremiah 17:5-8 166
Jeremiah 19:7-9 171
Jeremiah 23:1-8 137
Jeremiah 23:5-8 132
Jeremiah 23:10 166
Jeremiah 23:23-25 235
Jeremiah 24:8-10 166
Jeremiah 25:1-11 137
Jeremiah 25:8-14 143
Jeremiah 25:11-12 132
Jeremiah 25:15-21 114
Jeremiah 25:15-29 166
Jeremiah 26:4-6 166
Jeremiah 27:2-3 114
Jeremiah 27:4-11 143
Jeremiah 27:16-22 143
Jeremiah 29:1-14 137
Jeremiah 29:10 143
Jeremiah 29:15-23 166
Jeremiah 30 249
Jeremiah 30:1-17 152
Jeremiah 30:1-24 .... 137, 148
Jeremiah 30:1-31:26 167
Jeremiah 30:1-31:37 252
Jeremiah 30:7 218
Jeremiah 30:7-24 204
Jeremiah 30:10 178
Jeremiah 30:16 122
Jeremiah 30:18-24 152
Jeremiah 30:20 178
Jeremiah 31 .... 151, 152
Jeremiah 31:1 190
Jeremiah 31:1-9 204
Jeremiah 31:1-26 152
Jeremiah 31:3 187
Jeremiah 31:9 190
Jeremiah 31:15-17 176
Jeremiah 31:27-37 137
Jeremiah 31:27-40 .... 152, 167
Jeremiah 31:29-30 173
Jeremiah 31:31 150
Jeremiah 31:31-32 167
Jeremiah 31:31-34 .... 109, 148
Jeremiah 31:33 .... 149, 150, 152
Jeremiah 31:34 .... 149, 152

Jeremiah 31:35-36 188
Jeremiah 31:35-37 .... 149, 150
Jeremiah 31:36 107
Jeremiah 31:37 188
Jeremiah 31:40 150
Jeremiah 32:17-19 174
Jeremiah 32:40 .... 107, 150
Jeremiah 32:41 149
Jeremiah 33:20-21 188
Jeremiah 33:20-22 142
Jeremiah 33:25-26 188
Jeremiah 34:18 107
Jeremiah 42:18 166
Jeremiah 43:4-7 211
Jeremiah 43:8-13 143
Jeremiah 44:1-10 176
Jeremiah 44:7-10 166
Jeremiah 44:22-23 166
Jeremiah 46:27-28 178
Jeremiah 48:1-47 114
Jeremiah 49:13 116
Jeremiah 50:1-51:64 143
Jeremiah 50:5 .... 107, 150
Jeremiah 51:34-64 122

Lamentations

Lamentations 1:1 189
Lamentations 1:5 176
Lamentations 1:16 176
Lamentations 2-3 173
Lamentations 2:11-22 176
Lamentations 2:19-20 171
Lamentations 3 74
Lamentations 3:1 143
Lamentations 3:37-38 48
Lamentations 3:55-66 116
Lamentations 3:64-66 125
Lamentations 4:8-11 171
Lamentations 4:21-22 116

Ezekiel

Ezekiel 2:1-10 212
Ezekiel 3:1-27 212

Ezekiel 3:10-15 211
Ezekiel 5:5 .... 187, 189
Ezekiel 5:7-8 192
Ezekiel 5:7-10 171
Ezekiel 9:6 176
Ezekiel 11:14-21 212
Ezekiel 11:16-21 130
Ezekiel 14:1-24:27 212
Ezekiel 14:14-20 216
Ezekiel 16:1-60 186
Ezekiel 16:1-63 129
Ezekiel 16:14 189
Ezekiel 16:60 107
Ezekiel 16:60-62 .... 130, 148
Ezekiel 16:60-63 150
Ezekiel 18:1-4 173
Ezekiel 18:19-23 173
Ezekiel 20:1-32 251
Ezekiel 20:5 186
Ezekiel 20:23-24 133
Ezekiel 20:32 198
Ezekiel 20:33-38 137, 196, 218, 219
Ezekiel 20:33-44 .... 148, 204
Ezekiel 21:8-17 144
Ezekiel 22:17-27 137
Ezekiel 25:1-7 121
Ezekiel 25:8-11 114
Ezekiel 25:12-14 116
Ezekiel 28:11-19 247
Ezekiel 33:1-48:35 212
Ezekiel 34:25 152
Ezekiel 34:25-27 149
Ezekiel 35:12-15 116
Ezekiel 36:5 116
Ezekiel 36:22 251
Ezekiel 36:22-27 137
Ezekiel 36:22-32 192
Ezekiel 36:27 149
Ezekiel 37:1-14 .... 97, 137
Ezekiel 37:21-25 132
Ezekiel 37:25 142
Ezekiel 37:25-26 107
Ezekiel 37:26 .... 107, 149, 152
Ezekiel 37:26-27 149
Ezekiel 37:26-28 150
Ezekiel 38:1-39:29 122
Ezekiel 38:8 137

Ezekiel 38:12 .... 137, 187, 189
Ezekiel 38:16 192
Ezekiel 38:23 192
Ezekiel 39:7-29 137

Daniel

Daniel 18, 86, 215
Daniel 1:1-21 .... 210, 211
Daniel 1:1-2:3 212
Daniel 2:11 134
Daniel 2:49 211
Daniel 3:1-30 211
Daniel 6:1-28 211
Daniel 6:19-24 121
Daniel 7:13 134
Daniel 8:1-12:13 212
Daniel 8:9-14 144
Daniel 8:23-25 144
Daniel 9:1-27 210
Daniel 9:2 132
Daniel 9:3-19 211
Daniel 9:11-14 166
Daniel 9:24-27 .... 137, 138, 218
Daniel 9:26 144
Daniel 9:27 134
Daniel 11:15-35 144
Daniel 12:1 .... 134, 216
Daniel 12:1-2 242
Daniel 12:1-3 .... 137, 249
Daniel 12:11 134

Hosea

Hosea 2:14-23 130
Hosea 2:18 149
Hosea 2:19-20 149
Hosea 6:7 232
Hosea 10:14 176
Hosea 11:1 .... 190, 205
Hosea 11:8 196
Hosea 13:16 176

Joel

Joel 2:16 178
Joel 3:1-3 .... 122, 134
Joel 3:3 178
Joel 3:18-21 137
Joel 3:19 .... 116, 121

Amos

Amos 1:11 116
Amos 3:2 .... 44, 196, 197
Amos 3:7 210
Amos 7:1-6 .... 210, 211
Amos 9:11-12 137

Obadiah

Obadiah 8-14 116

Micah

Micah 4:11-13 137
Micah 5:1 144
Micah 5:4-15 137
Micah 7:11-20 137

Nahum

Nahum 3:8-10 177

Habakkuk

Habakkuk 1 74
Habakkuk 1:1-2:20 116, 122, 125, 144
Habakkuk 2:20 144

Zephaniah

Zephaniah 2:8-11 .... 114, 121

Zephaniah 3:8 122

Zechariah

Zechariah 1:12-15 144
Zechariah 2:8 258
Zechariah 2:8-9 122
Zechariah 3:1-2 216
Zechariah 5:1-4 166
Zechariah 8:11-15 167
Zechariah 8:13 190
Zechariah 9:11 149
Zechariah 10:8-12 137
Zechariah 12:1-14:21 .. 137, 168
Zechariah 12:2-4 122
Zechariah 13 249
Zechariah 13:2-3 178
Zechariah 13:7-9 148, 172, 178, 204, ... 218
Zechariah 13:8-9 .... 167, 219
Zechariah 14:1-4 122
Zechariah 14:4 134
Zechariah 14:16-21 249

Malachi

Malachi 1:2 187
Malachi 1:2-3 186
Malachi 1:2-4 113
Malachi 2:1-9 166
Malachi 3:5 232
Malachi 3:6 .... 188, 233
Malachi 3:7-12 166
Malachi 3:12 190
Malachi 3:17 191
Malachi 4:4 167

Matthew

Matthew 27
Matthew 1:1 193
Matthew 1:5 121
Matthew 1:18-25 206
Matthew 2:13-18 176

Matthew 2:13-21 217
Matthew 2:15 205
Matthew 3:1-17 206
Matthew 4:1-11 218
Matthew 5:1-16 206
Matthew 5:17-20 156
Matthew 7:13-14 206
Matthew 11:2-19 206
Matthew 16:13-17 206
Matthew 16:16-23 218
Matthew 19:28 204
Matthew 21:33-45 205
Matthew 22:15-22 218
Matthew 23:1-36 166
Matthew 23:1-39 166
Matthew 23:34-36 174
Matthew 23:37 175
Matthew 23:37-39 133, 144, 168, 219, ... 249
Matthew 24 249
Matthew 24:15 .... 138, 218
Matthew 24:15-22 ... 134, 148, 172, 218
Matthew 24:15-31 .... 137, 204
Matthew 24:19 178
Matthew 24:29-31 134
Matthew 25:31-33 122
Matthew 25:31-46 .... 117, 120, 134
Matthew 25:34 118
Matthew 25:40 124
Matthew 25:41 118
Matthew 25:46 242
Matthew 26:26-29 160
Matthew 26:27-28 151
Matthew 26:28 150
Matthew 27:25 176

Mark

Mark 1:12-13 218
Mark 7:18-19 159
Mark 8:27-30 206
Mark 12:13-17 218
Mark 13 158
Mark 13:17 178
Mark 14:24 150

Luke

Luke 1:5-25 206
Luke 1:26-35 193
Luke 1:26-38 249
Luke 1:26-56 206
Luke 1:32-33 142
Luke 1:37 235
Luke 1:57-80 206
Luke 1:72-73 157
Luke 2:8-20 206
Luke 2:21-38 206
Luke 2:32 206
Luke 3:1-22 206
Luke 4:1-13 218
Luke 9:18-21 206
Luke 11:37-41 159
Luke 12:32 204
Luke 13:34 175
Luke 19-21 158
Luke 19:37-44 133
Luke 19:41-44 .... 144, 176
Luke 20:20-26 218
Luke 21:20-24 ... 133, 144, 168, 170, ... 211, 219, 249, 252
Luke 21:23-24 176
Luke 21:24 .... 134, 158
Luke 22:3-6 218
Luke 22:19-20 160
Luke 22:20 .... 150, 151
Luke 22:28-30 204
Luke 22:31-32 218
Luke 23:27-31 176
Luke 23:29 178
Luke 24:25-44 193

John

John 3:1-8 251
John 3:3-8 250
John 3:16-19 .... 232, 251
John 4:22 193
John 4:25-26 193
John 5:39-40 193
John 6:69 206
John 6:70-71 218

John 8:44 218
John 10:14-16 206
John 11:47-52 144
John 14:6 193
John 15:1 205
John 15:26 250
John 16:7-11 .... 250, 251
John 16:14 250
John 17:12 206

Acts

Acts 2:14-41 212
Acts 3:12-4:31 212
Acts 3:25 .... 125, 185
Acts 4:12 193
Acts 5:12-42 212
Acts 5:31 206
Acts 6:8-7:60 212
Acts 7:2-3 185
Acts 8:1-4 206
Acts 10:9-16 159
Acts 11.5-10 159
Acts 13:13-41 212
Acts 13:16-24 206
Acts 13:34 142
Acts 13:44-47 191
Acts 14:15-17 236
Acts 15:14-17 132
Acts 16:1 206
Acts 16:35-39 207
Acts 17:22-31 236
Acts 18:2 206
Acts 18:24-28 206
Acts 20:7 159
Acts 21:20 206
Acts 21:39 207
Acts 22:3 207
Acts 22:22-29 207
Acts 23:25-30 207
Acts 24:17 207
Acts 25:13-22 207

Romans

Romans 1:1-4 249
Romans 1:3 193
Romans 1:18 230
Romans 1:18-32 .... 236, 251
Romans 2:14-16 165
Romans 2:28-29 .... 191, 206
Romans 3:2 192
Romans 3:9 208
Romans 3:21-30 154
Romans 3:21-31 164
Romans 4:17 185
Romans 5:2 251
Romans 5:3-4 251
Romans 5:20 247
Romans 7:4 170
Romans 7:12 156
Romans 7:12-16 156
Romans 8:1-2 163
Romans 8:2 159
Romans 8:16-17 250
Romans 8:17-18 251
Romans 8:26-30 250
Romans 8:28 247
Romans 8:28-39 230
Romans 9-11 .... 204, 212
Romans 9:1-3 211
Romans 9:3-4 207
Romans 9:4 .... 150, 190, 191, 204
Romans 9:5 193
Romans 9:6-13 186
Romans 9:10-13 113
Romans 9:13 187
Romans 9:29 210
Romans 10:1 211
Romans 10:1-3 164
Romans 10:4 .... 160, 161
Romans 10:11-13 154
Romans 10:12 208
Romans 10:14-15 154
Romans 11 249
Romans 11:1 .... 206, 207
Romans 11:1-2 188
Romans 11:1-7 199
Romans 11:2 157
Romans 11:5 152

Romans 11:7 152
Romans 11:11 154
Romans 11:11-12 212
Romans 11:11-24 181
Romans 11:13 208
Romans 11:13-14153, 207, 212, 252
Romans 11:13-21 206
Romans 11:15-27 137
Romans 11:25 158
Romans 11:25-27151, 152, 210, 219
Romans 11:25-29 .... 188, 204
Romans 11:25-36 .... 180, 198, 258
Romans 11:26 .... 157, 158
Romans 11:26-27 .... 129, 130
Romans 11:27 150
Romans 11:29 158
Romans 11:33 253
Romans 11:33-36 230
Romans 13:1-7 207
Romans 14:1-12 159
Romans 15:4 192
Romans 15:8-12 206

1 Corinthians

1 Corinthians 1:24 208
1 Corinthians 4:5 230
1 Corinthians 5:1-13..................251
1 Corinthians 7:20-24................208
1 Corinthians 9:19-22................209
1 Corinthians 10:1-13........ 192, 196
1 Corinthians 10:6 192
1 Corinthians 10:11 192
1 Corinthians 10:32 .... 231, 250
1 Corinthians 11:3-16................208
1 Corinthians 11:17-34..............251
1 Corinthians 11:23-25..............160
1 Corinthians 11:25 .... 150, 151
1 Corinthians 12:13 208
1 Corinthians 13:4-7..................242
1 Corinthians 13:12 230
1 Corinthians 14:34 208
1 Corinthians 15:3-4..................193
1 Corinthians 16:2 159

2 Corinthians

2 Corinthians 1:3-7 251
2 Corinthians 1:5 250
2 Corinthians 3:1-18 163
2 Corinthians 3:4-18 192
2 Corinthians 3:6 .... 150, 151, 160
2 Corinthians 3:7 164
2 Corinthians 3:9 164
2 Corinthians 3:11 164
2 Corinthians 4:16-18 251
2 Corinthians 4:17 247
2 Corinthians 5:21 248
2 Corinthians 11:22 207
2 Corinthians 12:7-10 251
2 Corinthians 13:11 235

Galatians

Galatians 2:3............................. 159
Galatians 2:7-9 206
Galatians 2:11-15 208
Galatians 2:14........................... 206
Galatians 2:14-15 207
Galatians 2:19........................... 164
Galatians 3:6-9 190
Galatians 3:7-8 151
Galatians 3:7-16 193
Galatians 3:8....................125, 185
Galatians 3:10-13 156
Galatians 3:10-14 ......160, 164, 168
Galatians 3:10-4:7 163
Galatians 3:13-14 151
Galatians 3:15-18 156
Galatians 3:15-22 188
Galatians 3:19-22 157
Galatians 3:23-25 156
Galatians 3:23-26 160
Galatians 3:28........................... 208
Galatians 4:4-5 193
Galatians 5:1-6 159
Galatians 6:2.....................159, 163
Galatians 6:16........................... 206

Ephesians

Ephesians 2:3 .... 247, 251, 252
Ephesians 2:11-12 150
Ephesians 2:12 191
Ephesians 2:13 151
Ephesians 2:19 151
Ephesians 3:1-12 151
Ephesians 4:18 247

Philippians

Philippians 3:4-7 209
Philippians 3:5 207
Philippians 3:10 250
Philippians 3:20-21 207

Colossians

Colossians 1:24 250
Colossians 2:13-15 .... 218, 248
Colossians 2:16-17 159
Colossians 3:11 208
Colossians 3:22-4:1 208

1 Thessalonians

1 Thessalonians 2:13-16 252

2 Thessalonians

2 Thessalonians 1:3-10 251
2 Thessalonians 1:3-2:12 .. 245, 249
2 Thessalonians 1:5-10 242
2 Thessalonians 1:6-10 230
2 Thessalonians 2:3-12 ..... 138, 218
2 Thessalonians 2:6-9 250

1 Timothy

1 Timothy 1:8-11 156
1 Timothy 2:1-4 207
1 Timothy 2:4 251
1 Timothy 2:5-6 193
1 Timothy 3:6 247
1 Timothy 4:1-5 159

2 Timothy

2 Timothy 3:16 193

Titus

Titus 3:1-2 207
Titus 3:4-7 250
Titus 3:5 251

Hebrews

Hebrews 1:13-14 247
Hebrews 2:10 251
Hebrews 2:14-15 248
Hebrews 2:17-18 250
Hebrews 4:13 235
Hebrews 4:14-16 250
Hebrews 5:8 251
Hebrews 6:13-18 .... 108, 188
Hebrews 7:11-18 163
Hebrews 7:11-28 160
Hebrews 8:6 .... 151, 160
Hebrews 8:8 150
Hebrews 8:10-13 150
Hebrews 8:13 164
Hebrews 9:15 .... 150, 160
Hebrews 9:15-17 151
Hebrews 10:19-25 250
Hebrews 11:31 121
Hebrews 12:5-6 235
Hebrews 12:5-11 251
Hebrews 12:24 .... 150, 151, 160
Hebrews 13:8 233
Hebrews 13:20 107

James

James 1:1 206
James 1:2-4 251
James 1:13 233
James 1:17 233
James 2:8-13 156
James 2:25 121
James 5:11 216
James 5:17-18 211

1 Peter

1 Peter 1:1 206
1 Peter 1:3-9 251
1 Peter 1:6-7 251
1 Peter 1:14-16 156
1 Peter 2:4-10 206
1 Peter 2:13-17 207
1 Peter 3:18 248
1 Peter 4:1-3 251
1 Peter 4:12-19 251
1 Peter 4:13-14 250
1 Peter 4:17-18 251

2 Peter

2 Peter 1:2-11 251
2 Peter 1:12-15 251
2 Peter 1:21 193
2 Peter 3:1-13 249
2 Peter 3:9 .... 246, 251
2 Peter 3:10-13 246

1 John

1 John 1:5 233

1 John 1:5-2:2 232
1 John 1:8-10 247
1 John 2:2 251
1 John 3:16-18 248
1 John 4:7-16 235

Jude

Jude 9 216

Revelation

Revelation 5:1-14 249
Revelation 6:3-8 172
Revelation 6:9-11 .... 205, 211
Revelation 7:1-8 204
Revelation 11:1-13 205
Revelation 12 217
Revelation 12:1-5 217
Revelation 12:1-17 148
Revelation 12:3-4 247
Revelation 12:5 .... 219, 249
Revelation 12:9-12 218
Revelation 12:10 219
Revelation 12:13 218
Revelation 12:13-17 218
Revelation 12:13-13:10 138
Revelation 12:17 205
Revelation 13 218
Revelation 14:1-5 204
Revelation 19:6 234
Revelation 19:11-16 249
Revelation 19:11-21 245
Revelation 19:11-20:3 222
Revelation 19:11-22:21 249
Revelation 22:3 167

Further publications from Ariel Ministries can be found at www.ariel.org.

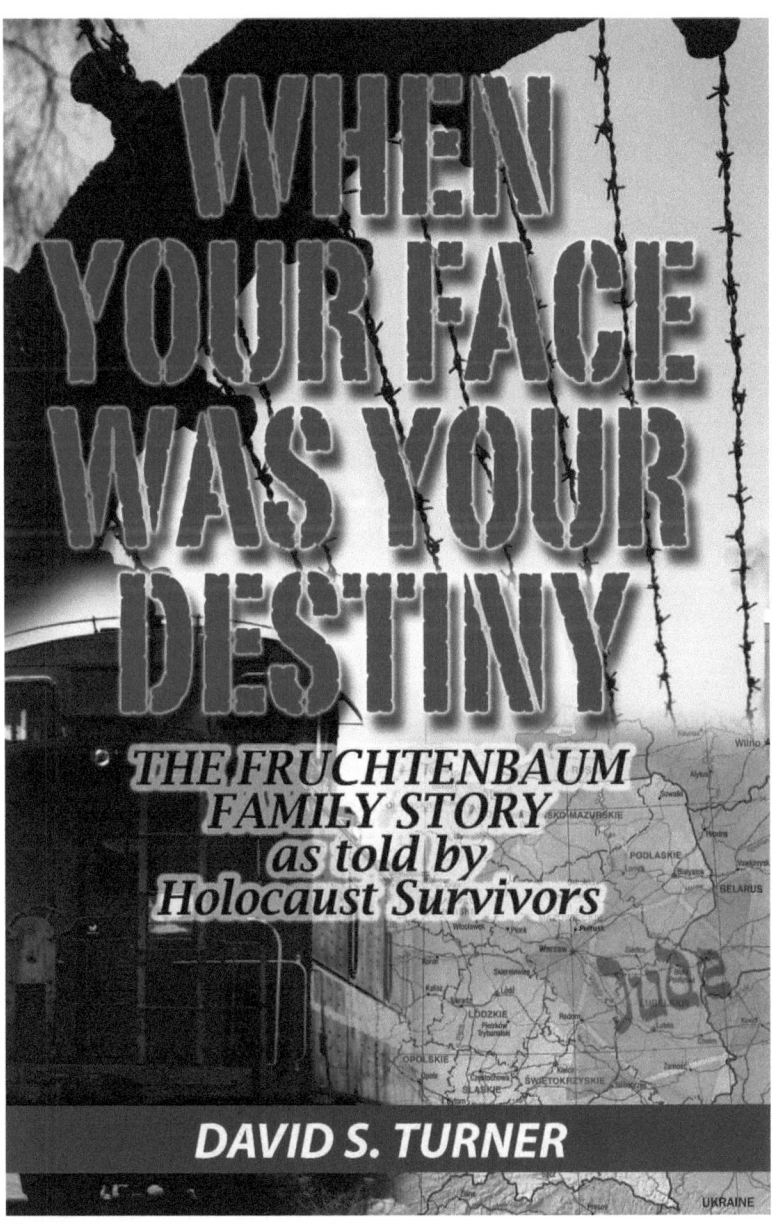

QUESTIONS

Ariel Ministries has you covered.

about Israel?

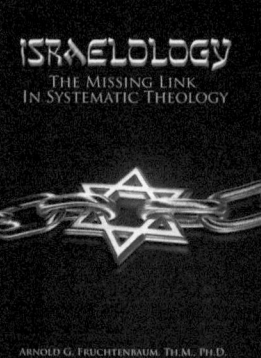

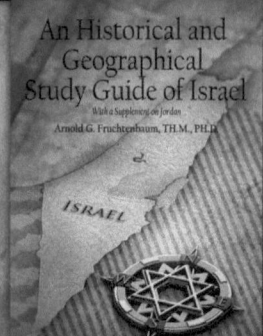

Solid...Comprehensive...Scriptural

Find these and many other books at...

ariel.org

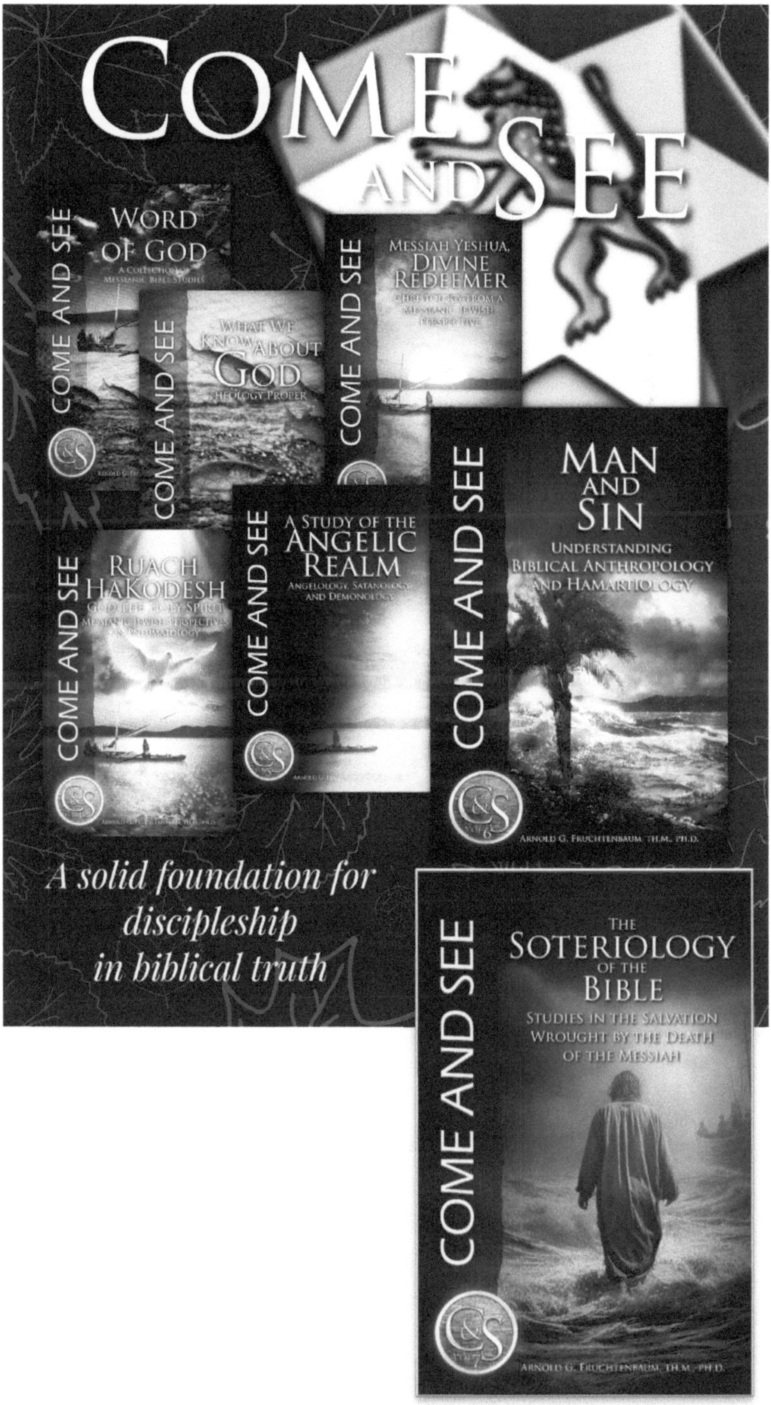
COME AND SEE
COME AND SEE
WORD OF GOD
WHAT WE KNOW ABOUT GOD
THEOLOGY PROPER
MESSIAH YESHUA, DIVINE REDEEMER
RUACH HAKODESH
A STUDY OF THE ANGELIC REALM
ANGELOLOGY, SATANOLOGY, AND DEMONOLOGY
MAN AND SIN
UNDERSTANDING BIBLICAL ANTHROPOLOGY AND HAMARTIOLOGY
ARNOLD G. FRUCHTENBAUM, TH.M., PH.D.
A solid foundation for discipleship in biblical truth
THE SOTERIOLOGY OF THE BIBLE
STUDIES IN THE SALVATION WROUGHT BY THE DEATH OF THE MESSIAH
ARNOLD G. FRUCHTENBAUM, TH.M., PH.D.

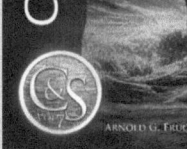

ARIEL COLLEGE OF THE BIBLE AND MESSIANIC JEWISH STUDIES
ONLINE COURSES

מכללת אריאל למקרא ולימודי יהדות משיחית

Improving & Expanding !

WEBSITE

We invite you to go to our new website, www.ArielCollege.com and watch the short introductory video. **Then read Steps 1-3**: "Overview," "Choose a Plan," and "How to Start." You can purchase a course on the "Course Catalog" page (for credit or non-credit).

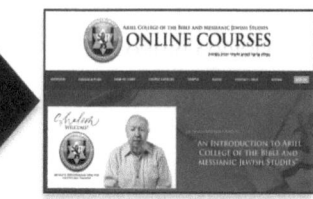

FORMAT

There are four study options for all of our courses. We call these "Tiers." Tiers 1-3 provide full course curriculum structured around "Modules." Typical courses have 16 Modules. Each Module is comprised of learning objectives, readings, videos, spiritual growth activities, open-book exams, and more.

VIDEOS

The video lecture presentations are professionally filmed in a closed-studio setting with high quality audio and video. We provide on-screen text, maps, images, and graphics that will keep you engaged. The lectures are very detailed and provide the full content.

WWW.ARIELCOLLEGE.COM